Straying
from the Flock

Straying from the Flock

Travels in New Zealand

Dr. Alexander Elder

WILEY

John Wiley & Sons, Inc.

Published by John Wiley & Sons, Inc., Hoboken, New Jersey.
Published simultaneously in Canada.

For general information about our other products and services, please contact our Customer Care Department within the United States at 800-762-2974, outside the United States at 317-572-3993 or fax 317-572-4002.

Wiley also publishes its books in a variety of electronic formats. Some content that appears in print may not be available in electronic books. For more information about Wiley products, visit our web site at www.wiley.com.

Library of Congress Cataloging-in-Publication Data

Elder, Alexander, 1950–
    Straying from the flock : travels in New Zealand / Alexander Elder.
       p.   cm.
    Includes bibliographical references.
    ISBN-13 978-0-471-71863-5
    ISBN-10 0-471-71863-7 (pbk.)
    1. New Zealand—Description and travel.   2. Elder, Alexander, 1950.   I. Title.
    DU413.E43 2005
    919.304′4—dc22

                                                                2005004691

Printed in the United States of America

10 9 8 7 6 5 4 3 2 1

*The only sure voyage of discovery would not be to visit strange lands
but to possess other eyes, to behold the Universe through the eyes of another.*
—Marcel Proust

To my favorite fellow travelers—Miriam, Nika, and Danny

CONTENTS

SECTION 5

SECTION 6

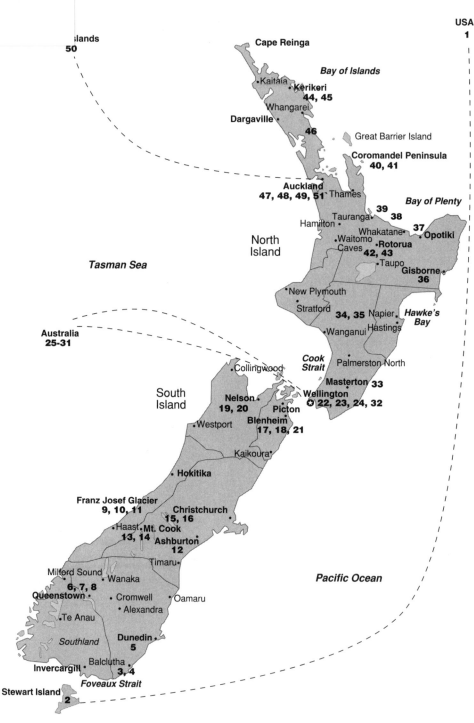

Each number on this map identifies the location for the relevant chapter of the book.

USA
1

lands
50

Cape Reinga

Bay of Islands

•Kaitaia

Kerikeri
44, 45

Whangarei•

Dargaville

46

Great Barrier Island

Coromandel Peninsula
40, 41

Auckland
47, 48, 49, 51 •Thames

Bay of Plenty

39 **38**

Tauranga•
Hamilton •

37 •**Opotiki**

Whakatane•
•Waitomo •**Rotorua**
Caves **42, 43**

North
Island

Tasman Sea

•Taupo
Gisborne
36

•New Plymouth

•Stratford
34, 35 Napier•

Hawke's Bay

Australia
25-31

•Wanganui Hastings•

Palmerston North•

Cook Strait

Collingwood•

Masterton 33

Wellington
✪ **22, 23, 24, 32**

South
Island

Nelson
19, 20

Picton•

•Westport

Blenheim
17, 18, 21

Kaikoura•

•**Hokitika**

Franz Josef Glacier
9, 10, 11

Christchurch
15, 16

•Haast •**Mt. Cook**
13, 14 **Ashburton**
12

•Timaru

Pacific Ocean

Milford Sound•
6, 7, 8 •Wanaka

Queenstown• •Cromwell •Oamaru
•Alexandra

•Te Anau

Southland

Dunedin
5

Balclutha•
Invercargill •
3, 4

Foveaux Strait

Stewart Island
2

Your Ticket to New Zealand

It is time to fly to New Zealand again. I planned this roadtrip from the bluffs at its southern tip to the cape at its northern end, where the Pacific Ocean crashes into the Tasman Sea. I'll be on the road for two months, taking quick side trips to Australia and the Cook Islands. My friends are waiting, their houses open to me.

I discovered New Zealand in the mid-1990s, around the time of my divorce, and this affair has been going on ever since. I had been telling my children and friends about New Zealand for so long, it became almost inevitable I should write this book. *Straying from the Flock* has helped me weave together all the strands of knowledge about New Zealand—its history and geography, sport and travel, business and culture, and above all its people with their quirky ways of life on faraway islands in the midst of the great ocean.

The land area of New Zealand is roughly equal to that of Italy or England, but while those countries have over 50 million people each, there are only about three million souls in New Zealand. There are more sheep running free on green pastures than there are people. It was the first country in the world to give women the right to vote. It is a sportsman's paradise where you can ski down the side of a volcano in August, swim in the South Pacific surf in January, and hike, fish, and hunt throughout the year.

But this book is not only about a country. It is also about the life and times of an aging baby boomer, single again after a lifetime of marriage, professionally established, with grown children, free to travel, and intensely curious about the life around him.

Now, as I go through my to-do list before the trip, I turn to you and say, "Come! I have enough frequent flyer miles for another business class ticket. There is a car waiting, a country road, people to meet, sights to see. I was going to fly there alone. Let's go together! Will you come with me?"

Dr. Alexander Elder
New York, 2004

SECTION
1

The Far End of the Earth

As the plane took off from Los Angeles and headed west over the Pacific, I leaned back in a comfortable seat and ordered the first glass of wine. My thoughts drifted back to the final days of my previous visit to New Zealand—it was March, an early autumn in the Southern Hemisphere. Auckland's harbor was dotted with islands where the ancient Maori built their fortified settlements on high volcanic hills. I had taken a high-speed catamaran to Waiheke Island, which used to be home to counterculture types who moved there to get away from it all and perhaps grow a little grass, but in recent years has emerged as one of the great wine centers in New Zealand. The island has 29 vineyards, and I was surprised to learn that the minimum size for a commercial vineyard is only five acres, although many are much larger.

I hopped off the ferry on a dazzling day—a hot sun in a cloudless sky, clean green water under the pier, blue water with whitecaps in the distance, groves of trees running up the hills, flags and canopies flapping in the breeze. A sleek blue motorcycle stood at the foot of the pier. I had to have it! I rented it and rode up the hill to the information center. A clerk booked me into a lodge in a vineyard whose restaurant was recommended by a friend.

The lodge crowned a hill in the middle of a vineyard, with panoramic views across rows of vines and spits of land interlaced by bays, all the way back to Auckland. The dining room was dominated by a table that could be set for ten—the maximum of four guest couples plus the owners. The pair that owned the lodge came out laughing, greeting me as I parked my motorcycle amidst expensive cars. Since a pickup at the ferry was included in the rate, I asked them to send a driver to pick up my flight bag at the motorcycle rental place and, while at it, bring an extra helmet—I was expecting a guest. I called Phyllis, my best friend in Auckland, and told her the place was exquisite: "Come, hop over for dinner."

I rode cautiously down the gravel driveway, gunning the engine on the asphalt. The little Japanese engine, running at high RPMs, sounded like a sewing machine gone mad. Riding on Waiheke was a joy. The roads were narrow and twisty, but well marked. The vineyards gave way to sheep grazing on hillsides and instead of asphalt there were smooth dirt roads, with gates between stations (ranches). I would ride up to a gate, hop off the motorcycle, open the gate, ride through, get off to close the gate, then continue to ride. Returning to the lodge in late afternoon, I sat on the terrace and read, listening to jazz, then drove down to meet the Auckland ferry.

Phyllis had recently celebrated her 71st birthday, but was so full of energy, curiosity, and laughter, that I often thought "If this is what 71 is like, take me there fast!" She stood on the front deck, craning her neck like a teenager. We hugged, and she pulled a helmet over her grey curls. I helped her buckle her helmet and rode to the lodge, leaning deep into the curves and tapping her knee to point out the views.

At the lodge, the owner opened a bottle of local Obsidian red and we drank it on the terrace, as we watched the setting sun. He emerged regally from the kitchen to report on his work in progress and served a plate of grilled mussels to tide us over. The four-course dinner, with more wine and cognac, was a poem. Halfway through the meal Phyllis leaned over to me and whispered, "May I come again tomorrow?" She went back to the ferry in a taxi, since the curves of the mountain road had grown much too sharp for motorcycle riding after we shared all that wine.

The next morning it rained, and after breakfast I listened to music in the library, leafing through an illustrated book on geography. I went for a jog, soaked in the hot tub, and went back to the library. The rain ended half an hour before Phyllis' ferry arrived. I gave the road 15 minutes to dry, took the second helmet and shot down to the pier. "I was so happy to see you standing there with the helmets," she said, clinging to me as we went through hairpin turns. "Riding is so much more fun than taking a taxi." After a gourmet dinner we lingered over cognac, and Phyllis had to tear herself away from the chocolate cake with berries when a taxi arrived to take her to the last ferry.

The next morning the sun was out. There was an amazing breakfast of fruits, jams, homemade cereals and breads, eggs, coffee, and tea. I ate more than I should have, but this was my last breakfast in the country. I had just enough time to ride to the far end of the island and walk through the World War II naval gun tunnels. Phyllis picked me up at the pier in Auckland. "I had breakfast with my granddaughter" she said. "When I told her about our dinners and the motorcycle, she said she envied me." I told her "Any time a teenage granddaughter envies you, it's a sign you're not living a bad life." I picked up my luggage at Phyllis' house, and she drove me to the airport.

1 Travel without Reservations

That spring I felt at loose ends. My latest book had gone to the printer, and I felt happy but also blue—that project, the new life which occupied most of my waking hours for the past three years—was out of my hands. The days felt mushy, melting into one another. I missed writing. On a flight home from a conference in New Zealand, I thought: "Let me fly back, drive from one end of the country to the other, and write a book about it." A few weeks later I called United to buy a ticket to Invercargill, the southernmost city in New Zealand, and a return ticket eight weeks later from Auckland in the north.

New Zealand lies in the South Pacific. Its shape and size are like those of Italy, only the boot is turned upside down and broken into two islands, with a three-hour boat crossing between them. The distance from the Bluff to the Cape—from the southern tip of the South Island to the northern tip of the North Island is under 1,300 miles, but because the country is so narrow, almost any point is within 40 miles of the sea. Since it lies in the Southern Hemisphere, the south is cold (closer to the Antarctic) and the north warm (closer to the equator). A northern exposure gets the sun, a southern exposure the cold wind. The seasons are reversed—July and August are the winter months, January and February the height of summer. The school year starts in February and ends in December.

When I told my friends in New Zealand that I was going to come in mid-July and stay through early September, several said it was crazy to come in winter. I persisted, and that decision worked out extremely well. The winters are very mild in New Zealand, and some days were so sunny and warm that I could wear a shirt outdoors, adding a sweater in the evening. Most tourist attractions were empty, and I found myself alone in stunning national parks that are filled in the summer.

In the middle of July, as a heat wave hit New York, I packed ski clothes and took a taxi to Kennedy airport. In Los Angeles I changed planes and flew for 12 hours across the Pacific to Auckland. Changing to Air New Zealand, I flew down to the colder South, where I could do a bit of skiing before driving up north. A year earlier I had returned from New Zealand only about 30 hours before the terrorist attack on the World Trade Center. This time I wanted to return to New York in time for the observance of the first anniversary.

I spent only one night in a hotel in New Zealand, using instead its excellent system of farmstays and homestays. Staying in locals' homes helped put me on the inside track. I had booked only my first night's stay in advance and improvised the rest of the trip, making up plans as I went. Most places are empty in winter, so locals are happy to see a rare visitor and show him or her around. In summer, good places get booked early. One homestay owner told me he earned 90 percent of his rental income in just three months, December through February.

Independent travel demands taking care of many practical details—tickets, accommodations, meals, cars, sightseeing, all with enormous ranges of options. A section in the back of this book, "The Practical Traveler," lists some of my favorite choices. I didn't tell any of the commercial operators I was writing a book, and they treated me just like anyone else. I traveled just like any other single traveler, but kept my eyes open and noted everything I saw.

2 Across the Ocean from the South Pole

On the flight from Los Angeles to Auckland I was reminded that the population of New Zealand is surprisingly small for such a large country. Its land area equals that of England, but while the UK is home to 55 million people, New Zealand has just three million. Whenever you talk with someone, you often find mutual acquaintances. My seat mate insisted on telling me his life story (born poor in England, got lucky, made quite a bit of money, quit while he was ahead, moved to New Zealand). Enjoying the anonymity of two strangers on a plane, he complained about his wife and kept talking about his transoceanic extramarital affair, which made him into a very frequent flyer. He even offered to fix me up with his girlfriend's girlfriend. When he went to the bathroom I turned off my reading light and put on noise-suppression earphones. When I woke up before landing in Auckland we talked again, and he asked whom I was going to see in New Zealand. Imagine his shock when he realized that one of my friends in a small New Zealand town was his neighbor! He blanched, then turned red, and swore me to eternal secrecy.

A sign at passport control in Auckland—"To deliver the best customs greeting experience in the Pacific"—plunges the visitor into the essential niceness of the country. A yellow line is painted on the floor at a distance of two feet from the luggage carousel, asking visitors to stand beyond it so that everyone can clearly see his or her luggage. New Zealanders' practicality and willingness to cooperate are apparent within your first minutes in the country. Phyllis was waiting for me at the gate—she came to say hello and take some of my luggage. We hugged, she loaned me a cell phone for the trip and drove me to the domestic terminal. Having a cappuccino with biscotti, I watched high dark windows light up as the sun rose across the green expanse of the fields. Seeing the blue bay beyond the runway, I finally knew I was in New Zealand.

Auckland, the largest city in New Zealand, is near the top of the North Island, and it took two Air New Zealand flights to get to Invercargill at the bottom tip of the South Island. Above South Island, the larger and less populous of the two, the pilot turned slightly to the left, showing a magnificent panorama of the Southern Alps on the right. Row after row of snow-covered peaks rose up from green valleys towards the sky. As the plane descended, I kept trying to see Mt. Hutt, where I had skied with my son on his first trip to New Zealand eight years ago, but couldn't make out the ski fields.

In the domestic terminals a rack of fresh magazines stood by each gate, allowing you to take what journals you liked and leave them on your seat upon arrival, where flight attendants collected them and put them back on the racks. I could not imagine such a system working in too many other parts of the world, where stealing freebies is the norm. The farther I got from New York, the smaller the planes were and the more homey the announcements. In a twin turboprop from Christchurch to Invercargill the captain announced "Hello, ladies and gentlemen, boys and girls. A few words about safety, and then enjoy snack service from Gary and Jimmy." In the Invercargill airport I stopped in front of a sign that was a clear indicator I was near the edge of civilization: "Four minutes to the world's most southern McDonald's."

My fifth and last flight of the day took me to Stewart Island, a speck of land occupied by a national park off the southern tip of South Island. There was no security gate and I sat next to the pilot. We flew south across the Foveaux Straight which eagle-eyed Captain Cook, making his first circumnavigation of New Zealand, had missed in bad weather, thinking Stewart Island was a peninsula. A grass airstrip was cut into the hillside, where small planes land uphill, shortening their run, and take off downhill, with heavier loads. At the bottom of the strip sat an empty shipping container that served as a waiting area in bad weather. The pilot unloaded our luggage and a waiting van took us into town, past a sign reading "Oban, population 350." With seven passengers on the flight, our arrival had just increased the population by two percent. I was as far away from New York as I was going to get. A huge rubber band was stretched to the max. My journey through New Zealand had begun.

Doug, the lodge owner, waited for me in the car. Throughout this book I use real names, except for descriptions of two visits. Most people in New Zealand are on a first-name basis—young and old, high and low. A respectful friendly informality is the mode of the land. When Helen Clark, New Zealand's prime minister, visited Stewart Island, she was introduced at a public meeting as Helen: "Good to have Helen here... And now Helen will tell us..." When one of her handlers chided the introducer that he should have used the last name, it was seen as uppity and out of touch.

Stewart Island was the only place on my journey where I made an advance reservation from New York. I had several preferences during this trip. I preferred farmstays to homestays, small places to large, and also any place whose write-up mentioned its owner's local knowledge or interest in history. All factors being equal, I chose more upscale places. On Stewart Island I wanted to stay at a one-room homestay run by the captain of a local water taxi, a fifth-generation islander. I found him on the Internet and called, but he and his wife were off the island until mid-August, taking advantage of the slow season. As a backup, I made a reservation at the best lodge on the island, which had six rooms and a Web site with beautiful photos.

Oban, the only settlement on Stewart Island, appeared dowdy—cheap construction, mounds of trash, dead motor vehicles by the sides of houses. The locals walked around with vacant faces, and when they recognized each other they made little hand signs, moving only their wrists. An outsider might as well be made of glass. We climbed to the lodge past its own trash heap. The rooms were small, with cheap plastic fixtures. This aloof island was absolutely unlike the New Zealand I knew from all my previous visits. The lodge had looked quite different on the Internet—whoever built Doug's Web site must have had a great way with Photoshop. I told him my plans had changed and I would be staying for only one night instead of two. The ability to make quick decisions is essential for independent travel. I did not regret starting on Stewart Island, but was not going to linger there.

Doug sat me on the couch and spread a worn map on the coffee table to review the island's history and geography. First came the sealers, then the gold diggers, then the lumbermen. The government planned to subdivide the island into lots of 80 to 100 acres to sell as farms, but the rugged nature held back development until finally the island was made into a national park. The village of Oban was zoned at a quarter acre per house, but some rare birds in the park required 100 acres each to survive. I started asking questions, but Doug told me not to interrupt since he was a person of vast knowledge. His lecture, interspersed with island jokes, sounded very well rehearsed.

I put on sneakers, grabbed a map, and went for a hike, stopping for a bite at the town hotel, which locals called "The place of culture and entertainment." The menu was limited to beer, chips, and nuts, and I hit the trail without lunch. Small islands tend to go seedy all across the globe, with piles of cannibalized motor vehicles parked years ago by thrifty locals who use them for spare parts. Even in Singapore, so clean you could eat from the floor of the subway, there are abandoned vehicles on the tiny offshore island of Pulan Ubin. They rust, lying on their roofs, only a few miles from the streets where jaywalking could get you arrested. Stewart Island was no exception, and the yards and roadsides of Oban held large collections of long-dead cars and boats.

The trail was well maintained, signposted, and absolutely empty. Everything was green, but in the shade a white coating of frost covered green leaves. The day was windless, empty motor boats bobbed in quiet, sunny harbors. As the trail climbed into the hills, I stopped, feeling something strange. I realized that for the first time in months I was surrounded by total silence, except for the occasional cries of birds and the pulsing in my ears from a hard walk uphill. Strange plants surrounded the trail. One had the trunk of a small palm, ending in a flat, broad, translucent canopy like a green disk, so sensitive it trembled even in the still air, while thick long straw sprouted from the center and hung all around the trunk. Coming down on the other side of the hill I could hear the surf, and soon faced the ocean. In the yards of houses lay batteries of lobster traps that looked like big black boxsprings.

Two girls coming up from the beach stopped to chat for a minute, unafraid of a stranger. The surf was loud, the tide was coming in. The waves, at the end of a long run from the Antarctic, hit the beach and broke into sheets of fine mist which drifted inland, lit by the setting sun. Rock pools had great piles of kelp, a brown leathery seaweed with green-yellow stalks as thick as arms. The Maori, the native islanders who arrived here before the Europeans, used to make pouches from dried kelp. On the walk back to Oban I passed an all-terrain vehicle with a helmet in the basket and a wetsuit on the handlebars, the owner nowhere in sight. Coming from New York, I was paying attention to such things. You see something like this and know you're not in a high-crime area. Doug told me the only reason to lock a house on the island was to protect the liquor cabinet.

The lodge looked like a $30-a-night motel in Alabama, but it was at the top of every tourist book, which could happen only on Stewart Island. Doug put on a big smile but had a mean streak. A kaka bird that looked like a parakeet twitted about his terrace. Doug said it was endangered, and when I said it looked pretty happy to me, he drawled, "It'll quickly become endangered if it starts picking on my furniture." I worked on a computer in the lounge and watched the setting sun when Doug brought in his second guest—Gerd, a German professor. Doug sat him down, spread out his map on the coffee table, and lectured him on the island, repeating word for word what he had told me earlier that day. Gerd tried to ask questions, but Doug jerked his leash. It sounded like he was playing a tape, with the same jokes in the same places.

Facing the audience of two, Doug told us that he was an intellectual with a great sense of humor, while his wife was an esthetician. Margaret was a quiet, mousy woman who rarely left the kitchen. I knew that Oscar Wilde was an esthete and I used to be friendly with a professor of esthetics at the university, but I never met an esthetician. Doug explained that an esthetician was a person who made others beautiful—cut their hair and did their nails. I could not resist the temptation to ask Doug several questions about his background, pulling out of him that he used to be a butcher and failed at farming. Here was an Archie Bunker trying to impersonate Masterpiece Theater. Doug offered us drinks before dinner, and this was my one and only time in New Zealand I could not finish a glass of wine; it was so sour that I switched to beer, a more reliable beverage in the Archie Bunker household. I wolfed down a seafood medley with sides of snow peas, baked tomato slices, and kumara, a sweet potato. It was 7 PM and I had had nothing to eat since an omelet on United at 5 AM and a cup of coffee in the Auckland airport.

I had great company. Gerd, a professor of near Earth space physics from Bonn, was a great lover of birds who had come to Stewart Island to photograph them. He looked like an exotic bird himself—long-legged and long-armed, with a beaky nose. He had many interests and passions. We spoke about space physics, and he told me that the Earth was not quite spherical, but 21 km shorter along the polar axis, wider at the equator because of its rotation. We talked about our children. We talked about his father whom he never met, killed in 1942 in Russia. He told me about the logistics of climbing Africa's Mt. Kilimanjaro, where I thought of going next winter with my kids. Meeting people like Gerd is one of the great attractions of travel. We never could have met in our everyday lives, but here, in a lodge at the southern tip of New Zealand, with nothing but the ocean between us and the South Pole, we were enjoying each other's company.

SECTION
2

The South Island

3 The Wrong Side of the Road

The next morning I watched an explosive red sunrise, then walked down to the harbor with Gerd. We had chartered a fishing boat for half a day. Gerd wanted to photograph sea birds; I came along for the ride and to split the NZ$200 bill.[1] The wooden boat was boxy, with a coal-fired stove, and its fast-talking captain told us to call him Squisy. Short for Exquisite, must have been a local name. The sky became overcast and the waters turned choppy as we chugged out into the Foveaux Straight between the South Island and Stewart Island. Squisy loaned me a warm jacket and I stood right behind him, near a coal stove, peering at the horizon to prevent seasickness. Gerd went back to the open deck, snapping away at seabirds with his telephoto lens.

Squisy turned on the fish finder, a great device owned by most commercial fishermen in New Zealand. He stopped the engine, pulled out a deep plastic dish with pieces of fish and baited his hooks. He would throw a line overboard and immediately pull it back with one or two fish. Seagulls began to gather, and a few albatross flew in. They were a joy to behold—hovering above the whitecaps, diving and rising, hardly ever flapping their wings, just catching the air this way and that. Soaring, the albatross could easily chase the boat at 30 miles per hour but flapping their wings they could overtake it. They glided at an angle, the lower wing just a few inches above the water, but no matter how choppy the waves, that wing always stayed a few inches above the foam. Their reflexes were

---

[1]At the time of this journey, the New Zealand dollar was low, about 40 U.S. cents. NZ$200 = US$80.

amazing. As they soared, their wings, many feet wide, swung right and left, but their bodies always stayed vertical, bellies pointing towards the water.

Squisy started throwing the fish he caught to the birds, who pirouetted, screamed, and fought. He was really a good charter boat operator. Gerd went into high gear clicking away; I took a few snapshots and wondered who had more fun—the birds with their fish or Gerd with his camera. I enjoyed the show but kept glancing at the horizon to keep myself in balance. By and by Gerd grew pale, asked me to tell Squisy to turn back early, then asked me to hold his camera. He got seasick and recovered only after we tied up at the pier.

We found the island abuzz—two cops had flown in from Invercargill and were writing tickets. Doug's daughter got a $75 fine for not wearing a seatbelt and $200 for an expired registration. Since none of Doug's cars were registered, he was grounded. The island had its own cop, but he never wrote tickets. "He's got to live there," said Doug with a nasty grin. Since the lodge was cold, Gerd and I went to the museum—two rooms of local memorabilia—and then found a bar that served lunch. The cops from Invercargill ate at the next table with local officials. The mood in the room was not happy. I tried to talk Gerd into joining me on the trip for the next few days, but he had his own plans. He was going to try to photograph the kiwi bird.

America has its bald eagle and New Zealand has its kiwi, a flightless brown bird. Some locals are as enthusiastic about kiwi as rugby, which is practically a national religion. The kiwi had been brought to the edge of extinction by an A-to-Z list of introduced predators, from domestic cats to weasels. A young kiwi can protect itself only by hiding, and when it grows to about twice the size of a chicken it can also run. There is something touching in this love for a flightless nocturnal bird (Stewart Island is the only place where kiwis may be seen during the day). New Zealanders track kiwis from the air, protect their habitat, kill their predators, and slap their image on every imaginable consumer item. I told Gerd that I had already seen a dozen kiwis the day before—on airport mugs, T-shirts, postcards, books, towels, clocks, pendants, you name it. I was not going to stay at Doug's lodge and hike for hours for an off-chance of seeing another one. Gerd walked me to the ferry, we shook hands and promised to stay in touch. From the deck I could see him walking down the trail, hunching slightly under his day pack, headed towards the birds at the waterline.

Many ferry passengers were returning fishermen, and when two fisheries officers came to distribute stickers for measuring legal fish length, I asked for one for my kitchen. The Foveaux Straight Express was a serious little boat, propelled by two 700 horsepower V8 engines. The chop was so strong I couldn't read during the crossing and watched the horizon again to avoid seasickness. We pulled into Bluff, a town at the southern tip of the South Island and the home to Bluff oysters, one of New Zealand's great delicacies. I planned to stay there since it looked beautiful on the Internet, but an object came into view that no Web site showed—a huge aluminum smelter whose towering smokestack dominated the landscape for miles. I changed my plans, caught a shuttle to the Invercargill airport, and rented the largest car I could get on short notice, a Toyota Corolla with a stick shift.

Most American rental car companies push optional insurance, which can easily add 50 percent to the rental price. The agents are trained to scare people into buying it despite the fact that most credit cards provide excess insurance at no cost. Here, in New Zealand, the sales pitch was mild and almost apologetic, and the Avis agent drove me back to the terminal to pick up some brochures and maps. It was getting dark, I wanted to hit the road, but did a quick spin through the few lit blocks of Invercargill's downtown. Its main attraction was a three-story former water tower. For a dollar you could get a key from a store next door and climb to the top. The town was essentially a supply depot for the surrounding farms. Its population was dropping when the city council came up with an ingenious scheme to pull in young people—by offering to pay the fees of any student who came to the local branch of the university.

I hit the road to the Catlins, New Zealand's newest national park, between Invercargill and Dunedin. The little Toyota handled like a dream, steering like a bicycle, but when I hit the brakes they gripped and all the brochures on the passenger seat flew to the floor. The passenger seat, of course, was on the left, the steering wheel on the right. Most of the Pacific drives on the left, which does not take long to learn. I had avoided driving on the left for years, until one night in Singapore a good friend, an old Chinese gentleman, picked me up at the hotel and drove us to dinner with his daughter at the Marine Parade. His night vision was terrible—he kept missing turns and hitting the curbs. It was so painful to watch him drive that I offered to take the wheel, and have been driving on the left ever since. Driving on the left is easy when you go with traffic—the left lane is slow and you pass on the right. Even intersections are easy, as long as you follow other cars. Difficulties arise when you drive up to an intersection alone at night and must think where to turn. The worst challenge is pulling out of gas stations or driveways. After doing it automatically for years, you must concentrate and think how not to turn against the traffic in a left-driving country.

I called the Catlins Farmstay on the cell phone after picking up the car. Murray told me his wife was out for the evening, but I could come; they were completely vacant. He asked for my name and gave me directions. It took some getting used to the fact that in New Zealand they never ask you for a credit card to hold a reservation. After getting lost a few times in the dark I found myself on a dirt road with herds of sheep behind wire fences and brown cows chewing cud. Whenever a high beam of light hit a flock of sheep, it looked like a small blue lake, the light reflecting in sheep's eyes.

The farmhouse was comfortable and neat. As a child in Russia I learned to expect poverty on farms, but here in New Zealand farmers lived very well. Murray was a stocky man in his sixties, with a friendly smile but few words. He showed me to a cozy room and turned on the space heater and an electric blanket. On my entire journey through New Zealand, staying in places that ranged from baronial to spartan, I never saw a house with central heating. The winters were so short and mild that central heating made no sense.

Murray's living room was lined with comfortable couches, family photographs were everywhere, a fire blazed at one end of the room, and a large TV played quietly in the other. Murray explained that his wife was away in Dunedin and offered me a beer or a cup of tea, but I just wanted to sit back and warm up. I drank in the warmth after Stewart Island, the boats, the drive in the dark. Murray went into the kitchen to make himself dinner and asked whether I wanted venison or lamb, but I was not hungry. We sank into comfortable couches, Murray with a plate of food on his lap watching the TV, me with a laptop near the fire.

There was the sound of car tires on a gravel driveway and Murray's wife and daughter-in-law came in. After another friendly offer of a drink, I got a cup of tea, and the four of us sat between the fire and the TV. I finished working on the computer, they caught up on family affairs and we chatted—about the history of their farm, their daughter-in-law's forthcoming trip to Germany, my plans to see the countryside. An easy companionable feeling hung about the room, hospitable and genuine. They asked me about my previous night's stay, and I told them of Archie Bunker with his esthetician wife. It turned out that Murray had gone to elementary school with Doug—New Zealand was indeed a small country!

4 Penguins, Pints and Pioneers

I woke up under a fluffy comforter and watched the sun hit the canopy of the forest on the hill across the road. Murray had been shifting cattle for several hours, but came to join me for breakfast. June's freshly baked blueberry muffins were the best I had tasted in my life—small, crunchy on the outside, with pools of moist, rich blueberries near the bottom. I was planning to shoot straight to Dunedin, but liked it here and asked June whether I could stay an extra day. By the time I finished working on my computer and checking e-mails the day had turned grey and cool. June marked up my map with places to see, gave me a banana, and I hit the road. The first stop she recommended was just a couple of miles away, at the neighbor's wool shed, where a traveling team was ultrasounding the sheep.

Raising sheep for wool, meat, or both is a major industry in New Zealand. The animals are raised in a natural environment, and most mountainsides have been turned into pastures. The lives of sheep farmers are dominated by the annual cycle of shearing, lambing, and weaning. A ewe (female sheep) normally carries one or two lambs, with twins requiring more food. If you put all ewes into a paddock whose rich grass is good enough for twins, those with single lambs will get big and fat without any return to the farmer. If you put all ewes into a more rocky, poorer paddock, perfectly sufficient for the those with single lambs, the twins will be born small and weak. To use pastures more efficiently, it pays to know which ewes carry a single lamb and which carry twins, and put them on different pastures.

Years ago farm service people began setting up ultrasound stations for sheep. A pulse of sound, harmless to the sheep and its fetus, is sent into the sheep's belly and a trained eye can tell from its reflection on the computer screen whether the ewe has one or two lambs. Pregnant women go to doctors' offices for an ultrasound, but pregnant sheep get house calls. A team comes to the farm with all its equipment in a pickup truck. The service is impersonal and rushed, but it cost only 50 cents per ewe (less than 25 U.S. cents). With thousands of sheep, the total bill can be high, but the farmer saves money by giving less feed to the ewes with single lambs and more efficiently managing his pastures.

Four guys were standing in the mud by the truck, drinking tea. I told them I was a physician from New York, and asked to see their operation. I told them the last time I saw ultrasound in action was when my ex-wife was pregnant. They invited me into the paddock, where two of them funneled the herd down a narrow chute. The ultrasound operator sat at the far end under a tarp protecting his machine from the drizzle. The fourth guy stood opposite him with a can of orange spray. Each ewe running past the operator was momentarily locked in a pen and a hand-held scanner shoved under its udder. The operator glanced at the image on his screen and called out a number. "One" meant the sheep could be released. "Two" or "three" got the ewe an orange dot sprayed on her back, while a barren ewe got orange spray on her muzzle. Afterwards the farmer could separate his ewes into two mobs (herds). Those carrying a single lamb were sent to poorer pastures, while those with twins or triplets got better feed. Those who were dry (not pregnant) went on the truck—a farming euphemism for being shipped to the slaughterhouse.

The young man with the scanner told me he had been doing this for two years and could scan over 200 sheep an hour with only a 2 percent error rate. He was in awe of his boss, who had been scanning for 10 years and could process 600 sheep an hour. A few weeks earlier the two of them, working two stations, had scanned 8,500 sheep in one day. The shape of New Zealand, narrow and long, stretching from north to south, lends itself well to this type of work. The teams start working in the warmer north where ewes get pregnant earlier in the year, and move south with the weather. The southern end of the South Island was still cold, and pregnant ewes had several months to go before giving birth, while in the far North the lambing season was about to begin.

The herd owner drove up on his mud-splattered all-terrain vehicle, like a quad bike with fat wheels, several dogs barking from the luggage rack. I recognized Peter, the man who helped me find the farmstay the night before. "It is a numbers game," he grinned, explaining how he sorted his sheep into two mobs. "Sheep farming is all about maximizing assets." Each sheep farmer had

several dogs, essential for moving large herds. There were two types of dogs—
"hunt-away" dogs barked and chased the sheep, while smaller "eye dogs" gave
the sheep such an evil eye that they started running in the opposite direction.
With an eye dog working the front and the hunt-away dog raging in the back,
the sheep could be compressed into a tight flock and moved in response to the
farmer's commands. Farmers controlled their dogs by special whistles, but a
very good dog could be let alone into a mile-square paddock, assemble all the
sheep into a mob, and move them near the gate. I mentioned to Peter that one
of his sheep-herding dogs was not much of a runner, with only three legs, even
though it was a prodigious barker. He laughed and said that the young dog was
so hyper, he stuck one of its front paws into its collar to slow it down, an old
herder's trick. My camera warning light came on, and I returned to my farmstay to recharge the battery. June offered me tea with one of her heavenly blueberry muffins and played a few riffs on her accordion.

The history of Murray's farm was typical of pioneer farming. When he
got his land almost 40 years ago, it was covered with virgin bush that he cleared
for pasture. Some old tree stumps could still be seen on the slopes—they took
over 20 years to rot. The timber industry came to virgin land, and then moved
on. I remembered the photographs of a "timber railroad" on Stewart Island,
with rails made of wood, and bullock teams hauling large trunks on carts. Camera battery recharged, I drove off to McLean Falls—a fun drive on a twisty road,
shifting gears, gravel flying from under the wheels. There were three cars in the
parking lot and a sign: "Lock your car, including the boot [trunk]; hide your
valuables." I knew I was not in New York, where a busted trunk was a common
occurrence. The trail, built by local high school kids, had informational plaques
by many trees; it ended near a cascading waterfall with reddish water, full of
sediment from the mountains.

June had promised to take me to watch the penguins when they came out
of the water at 4:40 PM. Her timing was so exact that I asked whether she called
them for information. I used the free time to drive to the nearest tavern, over
10 miles away, to buy wine for dinner. The place was lively on an early Friday
afternoon, with people hovering at the bar and sitting at the tables, while a
woman read a book by an open fire. Most locals took their beer in two-pint
carafes with a little glass on the side. I ordered a pint and was immediately
drawn into conversation with a few regulars, eager to compare the relative mer-
its of the Southland (the southern area of the South Island), New Zealand as a

whole, and the United States. We agreed that the Southland was the best part of
New Zealand, that local beer was very satisfying, while most American beers
were thin and sadly lacking in punch and flavor. We agreed that breathing was
easier in the open spaces of the Southland, but that New York was not bad
either, benefiting from its ocean breezes. I was getting ready to leave after the
second pint, when a big fisherman with huge, tattooed forearms stood me a
third beer, pushing my consumption way above my norm. After some more
free-ranging conversation I reciprocated with a pint, declined the offer of a
fourth, and made for the door, trying to walk straight and feeling sorry to leave
this warm place.

Back on the farm, June knew the name of every person I saw in the tavern. She ushered me into her Saab and we drove to the Petrified Forest—
a beach littered with petrified remains of prehistoric trees. There was a sign
"These trees have been here for 185 million years—let's keep them this way."
The flat, wide beach, all rocks and petrified trees, bordered on a broad, blue,
cold ocean. As the surf hit the rocks, plumes of white foam lingered in the
air, and a tangle of black and brown kelp bobbed at the water's edge. It was
windy and very cold. Out of the surf emerged a pair of small grey penguins
who ambled towards the rocks. Upon sighting two humans, they froze in place
and stood staring at us until we finally left. Penguins can die of stress if a human
or a dog comes near them, a sign warned. Those mutt-sized critters needed
their privacy, their space.

We climbed back to the parking area on a cliff above the beach, and June
drove to her son's beachfront house. He farmed rented land, while her
daughter-in-law, whom I had met the night before, ran a backpackers' hostel.
No one was home—June's son was practicing for the marathon—and she
showed the place to two young backpackers who had just arrived—one woman
from Switzerland and another from Britain. It cost just $18 (less than nine
U.S. dollars) to stay in a bunk bed, with five bunks to a room. On this winter
afternoon, they were to have the beach and the house all to themselves. Before
we left, June and I took the laundry off the lines and brought it to the covered
porch in case it rained.

A neighbor had invited Murray and June for dinner and told them to
bring me along. A farmer, another marathon runner, cooked up a simple meal
that we ate in the kitchen, washing it down with two bottles of red. Talk centered on farming and there was a wonderful sense of neighborliness and trust.

After we had an apple pie baked by June and coffee, we moved to the living room, where I dozed off on a couch near the fire until Murray and June woke me up to drive home.

5   A Hot Tub for Sea Lions

Murray and June were surprised when I asked for Vegemite at breakfast. Throughout this journey people told me I was their first American guest to ask for it. My friend Tony had introduced me to this pungent, black, salty spread years ago in Sydney. It was invented by beer brewers looking for ways to sell the thick black goo left at the bottom of their tanks after the brewing process was finished. Scientists found it contained no alcohol but was rich with minerals and vitamins, and they made it into a spread called Vegemite. Generations of local kids grew up smearing it on their toast. I kept a jar of Vegemite in New York, but it tasted better in the Southern Hemisphere where it felt like such a local food. When I spread jelly on top of Vegemite my hosts jumped for the second time because no locals did it, and I introduced them to the American invention of the peanut butter and jelly sandwich.

My next stop was to be in Dunedin, a city founded by Scottish immigrants in 1848, the home of New Zealand's oldest university. At the time of the Otago gold rush in the nineteenth century Dunedin had briefly become the richest city in the country. I asked June to recommend where to stay. It was a mistake I repeated several times before learning that the recommended places were never as good as those I left. None of my favorite hosts sent me to a place that was better or equal, only worse. I kept repeating this mistake—stepping on the same rake, as they say in Russia—until I finally learned I had to do my own research on the Internet or use guide books and follow up with a phone call.

I hit the road, stopping for a minute to say goodbye to Peter, who was working near the wool shed, separating his color-coded sheep into three mobs. Tall, craggy, with a white beard, surrounded by sheep and dogs amidst the mountains, he looked like a biblical prophet.

I kept stopping for short hikes along the road to Dunedin. There are very few roads in New Zealand that would be called highways in the United States, cordoned off from the surrounding countryside, with limited entries and exits. The main north-south arteries, well paved and with reflectors down the median, usually have just one lane in each direction, with an occasional passing lane. All traffic slows down whenever a road passes through some small town, becoming its main street for a few hundred yards. You can pull off wherever you like, and since the country is very mountainous each turn opens a new vista of mountain peaks, the ocean, and paddocks with cattle, sheep, or deer grazing on the hillsides. Driving in New Zealand is more fun than going to the movies.

Trails for hikers began at the roadside and led into the wilderness. Their approach was announced on the road signs, and when you pulled into a parking area, there was another sign, describing each trail and estimating how long it would take to hike. New Zealand is a walker's paradise. A 10-minute hike to Lake Wilkie went along a narrow wooden boardwalk that jutted into the lake, just a few inches above the water. The observation platform was flooded by an inch of water, and I was glad to be wearing waterproof hiking boots. It felt odd to be standing there in bright sunlight, surrounded by nothing but water, without out a human being in sight, just a few days out of the bustle of New York. It would have been a perfect scene for a crime, I thought, but this was New Zealand, and it was very safe.

At another stop I walked through a 900-foot-long, dark, abandoned railroad tunnel. It took 70 men two years to build it, using shovels and wheelbarrows at the end of the nineteenth century. They were local farmers who lived in the wilderness and needed a cash income. The project cost 9,300 pounds sterling, slightly over budget, but then sawmills moved on and the railroad closed the line.

I lunched on spicy green mussels and dark beer in Owaka, then drove to Suret Bay to take a look at a sea lion colony in the dunes. A spit of land protected a shallow bay from the ocean. As I walked on the sand in warm sunshine, a pair of sea lions played in the water further down the beach. I realized they were heavily into each other, like a couple in a hot tub. They would pop up their heads, rub their faces, playfully bite one other, then drop back into the water with their flippers whipping up foam. I looked at the sun and the dunes, then tested the water, and thought of my own hot tub at home. I decided the seals had a much better view, while I had a much more pleasant temperature. Trying to cut back to the car through the dunes, I beat a hasty retreat after a hissing grey sea lion rose from the grass to menace me. At the parking lot two men told me of having been chased by a sea lion; they escaped by climbing into the trunk of someone's pickup truck. This was New Zealand—up close and natural.

I drove past Cannibal Bay (named for its original inhabitants) to Jack's Blowhole, named after one Bloody Jack, a Maori chief. Like many attractions in New Zealand, it is on private farmland, with a sign admonishing you not to bother the livestock and stay on the trail. The path led me to a vertical drop of a couple of hundred feet to a rocky cove below. I tried to look down, but kept a respectful distance from the edge, feeling a strong wind pushing me in the back, towards the abyss. There were no guardrails. A warning sign at the beginning of the trail absolved the owner of any liability.

My last stop that day was at Nugget Point, reached by a vertiginous drive on a narrow gravel road cut into the side of a cliff, again with no guardrails. I hiked along the spine of a ridge to a lighthouse and small observation platform. Seals played on the rocks hundreds of feet below, ocean surf pounded kelp against the rocks. The grey-blue ocean curved as far as the eye could see— there was no land between this point and Chile, on the other side of the Pacific.

My cell phone rang near Dunedin—it was David, a retired dean of the medical school at Otago University. He was a friend of Bay and Shona, two New Zealanders I had met years earlier. We had become good friends and on this journey they generously gave me several useful introductions. Shona had roomed at the university with David's wife who at the moment was in the hospital recovering from an appendectomy. I invited David to a "bachelor dinner" after he visited his wife.

The homestay with Peter was a bit farther from the town center than I expected, but I liked the large, vaguely Norman house. June spoke highly of Peter's painting, but I saw immediately that he belonged to a school of painting that specialized in little urchins with big heads and oversized eyes thoughtfully holding blades of grass, rusty antique trucks in sunny fields, and other such hotel art. David came by and we drove downtown for dinner. He ordered a bottle of very satisfying Pinot Noir from a vineyard near his country house on Lake Hayes. I always enjoyed watching New Zealanders order their wines on the basis of local geography. We polished away a dozen Bluff oysters, then a second dozen before starting on the main course.

David told me about medical education in New Zealand—it took six years after graduating high school to qualify as a doctor. There was one year of general studies, two years of pre-med, then three years of clinical studies. The graduation rate for those who started their second year was 95 percent. The Otago University medical school accepted about 130 locals and 30 foreigners each year, most of those sponsored by their governments, often from the Pacific islands, Malaysia, and Kuwait. Locals paid $10,000 a year (less than $5,000 U.S. dollars), foreigners $35,000 (less than $17,000), and David figured that the real cost to the University was closer to $40,000. The training was excellent, the degree recognized through out the British Commonwealth, and many young graduates left for higher earnings abroad.

Dunedin was a university town, with students making up 15 percent of its population of 100,000. It was a pleasant and inexpensive city, with annual living costs for a student, including room and board, estimated at about $10,000 to $12,000 ($5,000 U.S. dollars). The streets and cafés were full of young people—the city felt young and energetic. It was so compact that David had a 10-minute rule—any place had to be within a 10-minute walk, or else it wasn't worth going. He drove me up the hill, I opened the front door with an ancient key, climbed into bed, and immediately fell asleep.

6 Stern Scotch Presbyterians

I thought of staying in Dunedin for two nights, but woke up thinking I would move on sooner—one was enough. Peter had a pleasant smile, but both he and his wife tried to run their homestay like a motel, with minimal personal contact. With June and Murray, I felt connected even when we sat together in their living room, with them talking among themselves and me working on the computer, but here the owners tried to minimize their emotional involvement. Later I learned this was fairly typical of homestays in the cities. I paid my bill, bought a copy of Peter's book on motorcycle touring, stowed my luggage in the car, and walked downtown in a silvery grey morning light.

Walking down to the Octagon, the central square of Dunedin, I rang up David and asked whether he wanted to go for a drive on the historic Otago Peninsula. Waiting for him to check with his wife, I stepped into the Anglican cathedral that loomed over downtown. It was nearly empty—parishioners at the Sunday morning service barely outnumbered the choir. My cell phone vibrated, and I stepped out—it was David. His wife was being discharged that day, sooner than expected. He apologized, but I told him that was the best reason to cancel our drive.

Dunedin is an old Gaelic name for Edinburgh, the capital of Scotland. The first group of settlers came from Scotland in 1848, led by the Reverend Thomas Burns. Like most areas in New Zealand, Dunedin was a planned settlement, with churches chartering ships. The early settlers were carefully selected, with free passage for the "deserving poor." One of the main differences between the settlement of New Zealand and Australia was that New Zealand was originally settled by religious farmers and tradesmen, Australia by convicts and their guards. England transported its criminals to Australia, but there was never a penal colony in New Zealand.

I walked up to the statue of Robert Burns in front of the cathedral—the great Scottish poet was the uncle of the Reverend Burns. It felt like meeting an old acquaintance, as lines of his poetry came into my mind—in Russian. When I was growing up in the Soviet Union, one of its best children's poets—Samuel Marshak—was a great admirer of Robert Burns and translated much of his work into Russian. During the Stalin era it was much safer to translate the works of a long-dead poet than to write an original work and be judged by political censors. An unexpected benefit of political oppression was that many talented writers and poets became translators and brought foreign classics to Russia (Boris Pasternak used to translate Shakespeare before he threw caution to the wind and wrote *Dr. Zhivago*). That is what led me to stand in the middle of Dunedin reciting Robert Burns in Russian.

The Dunedin Public Art Gallery in the Octagon opened at ten—its small eclectic collection was housed in a beautiful modern building suffused with light. The collection itself was very modest, but it was a pleasure to walk up and down beautiful stairways and through gallery passages, lingering inside the building. An exhibit on the social history of tea showed what happened after the leaves for this exotic beverage were brought to England at huge expense from India and China. At first only the very wealthy could afford it, but demand drove the market, so tea clippers were built. Gradually tea came within the reach first of the merely rich, then of the middle classes, and finally of the masses. The changes in porcelain and silver mirrored changes in tea consumption, as the service moved from solid silver, to silver plate, to pewter.

I walked down to Dunedin's railroad station, considered the finest stone building in New Zealand. Its contrasting light and dark stones, with balconies and balustrades, make it look sprawling and compact at the same time. Highways have killed the railroads, and today the only train still using that station is a twice-a-day scenic ride. It began to drizzle and I returned to the Octagon to meet with Len and Paul, local stock traders whom I knew from a financial conference I had organized several months earlier. They drove me to the Otago Peninsula just outside Dunedin. It was a pleasure to hand over the steering wheel, become a passenger, and just drink in the scenery.

There are two roads around the peninsula—one high in the hills and another low above the water. This circular drive could have been completed in 90 minutes, but it felt good to linger. We came in on the high road, with jaw-dropping views from the slopes. The peninsula is volcanic, its huge folds overgrown by grass and used for pasture. Rocks had been cleared from the pastures and turned into stone walls. They look like scars on a workman's hands, signs of a lifetime of hard work.

An albatross colony occupied the far end of the peninsula, but access to it had been recently limited for environmental reasons and we decided not to wait for a tour. We looked at a disappearing gun, one of several desultory coastal defenses in a country that has never been invaded. The gun—popping up to fire, disappearing underground to reload—was constructed after Britain became concerned with a Russian naval base in the Pacific port of Vladivostok in the late nineteenth century. In the end, Britain solved its problem by helping maneuver the Russians to war against the Japanese in 1905. A horrifying structure stood next to the gun—two tiny solitary cells for breaking the most recalcitrant prisoners. Built outdoors, these cells have no heat, no light, and only a stone bench for sleeping. I grew up in a country that had sent many of its most decent people, including some of my friends, to prison, so I rarely miss an opportunity to visit prisons that have been turned into museums.

We drove back on the low road, skirting coves and marinas. The stone seawall was built a century ago by prisoners doing hard labor. Paul and Len joked about the need to bring back old laws in order to fix up the wall. We had lunch on the waterfront, with waves breaking outside the windows and surfers in wetsuits carrying their surfboards on a windy winter day.

Paul and Len dropped me off in front of the Otago Settlers Museum. The area around Dunedin had been settled by Scotch Presbyterians whose strong stern faces still look down on modern visitors from the walls of the Early Settlers' Room. Otago was the farthest destination away from England, a three-month journey. Most emigrants had bid a final farewell to their relations, because only the wealthy could afford to go back to visit.

The new country followed England in many ways—first and foremost in being a country of laws—but it also rebelled against the parent country in very significant ways. There was a conscious effort to break down the class system. For instance, in England most streams were privately owned, and fishing was a rich man's pastime. In New Zealand all rivers and beaches were public property, even if they flowed across private land, with about 20 meters from the high water mark open to all, and no fishing license required. New Zealand was the first country in the world to give women the right to vote, it pioneered an eight-hour work day, and was the first country in the British Commonwealth to provide a universal old-age pension. I saw an exhibit about putting dental nurses into schools early in the twentieth century, to help families that could not afford dental care.

In the dusk I walked back to my car for an almost 200-mile drive to Queenstown. The road zigzagged through mountains, slowing down in villages, some of them with police cars parked by the roadside as a deterrent for speeders. I drove fast on the highways but slowed down to the speed limit in every village. At times I played my CDs, enjoying the contrast between the dark, unfamiliar road outside and the warmth of Chet Baker or Buena Vista Social Club inside the car.

I wanted to stay for a few days in Queenstown, one of my favorite ski areas, and looked for a place to stay on the Internet. I found Villa Sorgenfrei, which looked good on the web and had great feedback from previous visitors. I exchanged a few e-mails with the owners, and when I called, an attractive feminine voice at the other end said, "Hello, Villa Sorgenfrei, Micha speaking." I laughed. "Back where I come from Micha is a boy's name." She also laughed—"I can assure you I am a girl. Rounded in all the right places." I made a reservation, telling her I did not know exactly what day I would arrive, and then e-mails like this one started to arrive:

Alex,
Hope this amazing weather of clear skies holds for you. Holiday tips for
Invercargill—take the road past the airport to Oreti Beach (5 km). Look
at that expanse. In the Catlins: Curio Bay—petrified forest on the beach.
Porpoise Bay—$5 wetsuit hire. Waterfalls—can't remember the name.
Nugget Point—views. If schedule changes, don't hesitate to phone. We
look forward to meeting you then.
Cheers,
Micha and Klaus

I called Micha near Lake Hayes, and she guided me by phone (I often wonder how we ever found our destinations before cell phones). A slender, long-limbed blonde ran out to flag me into the driveway and hug me—Micha! The house looked like a very comfortable Alpine lodge. Klaus was German, Micha English, but they have been married for so long that she spoke with a slight German accent. She led me into their living room which had a fire roaring in a massive stone fireplace, behind fireproof glass. The heavy wooden beams came from a dismantled railroad bridge, but all furniture and fixtures and even the antique Mercedes Benz in the driveway came in a container from Germany.

Klaus opened a bottle of Pinot Noir—the wine for which this valley was becoming internationally famous. He and Micha had traveled all over the world and lived in several countries before discovering Queenstown and settling here. Klaus, a chef in a local hotel, was originally from Fulda in central Germany. He was surprised that I knew of that obscure town. That was because of the Fulda Gap—a break in the mountains through which Soviet tanks threatened to invade Germany, NATO's front line of defense. Klaus asked me whether I served in the American army. In the army, yes—but not in that one! I had compulsory military training in medical school in the Soviet Union and was commissioned as a junior lieutenant in medical service. Klaus told me he was a German paratrooper. We kept working on his bottle of Pinot Noir, sharing military stories from opposite sides of the Iron Curtain. Afterwards I ambled to a delightful bedroom. There were so many brushes, implements, and potions for taking care of one's hair that I wished I could grow some just to be able to use them.

7 Ski Trails above the Clouds

The sunlit kitchen had a stone floor, windows paneled in dark wood, and heavy Alpine furniture. Outside, the snowy bulk of Coronet Peak gleamed high above the valley. A single red grape graced the blood-red grapefruit. Yogurt was served surrounded by slices of five different fruits. An omelet cooked by Klaus was amazingly yellow, thanks to free-range eggs. He served it with a salmon sausage, raisin bread, and homemade jellies. The house felt like a work of art—each detail, from the furniture to the curtains to the silver to the food was just right and tasteful. I told Micha she was an artist. So much good stuff, so beautifully arranged, and so cheerfully served!

Micha pointed out the vines across the pond—the Pinot Noir we drank last evening came from their neighbors' vineyard. Wild ducks ambled across the green manicured lawn, pecking at the thin sheen of the morning frost. Klaus said they gathered in the morning outside the kitchen waiting for food, but left their droppings. The neighbors' dog loped across the lawn. I asked Klaus whether it could be used to chase away the ducks. No way, said Klaus. "If there is food, that dog will line up at the kitchen together with the ducks."

I put on my ski clothes and headed for Cardrona. I missed Nika, my younger daughter with whom I drove on this road so many times the year before. After graduating from Wellesley she fretted about not having a job, and I teased her that I was going to punish her for not working by dragging her to New Zealand and forcing her to go up and down snowy mountains. We had stayed near Queenstown for a week and had driven to Cardrona each day for her ski lessons. Now I zoomed past old barns where Nika had asked me to stop to take photos, past the paddocks with sheep and deer, past the fence where Nika had been frightened by an ostrich—the 10-foot black bird had spread its wings and charged the wire fence after she got near it with her camera. Some farmers use ostriches instead of guard dogs, but there were none this day—maybe they were in another paddock or perhaps already processed into low-fat ostrich steaks.

Near the mountain the asphalt ended and a dirt road zigzagged up the hill. The valleys in New Zealand are always green, and ski fields are up in the mountains because the higher you go the colder it becomes. You can walk out the front door of a house and see palm trees and roses, but after driving uphill for an hour you are on fresh snow. As the road climbed, the sky became cloudy, the road wet—I drove into a cloud. A few more switchbacks, and the car broke out above the cloud and into brilliant sunshine. The steep road became icy and I was shifting between second and third gears. I pulled over to the shoulder to take a few photos, but afterwards the wheels spun and the car would not go uphill. That light car was not the best vehicle for snow country. I waited for others to pass and when the road cleared rolled back downhill in neutral, touching the brakes and steering towards the clearings in the ice. Suddenly, the edge of the mountain road seemed very near. After some more slipping and sliding I found a clear spot, the wheels gripped, and I drove up to the top.

I bought a lift pass for the day and put it on top of the old one that had been hanging from my jacket since last year. I also rented "executive" skis and boots and paid for a half-day private lesson. I never carry equipment because most ski areas offer what they call executive level rentals for a few extra dollars, and that equipment is quite good, although I have never seen an executive in a suit and tie on the slopes. School holidays were over, lines gone from the lifts. Cardrona is the highest ski field in the area, with more reliable snow than Coronet Peak, Treble Cone, or the Remarkables. Because of its altitude, it has only natural snow and no snowmaking equipment. After the first few runs my physical memory returned, and I started picking up speed, lowering my body into turns, straightening up on the straightaways.

An hour later it was time for my lesson. My instructor, Kate, began by taking me up in an easy chairlift, watching me ski down, and diagnosing my moves. She set up the plan for the day—to work on my turns. "Press and roll" was the mantra for the day—press on the weight-bearing foot and roll the other foot, keeping both skis even and my nose over the weight-bearing ski. I was feeling increasingly comfortable under her tutelage, and by the end of the day followed her to slopes I could not have tackled in the morning.

Six years earlier, on my first visit to New Zealand, I had taken my 12-year-old son to Mt. Hutt to teach him to ski and to return to skiing myself after a break of almost 15 years. Most ski areas offer first-timers' packages—a lift ticket, an equipment rental, and a group lesson for one low introductory price. We picked up our gear, I helped Danny put on his skis, but he couldn't make a single step—he had never skied before. I felt a wave of rage rising within me, and was surprised both by the feeling and its intensity in the midst of a perfectly pleasant morning during a nice vacation. I figured out where the feeling was coming from—my father had taught me to ski in an experience filled with insults, fear, and the questioning of my masculinity. I thought I had worked through that relationship, but apparently not when it came to skiing. I knew that whoever taught Danny to ski, it wasn't going to be me—if I wanted to preserve a good feeling between us. I helped him take off his skis, carried them to where instructors assembled their groups, and promised to return in two hours.

I took my own group lesson and liked the instructor—Wanda. That was another shocker. Where I grew up, the idea of a man taking a sports lesson from a woman was unthinkable. I had never had a female coach. That afternoon I arranged private lessons for myself with Wanda and for Danny with another woman. He had half a day of private instruction each day, and by the end of the week we could ski together, trying different slopes, enjoying each other's company. Wanda, who lived with her parents on a farm below the ski fields, told us that she taught skiing on Mt. Hutt during the New Zealand ski season, late June through October, then went to teach at Mammoth Lakes in California from December through May. The next winter Danny and I had flown out to ski in Mammoth Lakes, but missed Wanda by about a week.

In the mountains it gets dark early and the ski lifts stop running soon after four. Driving to Villa Sorgenfrei I stopped for a beer at Cardrona Hotel, the first watering hole after coming down from the mountain. A year earlier, when Nika and I had first seen a mass of cars on both sides of the road, we thought there had been an accident, but no, it was a local tradition—to stop for a drink and a chat after a day of skiing. The hotel was over a hundred years old and looked ramshackle, with so much color and charm that it was featured in a nationwide beer commercial. There was a massive fireplace, and another big fire outdoors. A big cheery crowd in ski clothes milled and chatted, drinking hot wine and draft beer. The manager's father, in dirty clothes like a farm hand, came in from the construction site in the back and recognized me by my cigar—it was the same kind I had smoked the year before. He told me the hotel was being expanded from six rooms with bunk beds to 21 rooms with private bathrooms. It still looked cheerfully neglected, the yard littered with farm gear.

When I got back to Klaus and Micha's place, they had a guest, an old family friend who used to be an officer on a ship with Micha's father, but now worked as a diamond tool salesman. "If you don't have any dinner plans, please stay with us," said Klaus. We drank good wine and talked about everything under the sun, while polishing off Klaus's food, presented by Micha like a work of art—goose, trout, four or five different garnishes, local wines, and dessert.

8 Extreme Sports

The next morning was luminescent like the day before. Coronet Peak glittered like an enormous diamond over green fields and a soft blue lake. Klaus had a beautiful, pale wood rowboat that he invited me to use, but it was a bit chilly early in the morning. I was tempted to ski on Coronet Peak, but a warm front had come through the area and the day earlier I had met some people in Cardrona who told me so much snow had melted they called it the Concrete Peak. I decided to spend the day sightseeing and going to wineries.

Over an artwork of a breakfast, Klaus and Micha talked about the friendly and relaxed way of life in Queenstown. They had a friend who operated a hot air balloon and occasionally flew in for a cup of coffee, setting down in the field across the road. Klaus spoke of his concerns that their valley was being transformed. Million-dollar homes were going up where a few years earlier had stood only "baches"—cheap vacation shacks. One of Queenstown's most attractive aspects to Klaus was its egalitarian feel. When he had begun working here, he would go for a drink at the end of the day with his kitchen worker and his general manager, all on a first-name basis. He was now afraid that rising prices would change that way of life. A few years ago the valley had 9,000 residents, and now there were 7,000 building permits outstanding. Business leaders kept saying they would love to make Queenstown into another Aspen, Colorado, its sister city, but Klaus doubted that would be good for the locals.

I drove to nearby Arrowtown, followed the signs to an historic Chinese settlement, and stopped by a local cemetery where I noticed an old grave of someone named Methven. In a few days I was going to drive to the town of Methven at the base of Mt. Hutt, and thought it might be the same family. Near Main Street a video crew was setting up a shoot—a familiar sight in my neighborhood in Manhattan. This area, with its lakes and mountain roads, was especially popular for shooting car commercials. New Zealand received a boost among filmmakers after the success of *The Lord of the Rings,* shot by its New Zealand director on location in this country.

Driving to the wineries I saw a sign for a world-famous bungee jump and pulled into its parking lot. An observation platform was mobbed by a busload of American college kids watching a crew on the bridge strap together the legs of the next thrill seeker. Working on a bridge almost 150 feet above the river, they attached the bungee cord, guided the customer to the edge of platform, and encouraged him to jump. As I reached the front of the observation platform, a skinny young girl was having second thoughts, stepping forward and backward, with the bulky crew chief, dressed in black, holding her shoulder from behind with his gloved hand. The scene reminded me of a medieval hanging, except that the crew chief was a bit more patient than a hangman. There was the trembling victim, the executioner who had to make sure the business got done, and a crowd of onlookers yelling encouragement. Cords hanging from the platform and the tiny steps of the jumper whose ankles were strapped together reinforced the connection with the gallows. Once the body of a jumper stopped bouncing, it was lowered into the waiting boat below and laid out on a platform, like some unliving thing, a body taken off the gallows. Workers in the boat untied the feet, like helpers at the gallows untied the feet of the person who had just been hanged.

When I had gone to Queenstown a year earlier with Nika, I planned to sample many "extreme sports," for which the area is famous. We went skiing the first day, but I was hoping to talk my daughter into trying the extreme sports together in the days to come. Then we started reading local papers at breakfast in our hotel's sun-filled restaurant. News of the extreme sports were never on the front page, but the drumbeat of shocking news never stopped. That famous bungee jump took the face off an Irish girl, catching her head in the cord on the way down. In an interview, the operator blamed the girl for being too light to do the backward jump. I wanted to ask, "Didn't you take her money, sir, and stand with her on the platform." Then a world-famous jetboat ran into a canyon wall causing what they called minor injuries—a few broken arms. The driver lost control because the battery that powered his steering went dead. Oops! They closed the operation for a day to change batteries in all the jetboats. Whenever we drove into Queenstown, I was captivated by the sight of graceful parasails in the air, as people jumped from a cliff in the middle of town, in twin harnesses with their instructor, and glided gracefully to the ground. Then we read that the day before one of the instructors had dropped a teenage girl from the harness and she fell, breaking her spine and tearing up her intestines.

Those incidents were like pieces of a jigsaw puzzle that I had yet to put together. We took a gondola to the observation area on the cliff and a salesman came up trying to sell a parasail jump. When I asked about safety, he grew viciously angry—"If you're not gonna jump, don't bother me!" It wasn't me who initiated our contact. A woman working in the coffee shop told me the salesman worked for the company that dropped the girl. "I feel sorry for the pilot," she said. "He is so shaken now." We rode the gondola back down, past a bungee jumper having her ankles tied. There was mini-golf at the base of the cliff and the woman who ran it assured me they never had an accident. I paid and played a very pleasant round with Nika.

Then it came to me, a little slowly perhaps—the promoters of extreme sports told you how macho they were and how macho you could be, but they were money-making operations, with no risk of lawsuits. Some owners were rich, others operated on a shoestring, but none was financially responsible. We may love to complain about lawyers in the United States, but their lawsuits force insurance companies to demand proper safety measures. In New Zealand, however, there is no civil liability. You sign a release and take full responsibility. This freedom from lawsuits does make for a more vibrant society, but when you sign up for the "extreme sports' you put yourself at the mercy of an operator who has no lawyers to fear. The lack of external control makes commercial extreme sports a scandal waiting to happen.

After watching bungee jumpers from the platform I walked onto the bridge to see the operation up close. The crew chief turned around and asked whether I would be jumping. No, I answered. "Chicken, chicken, *ko-ko-ko*," he flapped his arms. This was typical behavior for an extreme sport operator. I had put my life on the line more than once, but always for a good reason and I certainly didn't pay for taking those risks. I asked whether it was his operation that took the face off that Irish girl. "Nah, not us, mate," he lied and immediately lost interest in me.

I drove from one winery to another, sampling Pinot Noirs. Klaus had told me that the discovery that led to growing vines in this cool valley was that a vineyard had to be on a mountain slope rather than on the valley floor. Whenever the valley was having a cold spell, cold air flowed down the slope, sparing the fruit. Before that they used to call in helicopters during cold spells to hover over the vineyards, pushing warm air down. I kept looking for a wine as good as the ones served by Klaus. One of the growers described his wine as having the flavor of a single malt scotch, but to my palate it tasted closer to saddle leather. I kept going on short hikes between visiting the vineyards—I walked down to the waterfall called Roaring Meg, then walked through the old gold works that Micha had recommended. The last winery at the end of the valley had good wine, and I bought their best bottle for Klaus and Micha.

In the evening we drank wine and ate local cheeses. Micha liked my bottle so much that instead of opening it she put a tag with my name on it and took it down into the cellar for my next visit. Klaus invited me to stay for what he called a simple meal but was in fact a gourmet experience. I enjoyed listening to his accent—he spoke highly literate English, but sounded Germanic because of peppering his speech with *mit* instead of "with" and *und* instead of "and"— "Alex, you go up the river *mit* the jetboat, *und* you'll see some wonderful sights." Klaus and Micha had a cat, Shimmers. At first I thought it was on opium— always puffy, with a perpetual half-grin, and an occasional moan. Gradually

I realized that Shimmers was a hard-working animal with an important role in the house. Klaus and Micha brought back carpets from the many countries that they visited and Shimmers made sure those carpets stayed in place. He moved from one carpet to another, following the sun throughout the day, and at night he held down the carpet in front of the fireplace.

9 Skid and Tow

In the morning Micha asked whether I had noticed anything unusual about my car. It did look a little strange, but I couldn't put my finger on it. She said that Klaus had washed it using his garden hose. The car had been splattered with mud from driving on country roads, and I joked that Klaus was ruining my image as a rugged driver of dirty cars. We had our last breakfast together— I couldn't figure out how Micha could find five entirely different fruits each morning, and the breads, cereals, and jams were always different, each one better than the last. I would have loved to linger, but had all of New Zealand ahead of me. We hugged, and I pulled out of the driveway, knowing with absolute certainty this was a place to which I would return.

The road ran west, towards the glaciers of the West Coast. New Zealand is the smallest big country in the world. Here you can ski in the morning in the middle of the country, then cross the continental divide and reach the West Coast in a few hours. It was equivalent to skiing in Colorado in the morning, then driving to the beach in Oregon in the afternoon. The road ran by the Cardrona hotel, and I stopped for a beer and a cigar. The room was uncrowded, the couch in front of the fireplace was empty, the skiers had not yet arrived. I could see the entry to a small gold mine through a window in the floor, but the real gold mine was a few feet higher—at the cash register. The ceiling was plastered with money from different countries. The manager told me that once every few years, after the ceiling became covered, they stripped off all the money, donated it to charity and started again. I brought a 100-ruble note from the car and, after the manager climbed on a short ladder to stick it to the ceiling, told him I would be returning to visit my investment.

I had a plate of fresh fish for lunch in Wanaka and read the local newspaper, lifting my head to gaze at the snow-covered mountains. A small, dark blue lake outside the window was the deepest in New Zealand. Kids were having a blast in a skateboard park, which looked strangely familiar. Its steps, sidewalks, and sturdy handrails reminded me of New York City, especially the area in front of the Public Library on Fifth Avenue and 42nd Street where local kids used to skateboard until the cops chased them away. Here I was, in front of New Zealand's deepest lake, watching a recreation of my hometown.

The road climbed through Mt. Aspiring National Park. Green and blue, the colors of New Zealand government forms, were all around me. The road was surrounded by green hills and blue lakes. That zigzagging road was an engineering marvel, but many bridges had only a single lane for both directions. First, you would see a sign to slow down and then another sign telling you which direction had the right of way. This system worked in an uncrowded country where people cooperated with one another. At the intersections, where in the United States a traffic light would be, in New Zealand you often came to a roundabout, here called a rotary. A roundabout was a more efficient means of speeding up traffic because no cars had to wait under a red light at an empty intersection. Many municipalities in the United States tried to use rotaries but saw an increase in accidents and went back to traffic lights because people tried to cut in front of each other. Trying to cut into a lane of traffic is considered bad form in New Zealand whose drivers move as smoothly through rotaries as across one-lane bridges.

All along the road there were short hikes to forests, waterfalls, and rivers, with well-groomed trails and signs about local geography and flora. Reading them felt like going through a museum of natural history, only outdoors. A breathtaking walk took me to Blue Pools, with a rope bridge over a river that swayed like something out of an Indiana Jones movie, except for a Department of Conservation sign—five persons maximum. After crossing the Blue River, its water the color of the bluest of eyes, the trail led to a natural pool where a mountain stream flowed into the river. Leaning over the barrier I could see fat brown trout, at least a foot long, leisurely flapping their tails against the current. Walking back to the parking area I met a cheerful blonde hurrying to the bridge and the trout pools. She was the only person I met on my hikes that day—I had this national park almost all to myself, but it was safe enough for an attractive woman to walk alone.

The road crossed the Gates of Haast—a mountain pass in the continental divide—and headed down to the West Coast. Soon I caught my first glimpse of the Tasman Sea. A sign at the beach read: "If you go west, you'll reach Australia in 1,700 km, but if you go South, there is nothing between you and the Antarctic. The full force of the Southern Ocean beats on these shores." The waves rolled onto the broad beach, which the early settlers used as their road. The red sun, setting in the ocean in the west, lit up the snow-capped mountains in the east, and for a few minutes their crimson flames made it look as if the sun was setting on both sides of the beach.

After sunset it became too dark for sightseeing, and I stepped on the gas. Micha had booked me into a homestay between New Zealand's two great glaciers, Fox and Franz Joseph. After passing Fox village I had to cross three valleys on a serpentine road. Within a few miles of my destination, eager to arrive, get out of the car and unwind, I momentarily lost my concentration while coasting along at about 50 mile-per-hour. A sign suddenly came into view warning of a sharp right turn with a 35-kph (20-mph) speed limit. I knew instantly that I would not be able to make that turn and hit the brakes. The wheels seized up and my little tin can of a car skidded straight onto loose gravel as the road veered right from under it. Grass, soft blow, bushes—I knew the car was about to roll into a deep ditch and gripped the wheel. The car slowed down, leaned sharply to the left, and stopped. I shut off the engine. It became very quiet. I could hear the gurgling creek. I slowly opened the door so as not to disturb the precariously balanced car and stepped out. The right front and left rear wheels were on the ground, the left front wheel was below the rim, with the right rear wheel up in the air. I could see the creek about 10 feet below.

Almost immediately a car with two girls stopped on the other side of the road. Are you hurt? Not at all. In a flash of enthusiasm they offered to tow me out, but the rope in their trunk was clearly not up to the task. My car was stuck in the waterlogged ground. The girls offered me a ride to Fox, but I preferred to stay and asked them to send me a tow truck. In the 45 minutes that help took to arrive only two other cars drove down that lonely stretch of road. Every driver, male or female, stopped to ask whether I was hurt and offered help. When I got cold and opened the door to get my ski jacket, I could feel the car bouncing slightly up and down. Had it skidded another inch, it would have rolled. I do not think I would have gotten hurt, but I would have probably totaled the car and lost at least a day dealing with Avis.

A long, bony pickup truck rounded the corner at which I skidded, made a U-turn, and backed up towards my car. Out stepped a tall bony man who stuck a yellow strobe light to his roof, locked his front axle, then came up to me with a length of cable. "How did you miss that pole?" he grunted, before wrapping the cable around the rear axle of my tiny car, getting back into his truck, and gunning the engine to pull the car from the edge. He then walked around my car and cleaned off the dirt where the left fender had plowed through soft ground. Getting on his hands and knees, he shone his high-intensity lamp under the car. He got up and growled "Damn, not a scratch," sounding very disappointed. "The fool got lucky," I said. "That will be $80, thank you." When I told my friend Tony about this a few weeks later, he laughed—cheap at twice the price.

Five minutes later I was at my homestay. A petite well-dressed woman in her early sixties came into the driveway, trembling. "My husband is not here." Her niece was staying with her upstairs, she said, and the guest room had a separate entry downstairs. It was as if Jack the Ripper had shown up unannounced on her doorstep. I had anticipated sprawling in a comfortable armchair and having a drink and a chat with a family, but now I was consigned to an isolated room. Suzie had to have known her husband would be away when she took the booking and it was her friend who had called on my behalf. Had I not been shaken by the accident, I would have turned around and driven away. Suzie led me into an attractive room, stressing how everything was organic and showing me the books to which her husband had contributed. "You will love these pictures," she said, and then added, "but one can only love a woman," and blushed. When she asked me whether there was anything I wanted, I asked for a beer and fell asleep.

10 Paddling under the Glaciers

The next morning the sun rose over a beautiful green valley, with not a single house in sight. Suzie's horses picked their way slowly through the dew on the pasture outside the window. The winter morning was warm enough that I wore only a shirt and sweater. Suzie invited me upstairs for breakfast, telling me her niece had already left for school. She laid out a beautiful all-organic spread of home-grilled cereals, freshly made yogurt, and exotic fruits, and I ate all her lychees. Suzie knew the area inside and out, had a rating for every guide and drew a surprisingly interesting day plan for me. She recommended a scientist who did private guiding, but he was away at the moment, and she sent me out with a professional kayaker for a private tour of the lake and river.

One of the great attractions of traveling in New Zealand is the easy availability of enthusiastic and intelligent people who serve as private guides at very modest rates. There are many people who love the area where they live and advertise their guiding services. They can show you around, teach you, share their enthusiasm with you, and when at the end of the day you hand them a credit card, the charge is surprisingly low, considering the value received. A few days earlier, half a day of private ski instruction with a complete equipment rental and a full day's lift pass cost me 140 U.S. dollars. This day, since I came alone and Wayne had a minimum of two persons per trip, I had to pay double, which was still under 50 U.S. dollars for half a day.

Wayne told me to hurry so we could catch the morning mist. I mentioned I was a rower, but he laughed and said that in a kayak I would be facing forward instead of backward. No prior experience was required—only a modest level of physical fitness. We carried two kayaks to the beach of Lake Mathieson and pushed off in an amazing silence. We were the only people on the lake, created by a glacier that pushed the ground 270 feet down before melting away. Mist swirled above mirror-like water. Ducks flew out of the mist and faded into it again.

"This is the best time of the day," said Wayne as we paddled quietly. He had a wealth of knowledge of local geography, flora, and fauna, all of which he eloquently shared. He explained that moisture-laden winds from the Tasman Sea hit the mountain ranges on New Zealand's West Coast, dropping an enormous amount of rain on the narrow coastal strip. They sometimes had two feet of rain a day, and a few years earlier they got five feet of rain within a 36-hour period. The geography is similar to Sierra Nevada, which drains the Pacific winds in the United States—only in California the coastal plain is broad, while here it was narrow, compressing the effect of the rain.

The water in the lake was so clear I could not tell where the air ended and the water began. As the mist disappeared, we crossed the lake and glided into the river that fed it. We could see every blade of grass, every pebble on the bottom of the river, even though the water was a brownish red from the nutrients carried from the mountains. The trees on both sides were overgrown with moss, creeping vegetation and lianas, like those in a tropical forest. Even on this sunny morning the trees and the bushes were laden with moisture, and bumping into the shore released a cool shower of dew.

The river became too narrow for paddling and we returned to the lake. Glacier-covered mountains crowded one shore, while the other was relatively flat, with lush green forests. The sun became hot, and we took off our sweaters. Neither Wayne nor I could find a verb to describe the movement of our kayaks across the lake. "Gliding" came to mind, but gliding produces some noise, like when you glide on skates. Here our movement was totally and absolutely silent, the water perfectly flat, reflections merged with reality. "It is hard to believe," said Wayne, "but this is a fairly typical winter day." He told me that in summer he took three groups of ten kayakers on the lake each day. This is how he earned a living, but his favorite way of showing the lake was private guiding with a single person or a very small group.

Wayne kept clicking away with his digital camera—a photo CD was included with the trip. He explained that it was unusual to have so many glaciers in such a temperate climate. The glaciers of Alaska were at 62 degrees latitude, but in New Zealand they were at 47 degrees, much closer to the equator. This was the only area in the world where a rainforest bordered a glacier. The beaches were just a few kilometers away. Sometimes in summer Wayne went skiing on the glacier in the morning, then surfed in the Tasman Sea in the afternoon. This was his favorite area in New Zealand—he loved the outdoors so much that he did not own a TV.

After we returned from the lake, Wayne recommended that I spend the rest of the day hiking to the face of Fox Glacier and then around lake Mathieson, timing my hike to arrive at the far end at sunset, about 5:30 PM. I drove back to Fox Village, up and down three mountain valleys, passing the spot where I had gone off the road the night before. The glacier trail was typical of New Zealand—well maintained, signposted, leading to interesting views, but not insulated from danger—you've been warned, mate! The streams of glacier melt forced me to jump from rock to rock, and I met a woman in dress shoes and then a man in low moccasins who could not hike the trail and had to return. The glacier melt was the color of dirty laundry water, grey from suspended particles of stone ground into dust. These glaciers used to reach the sea, but had become shorter and fizzled out in the valley due to global warming. At the end of the hike the face of the glacier looked like a pockmarked, high wall of ice.

A huge naked rock, hundreds of feet high, that looms over the glacier valley used to be covered by the glacier. The ice killed all vegetation, but when the glacier receded a thin film of red lichen (similar to moss) appeared on the rocks. Red lichen was followed by green lichen, then grasses, bushes, and finally trees.

An area cleared by a glacier went from red lichen to fully grown trees in about 150 years. A sign quoted the lines by a New Zealand poet who hoped that his words would be like spores of red lichen falling on inhospitable rock and rendering it into soil.

Driving from the glacier to the lake, I saw a woman walking with a backpack and pulled over to offer her a ride. She was a tourist from Germany, walking to the lake a few miles away. We drove and then hiked together to its far end, comparing travel notes along the way. From a bench on an observation platform we watched the mountain with its glacier change color from green and white to red, then to silvery grey as the sun disappeared behind the peaks. The lake reflected those colors like a mirror, the air was absolutely quiet, and the loudest sound in the wilderness was the click of a tourist's camera. In the dark we hiked back to the car and I invited Sabine for dinner. She was a student, making a career change in her 30s. She was a strict vegetarian, would not even eat fish, and we shared a vegetable stir-fry with nuts and a bottle of wine in the village restaurant. We kissed each other on the cheek, and Sabine walked to her motel, while I drove cautiously across three dark valleys, and closed the gate to the ranch before parking my car.

11 Crampons and Crevasses

Suzie invited me upstairs for breakfast, saying her niece had already left for school. Strange, I saw no cars other than Suzie's and mine the night before and I had been writing in bed since six in the morning and did not hear an engine. The green valley was flooded by soft sunlight, smooth pastures on all sides of the new, square, two-story earthquake-proof building; beyond the pastures were mountain ridges and glaciers. The table was beautifully set and laden with fruits and cereals, but Suzie, who seemed a little less afraid today, asked me to wait while she cooked up a storm in her modern kitchen, separated from the dining room by a low partition.

I went to the window and picked up a set of binoculars from a flat pillow on a wide low windowsill. Many houses in New Zealand had binoculars by the windows because the views were intoxicatingly attractive. I followed the lines of glaciers, the horrible scars they left on mountainsides centuries earlier; the fresh growth of trees. The pattern of rock crevasses, pine groves, and sheets of ice was more hypnotic than the images in a kaleidoscope.

Suzie brought out a large organic frittata, its multicolored vegetables shining through the brownish crust, puffy from the moisture trying to escape. A trail of delicious vapor followed in her wake. I urged Suzie to join me and as she tucked into her slice, I looked again at the table—different fresh fruits from the day before, a different yogurt, different jams and condiments—only the massive glass jars of homemade cereals had not changed. I resisted the temptation to try them all.

Suzie was shocked to hear that the day before I had left a small deposit with a guiding company at Franz Joseph to go heli-hiking today. Heli-hiking involved flying to the glacier in a helicopter and walking on the ice with a guide. She pursed her lips and intoned that her husband thought Franz Joseph guides were not up to snuff on their safety training. He trusted the Fox people whose training was fully in gear with the Department of Conservation. Later I found there was a bit of a struggle between the DOC people and the entrepreneurs in many national parks, and Suzie's husband used to work for the DOC. That morning, however, she had me concerned about safety just enough to ask her to call Fox and switch my reservation. That little birdlike woman certainly knew how to move the world to her liking.

Driving to Fox, up three mountains and down three valleys, I again passed the turn where I had gone off the road. At a sharp turn above the ravine on the other side of the road stood a foot-high white cross with a fresh flower garland. It could have been mine. I could feel the terror of some kid somersaulting down the cliff and the grief of parents for whose son the Earth stopped just a few feet short.

At the heli-hiking place there was a minute of easy New Zealand formalities—credit card, last name, sign the disclaimer. At Franz Joseph they had asked for the name of the next of kin, but not here. A dozen of us got on a bus for a short ride to the helipad which looked like the backyard of someone's house. We had two guides: a wiry older guy who had seen it all, and a young strong kid with an ice axe who was in his first week on the job. They told us to tuck in any loose clothing before flying and issued hobnailed boots. I never knew what those were until that day, even though I had often read about foreigners invading Russia in hobnailed boots and going back dead. They had thick soles studded with nails whose ball-like heads stuck out of the sole, providing a firmer grip on the ground.

A Squirrel helicopter is the workhorse of New Zealand tourism, a little fiberglass ball with a rotor and a tail. It takes to up six people at a time, including the pilot—three in the front seat and three in the back, packed tighter than in a subcompact. It took three flights to get our group on the ice. The eager beavers went on the first flight, the apprehensive hung back, and I stayed with them because the older guide, the more interesting of the two, was going on the last flight. He sent the kid up on the first flight with orders to chop steps in the ice with his axe.

Tourists swap stories, and here I heard for the first time the one that would keep coming up until my last week in the Pacific. The year before, the captain of an Australian dive boat had accidentally left two divers on the Great Barrier Reef. The next day the company noticed they were missing two air tanks and had an extra car in their parking lot. Rushing back, they found only a few bits and pieces of gear on the bottom. The sharks must have gotten the rest. From my experience of traveling with children, I suggested it would have been a simple matter to establish a chain of safety, to make sure that each person was responsible for someone else. Colin, the older guide, came out to the helipad and changed the topic.

The helicopter took off more softly than an elevator in a tall Manhattan building and floated above the trees on an invisible air pillow. Colin, sitting next to me, said that the flying style depended on marital status. Our pilot, a young Canadian, had two babies, and flew very gently and carefully. Single guys were more likely to be cowboys. We flew over a waterfall—the melt from Victoria Glacier, one of 200 in this national park, had nowhere to go but cascade from a high cliff. I snapped photos—Colin had warned to be quick on the trigger, joking that the nine-minute flight lasted about 30 seconds. As we came in to land, the earlier arrivals looked like miniature chess figures on ice. We hopped out and ran forward like paratroopers in a war movie, then crouched when the rising machine sent down a sharp blast of wind.

Once the *twock-twock-twock* of the helicopter faded away, we were surrounded by total silence. We were cocooned by the blue and white ice below, grey and green mountains on the sides and the blue sky above. The guides handed out crampons—small metal plates with inch-long stainless-steel teeth, which we attached with leather straps under the arch of each boot. When you step flat down, crampons bite the ice and hold, allowing you to walk on sheer ice, even when it is at an angle. I felt like a fly on the glass and expected to slide down any moment, but kept walking.

The glaciers form when snow at high altitudes compresses into ice under its own weight. A glacier can be a mile thick, and its enormous weight causes the bottom layer to melt, lubricating the glacier, and helping it slide down the mountain. Alaskan glaciers move about an inch a day, but glaciers in New Zealand are smaller and faster, moving up to 15 feet a day. Fox moves about three feet a day, causing the ice to buckle, so our makeshift helipad demanded constant maintenance. Glaciers are quick to respond to changes in weather. In 1990, after several years of high snowfall, Fox glacier gained 200 meters (almost 600 feet) in thickness, but by now it had receded to its previous size. We know this for a fact, said Colin, from our helicopter pilots—they land in pretty much the same area, but their altimeters have gone from 700 meters to 900 meters and back.

The Fox glacier was a huge sheet of ice, several kilometers wide and hundreds of meters deep, sliding from the top of the mountain towards the sea, buckling and cracking, grinding pebbles into dust, producing ice arches and crevasses. In the middle of the day, with the sun high in the sky, innumerable little springs appeared on the surface of a glacier and ran into crevasses, producing vortexes—a complex, shifting system of plumbing that froze at night. "The glacier had to be lubricated to move down," Colin kept repeating, sensuously smacking his lips whenever he said "lubricate."

He pointed his arm to the sea and said, "There is a landmass on the other end of the Tasman Sea that produces a lot of hot air," and the Australians in our group howled. "That warm air blows across the sea, picking up moisture, hits the Southern Alps in New Zealand and is forced up, rapidly cooling off, generating snow, producing glaciers. These glaciers exist because of a unique combination of warm, moisture-laden wind and high mountains close to shore. There is only one other place on Earth where glaciers exist at such low altitudes—in Chile. What makes the local picture so different is that glaciers are bordered by temperate rainforests. You can go on a hike in the rainforest and cross onto glacier ice. Last year a hiker took a shortcut across the glacier in hiking boots without crampons, slipped, and fell into a crevasse. They found his remains a month later—nobody knew where he went, there was only an abandoned tent in the campground."

Colin and the younger guy carefully shepherded us between crevasses. "They become narrower as you go down," said Colin, "and you get wedged in.

We haven't lost anyone yet; let's not make today the first day. Still, if you have to go down, make sure you go head first—we'd like to be able to reach down and remove our boots and crampons. The company is very particular about that." We took turns photographing each other in front of ice formations. Colin was enjoying himself, sending the kid forward to chop steps in the ice with his axe and regaling those of us in the back with his tales. He had come to the valley with his wife 10 years ago, ran an auto service station, then sold it. A friend had asked him to guide for one season—and now this was his eighth year.

Colin said that a heli-hike was much better than a plain hike—you were whisked immediately to the glacier instead of spending an hour walking from the parking lot and then an hour back. The ice formations were much nicer at higher altitudes—the caves, the arches, and the springs. A foot hike cost about NZ$50 (less than US$25) and a heli-hike NZ$150–200 (under US$100 for half a day). After listening to him I decided that if I ever came back in summer, I would take a two-day heli-hike—they helicopter you in, you hike to a hut above the glacier, overnight there, hike some more the next day, then helicopter out. Colin said that the colors when the sun went down were just incredible, and all night long you could hear the creaking and breaking of the ice sheets below.

At the helipad I turned in my hobnailed boots and received a breathlessly phrased certificate. "This is to certify that Alex heli-hiked the fantastic Fox glacier, whirled over the rainforest and looming ice towers, mastered the art of cramponing, teetered on 1,000 feet of solid ice, squeezed through ice tunnels, peered into bottomless crevasses, subjected his leg muscles to the wearing of 15-lb. nailed boots and endured the rambling discourse of the guides." Colin drove the bus back to the village, and turned around to face the people leaving the bus. Many said thanks, but there was not a single cash tip given or expected—this was New Zealand. People got paid a fair wage and did not look for tips. Colin chuckled. "If you cannot bear to leave your guides, come and help us wash the socks." They washed them every night and issued a clean pair with every pair of boots, which was another typical feature of New Zealand—it was very clean.

The sun was still out when I returned to my homestay to find Suzie a bit shaken. She stood with an empty syringe, having just given a horse an injection for the first time in her life—usually her husband did it—and she had pricked her finger with a needle. I told her she should have asked me to do it. I have been giving people injections since the age of about 13 when my grandfather, a professor of orthopedic surgery, started teaching me a few things. Suzie warmed up a little, and from that point on I never heard another word about her mythical niece who supposedly was staying with her while her husband was away.

She took me for a walk in the pasture to pet her horses and hand out carrots. A 25-year-old horse was her "nurse" for other horses dying of old age—she attached herself to a new oldster after the previous one died. Another carrot went to a horse who Suzie said was the best judge of character. That horse seemed to like me a lot, to Suzie's great reassurance. She told me she had taught over 5,000 people to ride before a bad back forced her to stop. She once hoisted a very ill man with an artificial heart valve atop a horse—he was so ill, he could hardly walk, but he was happy to ride.

As I headed out for dinner, Suzie asked me to close the gate when I returned, same as I had done the night before, because she was afraid to step out in the dark. I had invited Wayne, my kayak guide, for dinner, but he canceled claiming overwork. When I stopped by to say hello, my reading of it was that he had a partner who did not like the idea of Wayne having dinner with a stranger. One of the charming pieces of the New Zealand vocabulary was the word "partner." People used it instead of spouse, regardless of marital status, gender, or sexual orientation. I went alone to the best restaurant in town, marked by two gas torches burning in front, ordered grilled trout, and read the local newspaper while sipping dark beer.

12 Across the Southern Alps

Suzie had cooked another delicious breakfast with colorful condiments, fresh juices, breads, and lychees. (She will probably remember me as the man who ate up all her lychees.) My plan for the day was to drive up the West Coast to Greymouth and catch the train across the Southern Alps to the East Coast. There I would pick up another car, drive down to Mt. Hutt and overnight near the ski slopes.

Suzie wanted me to stay with one of her friends in that area, but I pulled out a bed-and-breakfast book and reserved a room on a farm. My bill from Suzie was the second highest for the entire journey, and she took pains to add four dollars for a bottle of beer on the first night. She was my only host in New Zealand besides Archie Bunker on Stewart Island to charge for a drink. I packed, extended my hand, but Suzie came in for a hug. It was the strangest hug of my life—we stood far apart, leaning forward, and only our forearms touched, there was certainly no contact between facial skin.

She was really not a bad sort, I thought, only very fearful. When I come back to the area, I'll probably stay someplace else, just out of curiosity, but if a friend asked me for a recommendation, I would not hesitate to send him or her to Suzie, with her breathtaking views, interesting breakfasts, and excellent local knowledge. I would only tell them to make sure her husband was going to be there when they visited.

I stopped for the last time at Franz Joseph glacier for a 20-minute hike to the viewing platform. The Sentinel Rock protruded from the lower part of the glacier, one of several *roches moutonnées* in the valley. This French name, meaning "sheep-like rocks," describes large rocks that have withstood the scrapings of glacial ice. Now clothed by forest and surrounded by ice, these were covered in ice during the Ice Ages.

I passed the lake where I had kayaked with Wayne and headed to Greymouth. Colin, my glacier guide, said the day before it was such a depressing place that locals called it Grimmouth. The town stood on Maori land. "We have only one tribe here on the South Island," said Colin, "and they are pretty reasonable to deal with. On the North Island they have 13 tribes and they were still eating each other a hundred years ago, so negotiating with them is much harder."

There were no humans in New Zealand until approximately a thousand years ago. The great Polynesian explorer Kupe had visited New Zealand during the first millennium in his large canoe, explored its coasts, and returned to the Pacific islands to tell his people about the land farther south. To appreciate the greatness of his achievement, you have to remember that Kupe lived during the Stone Age. He cut the trees for his canoe with a stone ax, built a catamaran without a piece of metal, and sailed across the ocean and back without a compass. He must have been not only amazingly imaginative to come up with this idea and brave to execute it, but also very observant: He navigated by the stars, tracked flights of birds, and noted the swells of waves whose shape changed depending on the closeness of the land.

The Polynesian societies were cannibalistic. They harvested coconuts, fished, did a little farming, but whenever the population increased and food became scarce, intertribal conflicts led to cannibalism. A tribe that was losing a fight on an overpopulated island, many of its warriors already killed and eaten, faced a stark choice—to go into the pot or into a canoe. Think of the horror of a small band of warriors having to choose between staying on their ancestral island to face an almost certain murder and pushing off into the ocean with their relatives and a bit of livestock, hoping to find empty land far beyond the horizon. This is how most Pacific islands became first inhabited and then over-populated over several centuries, each overpopulation creating a new wave of migration. The two big islands of New Zealand were at the end of that trail.

Most ocean-going canoes, some carrying dozens of people, perished in the ocean, but a small fleet, sailing through the cloudless Southern Pacific, saw a long cloud on the horizon. It was a sign of the land which afterwards they called Aotearoa—the land of the long white cloud. The Polynesians who came to New Zealand evolved into the Maori over the centuries. They had no writ-ten language, but such a strong oral tradition that to this day many Maori can tell you on which canoe their ancestors arrived. Since people traveled in tribal groups, different tribes in New Zealand trace their ancestry to different canoes. The oral history includes the names of people in the canoes, who first saw the land, who was the first to step out of the canoe and what he said, and so on.

When the people first arrived here, Aotearoa must have seemed like paradise. There were no humans, no mammals other than two small species of bat, no predators other than eagles, and no snakes. The rivers and coastal waters teemed with fish and shellfish, while in the forests were walking meat lockers— the moa birds, rising over three meters high. The bones of these huge flightless birds, similar to ostriches, only much bigger and meatier, dug up centuries later by archeologists, provide a record of the Maori society. In the early era, when the birds were plentiful, the Maori ate only the best parts. As the population grew and the moa population thinned out, they chewed the birds down to the bone. As the moa became scarce, the Maori returned to cannibalism.

By the time the Europeans came to Aotearoa, the Maori tribes lived in heavily fortified settlements called *pa*. A hilltop *pa* was circled by a complex sys-tem of ditches with sharp spikes and defensive breastworks. The Maori were such experts in trench warfare that the British infantry, armed with rifle and cannon, found their *pa* a very hard going. The safety lay inside the *pa*, but the food was outside—birds in the forest, fish in the rivers and the sea, and fields of kumara (sweet potato) on the hillsides below. The Maori tribes lived in a state of more or less permanent warfare, fighting each other for limited resources— territory, slaves, women. They fought with clubs made of heavy wood, while a chief or an important warrior could have a club made from very heavy gemstone. They had spears for hand-to-hand combat but not for throwing, nor did they have bows and arrows—all their fighting was hand-to-hand. The Maori had a strong tribal structure, with hereditary chiefs and a strong sense of belonging to a tribe. That, combined with their fighting ability, stood them in good stead when they fought European invaders—Maori came out of that struggle better off than most native people anywhere in the world.

The first European to sight Aotearoa was Abel Tasman in 1642. He sailed in two ships from Batavia, the capital of the Dutch East India Company, near what is today Jakarta. Sailing south, he discovered the West Coast of Australia and the island we now call Tasmania. He thought it was a peninsula of Australia and named it Van Diemen's Land. Tasman was a cautious mariner who took no chances. To claim Van Diemen's Land for his Dutch East India Company, he had his ship's carpenter swim ashore with a flag and attach it to some rocks—not the most assertive way of taking possession of a new land. From there Tasman turned east, crossed the body of water we now call the Tasman Sea, and saw the West Coast of the South Island of New Zealand. Sailing north, he brought his ships into a sheltered bay, one of the richest areas for seafood in New Zealand, jealously guarded by the Ngai Tahu tribe that lived on its shore. Tasman dropped his anchors opposite one of the settlements. The Maori saw that as a threat, sent out a fleet of *waka*—war canoes—which attacked, killing four sailors and a boatswain. Tasman named it The Murderers' Bay and left without landing. From the Maori point of view, the encounter was highly satisfactory. The invaders were repelled and the local way of life preserved for another century and a half.

127 years later, in 1769, British Navy lieutenant James Cook, commanding a converted collier called the *Endeavour,* sailed into the South Pacific with a scientific expedition to perform astronomical observations in Tahiti. There he took on board Tupaia, a local chief who knew the ancient methods of navigating by reading the flight of birds and the shapes of the waves. With his help, using Abel Tasman's old chart, and trusting his own superlative seamanship, James Cook rediscovered New Zealand. He circumnavigated it, drew very good coastal maps and made repeated landings, creating a base for repairing and servicing his ship in the straight between the two islands. Once Cook returned to England with his maps, New Zealand became open to European settlement.

Driving to Greymouth I observed the speed limit, aware of white crosses at sharp turns above the ravines. I skipped most scenic bypasses, having to make the Tranz-Scenic train at 2:05 PM. This green coastal land, lazing in the winter sun, reminded me of summers near the Baltic in Estonia, where I grew up—green flatlands and pines running to the sea. As I passed historic West Coast villages—Ross, Kumara, and the whaling port of Hokitika, I promised myself I would come back and spend more time here.

A yellow "low gas" light came on, and I stopped in a village that consisted of just a few blocks of neat, one-story houses, with sheep grazing on sunny front lawns. A plump guy waddled in from across the road and started pumping gas. I asked how far it was to Greymouth, and he said, "An har an a but." What? After he repeated himself a few times, I found he was saying "an hour and a bit." Another customer stopped by, said a few words, my guy answered, collected the money, and the customer left. I asked what the conversation was about, and he said that the customer bought milk. I never once heard the word milk during the conversation! The southern part of the South Island had been settled by Scots, and many people in the villages have preserved their distinctive patterns of speech to this day.

There were polling stations all along the road that day—New Zealand was having its parliamentary elections. Two farmers trotted on horseback towards a polling booth. New Zealanders take voting and public service very seriously. Year after year the country comes up on the top of the list as the most transparent in the world, meaning the most honest. New Zealanders love picking on their politicians, but it is comforting to know that as a group they are the least corrupt in the world.

I rolled into Greymouth, topped up the tank, and returned the car without a hitch. I recognized several people at the platform; they were waiting for the same train. I shook hands with an Australian couple who were on my heli-hike the day before, and then Sabine, the German student with whom I hiked near the glacier lake, came from another car and sat next to me. We kept buying each other drinks and taking them to an open observation platform. I drank wine, but Sabine kept hitting a popular New Zealand drink called KGB—a vodka cocktail. She offered me her bottle, but I told her I would pass because for me the KGB was no joke since years ago those guys had tried to catch or kill me. The experience, which I described in my book *Rubles to Dollars*, was more extreme than bungee jumping, and even though I escaped, I was not going to drink anything named after them.

The four-hour ride across the Southern Alps is rated by connoisseurs as one of the ten most beautiful train rides in the world. It starts on the western coastal plain, passing sheep in the meadows, deer prancing in broad paddocks, fishermen sitting above the streams. The track heads up into the mountains, slicing in and out of tunnels, and the train stops to attach an extra locomotive for the final push towards Arthur's Pass, where the track gains a meter of altitude for every 33 meters of distance.

The conductor kept making announcements: "On your right are the houses used by the Canterbury University, where their students stay when they come here to study about the Alpine plants, the birds, and the bees." We approached the longest tunnel of 8.55 km (almost five miles) and the observation deck was locked because of the danger from engine fumes in that narrow space. Before we entered the tunnel, rivers flowed west, and after we emerged they flowed east. A restored ghost town came into view, grassless front yards littered with odd bits of metal, and the conductor said, "The people of Otira lead busy and productive lives and have no time for pleasures such as gardening."

In the dark we pulled into Christchurch and I said goodbye to Sabine. She took a shuttle to catch her flight home while I had ordered a car to be delivered to the rail station. The best I could get was a four wheel drive Subaru station wagon, a sturdier vehicle for mountain roads. It was brought to the train station by a grandma, who amused herself by flirting with me, then looked at my driver's license and called me a baby. On the drive towards Mt. Hutt my cell phone rang—it was a follow-up call from tech support at Maxnet, an Internet service provider with whom I signed up in New Zealand. In the glacier area I had a problem connecting, and even though the problem lay in Suzie's phone line, Maxnet was extremely supportive. I thanked the guy who called me and told him that in many years of calling tech support this was the first time that tech support rang me up.

The road from Christchurch to Methven, the town at the foot of Mt. Hutt, was probably the worst signposted in New Zealand, and that's saying a lot, because the New Zealand roads are not nearly as well marked as in the United States. This was my third time on that road in six years, and every time I get lost. My host, Sandy, whom I had called on the cell phone for directions, was geographically challenged—this disorder is forgivable in a customer, such as myself, but inexcusable in a host. I pulled over to the Abisko Lodge, where I had stayed twice with my son and knew the owners, but I saw a "no vacancy" sign and kept driving. Further down a country road there was another farmstay, but when I got out of the car, I noticed a sign on the gate: "Never mind the dog, beware of the owners." I took that for a bad omen in hospitality and got back in my car. Finally I found my farmstay, but I must have pulled out a poor ticket in the bed and breakfast lottery—the décor and the owner were both dull. The woman offered me tea and we sat in front of the fire, watching the election returns on TV. Atypical for New Zealand, she did not know the parties and only could tell that Helen Clark, the prime minister, was a nice lady who did not get flustered when challenged.

13 Heli-skiing? Heli-no!

In the morning Sandy served me a pot of tea with three slices of white toast and two packets each of Vegemite, butter, and jelly. Breakfast was included at every place I stayed, but the menus differed widely. Her price matched the menu—Sandy charged me the second lowest rate of the whole journey, about 20 U.S. dollars for the room and breakfast. In brilliant sunshine I scraped the frost off the windshield and headed towards Mt. Hutt, one of several peaks towering above the valley. Flocks of big fluffy sheep ambled across green paddocks and the snow higher up on the mountains was so bright I needed sunglasses. The ski season at Mt. Hutt is the longest in New Zealand, thanks to its high altitude, the location behind the opening in the Southern Alps which funnels moisture to its slopes, and extensive snow-making equipment. Methven, the town at the foot of Mt. Hutt, is small and sleepy and does not have the glitter and the nightlife of Queenstown, but it is a good, quiet, reliable place to ski.

My heavy Subaru hugged the mountain road, and it was a pleasure to feel the return of the physical memories of the switchbacks on the way to the ski fields. This was my third time in this area, and I had driven up and down the mountain about ten times. During the first visit my son learned to ski and I had reconnected with skiing after a long break, but at that time, there had been more snow. I carried chains in my trunk, but the shack where for a few dollars they put them on your wheels was closed. Nor did I see any hitchhikers—raggedy kids who used to catch a bus to the foot of the mountain and stand there with their snowboards. I drove to the top, and in the parking lot saw a familiar sight—colorful kea birds, the only snow parrots in the world, hopping from car to car. They were so curious and their beaks so strong that sometimes they pulled out rubber seals between the car window and the body of the car.

I rented "executive" skis and boots and hit the slopes, where the lines were short and the trails familiar. The entire ski area, from beginners' trails to double diamond expert runs, was surprisingly compact—it was a perfect mountain for beginners. At the instructors' shack I asked about Wanda, but she was leading a group, and I could not find her on the slopes. I guess the ski field was not so compact after all. Riding a chairlift I met a local woman who was Wanda's neighbor in the valley and had known her since she was a little girl. She told me of her own happy winter on this mountain before she had her daughters—two little girls who bickered in a chairlift ahead of us. That winter her husband was the chief groomer, driving the huge snow-cat each night, while she cooked for the maintenance crew and they skied together each day. Now her husband was a contractor and she had an "ordinary job" in the valley. On another ride to the top I spoke with a local farmer who skied on his day off. The day before he had been shearing the bellies of his sheep—they were about to start lambing and he did not want newborn lambs to have dirty hair in their faces. In September, when things got slow on the farm, he was going to fly to Northern Italy. Vacation? No, he imported Italian tiles.

I stopped by the heli-ski shack where they had a helicopter that whisked skiers up a mountain with no lifts or roads. It took six persons—the pilot, three skiers, and two instructors who guided the small group on its way down, one leading, the other bringing up the rear. A few years earlier I had asked Danny whether he wanted to go heli-skiing. The little kid looked up at me and said: "Heli-skiing? Heli-no!" Today I would have been the only client, and their minimum was two skiers. I didn't feel like paying double, however, and went to the slopes where I had skied with Danny.

This time around I noticed the near absence of "beautiful statues"—exquisitely dressed Japanese tourists, who used to stand on little flat patches near the lifts. There had been lots of them when Danny and I first came to Mt. Hutt, wearing gorgeous outfits, matched and color-coordinated, beautiful new boots, top-name gear—and an expression of fear. They spent thousands of dollars on stylish outfits, managed to hoist themselves onto a chair-lift, but could not ski down and just stood there. Danny wore his cousin's hand-me-down ski pants of a vaguely fecal color, with a big tear on the left knee stitched with dark thread and an old New York Jets winter jacket—but he had a private instructor for half a day each day and was rapidly becoming a competent skier, while also receiving a lesson in asset allocation and choosing substance over style.

By 3 PM the sun hid behind the tallest peaks, the air became colder, and I headed down into Methven. The "no vacancy" sign was still in front of Abisko Lodge, while most other places advertised vacancies. Evan and Heather were pleasantly surprised when I walked into their office and invited them for a drink. They could not leave the lodge, so they pulled up a wooden roll-up curtain at their bar in the dining room, and treated me to a beer, then another. We had not seen each other in a few years and had a lot of catching up to do. I had first come to the lodge with Danny at the time of my divorce, and these two former teachers had created a great environment for a child. He had free run of the lodge, going from its dining room to the hot tub, to the office to hang out with Evan while he was installing a new computer, always feeling at home.

Evan and Heather had a funny local woman who came in daily to cook breakfast and dinner for the guests. One morning, unable to pull Danny out of bed, I left him sleeping and went to breakfast alone. "Where's the juvenile delinquent?" inquired Sue. "In the room, unconscious," I answered. "Perhaps something he ate last night?" "Oh my, oh my!" exclaimed Sue. "Let me call the vet." Danny loved her grilled salmon but also chocolate and one morning Sue promised to make him chocolate fish for dinner. As the day went on, Danny grew worried—he didn't want to miss Sue's regular fish, but she was adamant—he was getting chocolate fish, and that was that. The kid grew apprehensive over his salad and soup, but then Sue brought out his main dish— a piece of baked salmon with all the trimmings and a piece of chocolate shaped like a fish on the side of the plate.

Evan and Heather ran their little lodge at nearly 100 percent occupancy partly because of repeat business and partly by attracting many Japanese. They had a Japanese Web site and a young Japanese man to answer emails. When I told them Danny was planning to come back they were glad but said to tell him to book well in advance. We shook hands, I lit up a cigar and headed back to my car, past a small group of Japanese kids spilling out of a minivan and setting their skis against the outer wall of the lodge. Driving away, I thought that a big part of the pleasure of travel was meeting people to whom one wanted to return. I was sorry I had not booked a room there the night before. I could find accommodations that were more luxurious or less expensive, but I would not be able to find nicer people in Methven.

My next destination was Mt. Cook, New Zealand's tallest mountain, in the midst of a national park. The road climbed through broad pastures—cows grazed under the fading sky, the deer stood on mountain ridges like statuettes, green and brown slopes with off-white sheep looked like patterns of handmade rugs. There was jazz on the radio: Last night the local station played Mahler, in the morning on the way up the mountain Leonard Bernstein and on the way down Prokofiev. I drove fast for about three hours. Occasionally a sign— "Speed camera area"—came into view, reminding drivers to slow down to the legal limit of 100 kph (about 60 mph). It was very decent of New Zealanders to warn you before taking your picture. On my first day I ignored this sign and saw a flash in my rearview mirror, but never received a ticket—a friend told me those cameras sometimes ran out of film.

The road climbed into high desert country, ringed by snow-capped mountains; my silver car seemed like an insect racing across the bottom of an enormous brown dish. Other cars started turning on their lights. A narrow string of red clouds appeared across the mountains, cutting them in half at the waist. I turned on the headlights, beaming at patches of fog. Huge lakes of fog filled the valleys below the ridge, looking more like lakes than mere mist. Those lakes began to spill over the road, forcing me to slow down a bit. There was Hawaiian music on the radio, but the sound came through more and more crackly as the mountains grew taller. At the turn towards Mt. Cook village I shut the radio off and focused all my attention on the short black strip of road still visible in front of the car. Other cars tried to follow, but their headlights kept disappearing in my rearview mirror. As the road climbed and the car roared out of the fog I saw a mass of lights, like an ocean liner amidst a black sea, and knew I was home for the night.

When Phyllis heard I wanted to visit Mt. Cook, she mentioned that her daughter was dating the man who ran its Department of Conservation (DOC, pronounced "dock"), in charge of the national park. It seemed at times like everyone in New Zealand knew one another. A few days later Phyllis emailed me, saying that Bob had invited me to stay with him. He had a house next to the locally famous Hermitage Hotel in the middle of Cook Village and had a guest room waiting for me. I invited him for dinner that evening at the hotel, which is why I raced to get there by 7:30.

At this altitude there were patches of snow on the ground. I navigated to a boxy, one-story house with a dirty white jeep out front and an aggressive-looking red sports car in an open garage. Bob came out to shake hands and grab one of my bags. He was a powerfully built square-shouldered man with closely-cropped grey hair, attentive eyes, and an easy half-smile. He pointed with pride to a pile of freshly chopped firewood that lined the outer wall of his house and smiled when I told him of the essay by Henry David Thoreau on the manly pleasure of contemplating your woodpile. It was a perfect house for a single guy—deep old leather armchairs, a good stereo with a collection of CDs, a library, working fireplace, big windows opening to the mountains, and framed photos and travel souvenirs on the walls. Everything was in place, but not too neat—the house had a strong, comfortable, lived-in feel, plus a beautiful blonde flew in on weekends. It was heaven.

Bob put my bags into a simple but comfortable guest bedroom, turned on the heater and the electric blanket, then led the way to the hotel restaurant through the cold night air, briskly maneuvering between snow banks. He ticked off a few facts about the DOC. It controlled about one third of New Zealand's territory and 17 percent of its territorial waters, but had only 1,500 employees. The Labor government, which had won reelection the day before, had been pouring money into the DOC—they had just received over NZ$300 million for upgrading the network of backcountry trails and huts. I told Bob of the exquisitely maintained walking trails that I had hiked in other parks but told him I had seen few, if any, people. He said there were many more people in summer and the government saw funding DOC as an investment in tourism.

The windows of the hotel shone like trays of jewelry against the black night, and a huge fire roared in the lobby. One of the walls had a waterfall, with a flat sheet of water running down two stories, a few silvery metal salmon swimming upstream to spawn. The hotel was privately owned by two families that had just completed a million-dollar upgrade. We ordered salmon and Bob chose a very good local Cabernet. The staff hovered over him, with the Maori dining room manager coming to the table to tease and joke. New Zealand was such a small country—it turned out that while I had been staying with Suzie near the glaciers, her husband was here, meeting with Bob. I told him of my crazy experience there, and he said it was too bad I had missed her husband. "You guys would have liked each other."

Bob used to work for an old forestry service, served four years as a policeman, taught high school, managed New Zealand's Antarctic base, and now worked for the DOC, but still went to the Antarctic once a year as an inspector aboard a Russian icebreaker. While teaching, Bob became eager to get a job in the Antarctic and scoured the list of vacancies in the newspapers. When he decided to apply, he thought he would start at the top and got the job. He spent a year running New Zealand's Scott Base in the Antarctic, a few kilometers from the U.S. McMurdo Base. He described how everything in the Antarctic was dominated by the weather. You could make any plans, but whether they worked out or not depended on the weather. Also, nothing ever rotted away there—the equipment left behind by the original explorers more than 100 years ago was still on the ice. That's why everybody was obligated to take out every last piece of their own garbage.

The year before, when the ice suddenly receded in front of his icebreaker, Bob was able to make an inspection visit to a Soviet base, Leninskaya, evacuated in 1987. It was very dirty, with abandoned vehicles, spilled chemicals, and a huge hall full of electronics that looked like an electronic intelligence gathering station—this would have been completely against the rules because Antarctica had been demilitarized by an international treaty. He said walking through Leninskaya felt like a throwback to the Soviet era, with busts of Lenin and Soviet propaganda on the walls. Bob thought they abandoned it in a hurry because the Soviet Union was collapsing and suddenly the weather changed, allowing for an evacuation. Possessions had been strewn about and some beds were neat, while others had been left unmade. Bob wrote a report on his visit and forwarded a copy to the Russian government, which will have to clean up the area.

I was surprised to hear that Bob used to be a policeman because he lacked that edge of harshness, bordering on brutality, one often sees in cops. Also, it seemed strange that he served for only four years. In the United States they take kids in pretty young, make them into cops, and once a cop always a cop. Bob smiled—that was not the New Zealand way. He worked as a crime scene investigator and a cannabis control officer, and learned some useful skills, such as how to diffuse situations and to read people. It was not uncommon in New Zealand to do this kind of work for a few years and then move on to something else.

The policemen in New Zealand patrol unarmed. In the rare instances when they think a suspect could be armed, they call in the Armed Offenders Squad. Some police cars have a floor safe with a gun, which a sergeant can open in an emergency. The level of violence in the society is low. The prime minister travels with a single policeman from the diplomatic protection service who carries a pistol, and occasionally a policeman is detailed to one of the ministers. Bob was amazed at my description of what happened in New York when the president of the United States visited—even before 9/11 officials had blocked the highways on which he traveled, with a police car blocking each exit ramp and another sitting on top of each overpass. There could be 40 or more vehicles in a convoy, some of them SUVs with heavily armed men, sharpshooters, Stinger missiles, the works. Bob said that if the prime minister came into the restaurant where we were, there would only be one policeman as an escort and nobody would pay much attention. The pace of life was especially peaceful here on the South Island, which had only 800,000 people—fewer than in the entire city of Auckland.

I started asking Bob about the Maori. He said that the first Europeans in New Zealand were mostly whalers and sealers, a pretty rough bunch. They introduced muskets into a Stone Age cannibalistic society that lived in a state of semipermanent warfare, fighting with clubs. A small tribe that played host to a whaling station could obtain enough muskets to take on much bigger neighbors and wipe them out. There had been a Maori chief who traveled to London, was received by the King, feted by the nobles, and given expensive gifts. Stopping in Australia on the way home, he heard that his son-in-law had been killed. The chief sold all his gifts except for the sword and the body armor given to him by the King, bought muskets, brought them home, armed his tribe, and proceeded to wipe out several neighboring tribes. That period of Maori-on-Maori armed violence came to be called the Musket Wars. The chiefs saw the writing on the wall—the old era was over and unless something was done, many Maori tribes would be exterminated. At the prompting of the missionaries who settled among them, the chiefs came to Waitangi in the Bay of Islands to sign a treaty with a British naval officer representing the Crown. The Treaty of Waitangi gave New Zealand to England, established English law in the land, guaranteed the rights of the chiefs and protected Maori land ownership by prohibiting direct sales to the settlers.

When I asked Bob about the Treaty of Waitangi, he grinned—which version? The English original and the Maori translation had subtle differences. The Maori had only an oral language, and the missionary Reverend Henry Williams translated the English version into the newly created Maori written language as best he could. In any event, the Treaty of Waitangi did not put an end to violence. The settlers, whose numbers were growing, were dissatisfied with the slow pace of land sales, while the Maori held back, leading to wars between them, followed by illegal land seizures. In the 1970s the government established the Waitangi Tribunal for addressing old grievances, mostly over illegally taken land. The tribes were receiving financial settlements that could establish their prosperity in perpetuity, but there were differences between tribes. The only tribe on the South Island was practical and savvy, but the farther north, the more militant the tribes. The tribe in the south had invested its settlement in income-producing businesses and insisted on several symbolic measures. For example, they took over all Crown (government) land on the island and held it for two hours before turning it back. They got the government to rename Mt. Cook Mt. Aoraki when the next generation of maps comes out. While this was happening in the south, many tribes in the north still argued among themselves about their old boundary disputes; they also refused to cooperate with the government simply to show their power, even on those issues that were to their obvious benefit, such as pest eradication programs.

14 Mountain Rescue

In the morning I worked on my computer in front of windows that framed enormous mountains nearby, skipped breakfast, and went to the information center for an audiovisual presentation. The Maori name of Mt. Cook was Mt. Aoraki, from a legend in which four brothers went out in a canoe and after it overturned, climbed up and sat on its hull, some higher, some lower, gradually freezing and turning to stone. Aoraki was the fellow who sat the highest. From this charming tale some anonymous hack reached the conclusion that the Maori knew that New Zealand was created by a tectonic plate rising from the sea. This was one of very few instances of political correctness gone wild in an otherwise very sane country.

Mt. Cook is the highest mountain in New Zealand at 3,750 meters (12,303 feet) high, its top perpetually clad in snow and ice. Its steepness and unstable snow make it one of the most challenging mountains for climbers. Bursts of bad weather come suddenly in summer, creating blinding snowstorms and avalanches. Here Sir Edmund Hillary trained for his ascent of Everest, 29,035 feet high. In this country of inveterate hikers, climbers, and kayakers, the local man who went to Nepal and became the first to climb the tallest mountain in the world is the closest figure to a national hero.

The first people to attempt to climb Mt. Cook were Reverend Green, an English clergyman, and his two Swiss guides in 1882. They were caught in a storm and had to turn back for their lives, 200 meters short of the peak. On the way down the storm grew fierce, blocking the trail and forcing them to spend the night holding onto the rock while standing on a two-foot-wide ledge leaning out over an abyss. They were exhausted, but to fall asleep would have meant to fall to their death; to survive they kept themselves awake by singing and talking.

When the newspapers announced that more European climbers were sailing to New Zealand to conquer its tallest mountain, a group of local young men—Tom Fyfe, Jack Clarke, and George Graham—beat them by climbing the peak in 1894. All that was left for those who came later was to climb the peak by other routes, claiming those firsts as their consolation prizes. More than 130 people have died climbing Mt. Cook or descending after a successful climb—there has rarely been a year without a fatality.

After a morning without breakfast I felt hungry and headed back to the restaurant where Bob and I had eaten dinner the night before. After an ample buffet lunch of fish, shrimp, calamari, salads, and desserts, I took myself on a much less ambitious trail, hiking to a glacier in the Hooker Valley at the base of Mt. Cook. I hiked past a memorial to dead climbers, across two swinging bridges over a rushing river, then along an icy ledge wide enough for only one person. A waist-high wire fence separated hikers on the ledge from an almost vertical drop to the roaring river below. A wooden walkway led to the glacier, protecting the fields of tussock grass. It took an hour and a half of fast hiking to reach the icy lake of glacier melt. I tossed several heavy rocks to test the thickness of the ice, and by the looks of it I was not the first one to have had that bright idea.

At about 3 PM the sun hid behind the mountain peaks, and while the glaciers up in the mountains remained brightly lit, the valley suddenly became grey and cold. A minute earlier I had been sweating from a fast hike, with a ski jacket slung over my arm, but suddenly my sweat felt icy, and I put on a scarf, jacket, hat, and gloves. Back at the parking lot I glanced at my watch—the entire hike had taken three hours, and during that time on a popular trail in a major national park I met fewer than 20 people. Bob told me that in summer the trail became so clogged that the DOC had started counting hikers and planned to introduce trail capacity controls. Winter was clearly the best time to visit the park.

Bob invited me to a staff event—the presentation of a documentary about the mountain rescue unit on Mt. Cook, filmed last summer by a local company for National Geographic. The visitors' center had been closed to the public for the event and filled with displays of rescue gear and tables laden with beer and wine, cheese and crackers. The rescue team had four permanent members, including a helicopter pilot, and four seasonal members, hired for the summer climbing season. All were experienced climbers who constantly trained in crevasse rescues and aerial evacuations, where a pilot pulled a stretcher with an injured climber up on a rope, while a rescuer guided it, clinging to its side as it flew above the rocks and ice.

Rescuers were on call 24 hours a day, waiting to fly into places where no person would want to go, into some of the most dangerous spots on the globe, into situations where the best—you had to be the best to climb Mt. Cook—had already failed. These people did it for the sheer sport and for so little money that when they were not flying rescue missions the DOC used them for trail maintenance. It also sent them rappelling down from their helicopter to evacuate toilet tanks from remote mountain huts because refuse could not be left there. On those evacuations the heroes wore surgical masks and gloves, like airport toilet cleaners. They lived for the emergency calls, and when those came they raced to the helipad.

Much of the movie was shot with cameras attached to helmets, tracking the rescue of a climber who had lost his footing, fell, and slid down an ice field. He picked up speed and shot through a narrow crevasse, down into a deep ice and snow cave where he lost consciousness, unable to respond to the rope pull. His partner hiked to a hut and called the rescuers. When the helicopter flew in, the crevasse leading down into the ice cave was so narrow that the two skinniest members of the rescue team had to take off their safety gear in order to squeeze down the hole. They attached a set of pulleys to the injured man and hoisted him to the surface, while the cave could have collapsed at any moment, burying them all.

The men who did this kind of work were hard and straightforward—the danger rubbed away any fluff. Asked to introduce the movie, their team leader called their work perfectly ordinary. They were people of action and dedication, but the movie crew was slick and gave clever speeches. The director patted his big fat stomach, blaming it on the good cooking on the mountain during two months of shooting. When he asked me what I thought of the movie, I told him that the camera work was impressive, but when it came to the script, they really scratched the bottom of the cliché bin—"treacherous mountain," "precious cargo," "lasting scars" (are there any other kind?). He said they used that kind of language because the movie was shot for the U.S. market; they would have done it differently for a New Zealand audience. "Don't think that Americans are stupid," I suggested. "They know quality and reward it"—but the director was already looking for another project.

I went back to the Hermitage for dinner with Bob and Mike, his regional manager, one of six such managers in New Zealand. He had supreme political reflexes, running circles around those who wanted to commercialize the wilderness and I got the distinct feeling that anyone who wanted to despoil the Canterbury region would have an extremely hard time with Mike. He was a very tall, imposing man who had an easy laugh and enjoyed a good story. He told us how his son was found unfit by the Navy—the first in a family with a long tradition of service. It turned out that the boy was even taller than the father and there was no naval vessel in New Zealand with a bunk big enough for him.

We were having dessert when Gilbert and Marian joined us, an elderly ranching couple whom Mike jokingly but respectfully called the local gentry. Gilbert was the only man in the restaurant to wear a tie under his zippered jacket. He reminded me of the photos in the visitors' center, in which old-time climbers stood on glaciers in hobnailed boots wearing ties and hats. Gilbert had climbed Mt. Cook in 1959, walking all the way up from the valley rather than taking a helicopter half way up like many climbers do today. Being able to read the weather and knowing local conditions were absolutely essential skills. On the last leg of his climb, in fine weather, two hours from the last hut, his companion saw a few wisps of white in the sky. "I think we've done enough climbing today," he said, turning back. An hour after they returned to the hut the mountain was hit by a severe storm. Those white wisps had been the first signs of a weather front on its way in from the Southern Ocean. Gilbert said one of the advantages people had in his day was not living in such a tense time. Climbing today, tomorrow, or next week made little difference. Now a guy comes to the mountain on a five-day vacation, and if the weather is bad for four days, he is going to push on the fifth.

I kept pouring the cabernet, even though both Gilbert and Marian tried to prevent me from filling their glasses. When Marian mentioned it was Gilbert's 74th birthday, I asked about his favorite after-dinner drink and brought it to him from the bar. He grinned, drank, and sat back enjoying the warmth, while Marian, who had very strong opinions on just about everything, was making them very clear to Mike. He was starting to fade a little when Bob and I said good night and walked back to his house in total darkness.

15 The Country of Second Sons

Bob and I shook hands and I invited him to come and stay with me in New York any time. The highway, so foggy and dark two nights earlier, glistened in the morning sun, snaking between a blue lake and brown and green mountains. The patches of snow melted away at lower altitudes, making the sheep the only white spots on the hillsides. At the main highway I turned south and drove to the Ohau ski area, taking a dirt road and crossing a bridge partly submerged under a swollen creek. I was lucky not to have met a single car on the way up because that road was too narrow for two, and there was no guardrail above the ravine. As I climbed higher, the road became slick with ice and the sky grey with clouds. Looking back felt like looking down from an airplane. It was 1 PM, but the ski field was already in the shade and the snow looked icy. A few skiers were out, but I decided not to join them, deciding instead that this was a place to return to on another trip, only earlier in the day and after a fresh snowfall. The lodge at the base looked cozy and had great views over the lake.

I felt a tinge of sadness turning back north. Ohau was the farthest point on my backtrack south after the train ride across the country. Driving back north felt like glancing at a calendar during a vacation. There was still a good stretch ahead, but it would not last forever.

I stopped at a fish farm where huge masses of salmon in rectangular netted pens lazily beat their tails against the slow current of a canal. The neat square pens, each about the size of a tennis court, looked oddly unnatural in the stream amidst the fields. A fishy smell hung over the operation, which charged a dollar to read a two-page advertisement and walk by the fish pens. A plump girl in the office wanted to sell me fish food to feed the salmon, but I said to her, "Let me feed myself, and let the salmon feed themselves." Her jaw dropped and stayed that way until I left the office. Those salmon ate one percent of their body weight each day, mostly ground anchovies. Oddly enough, on my flight back to the U.S. many weeks later, I sat next to an unfriendly American decked out in the bizarre combination of a formal tie, gray pony tail, and earring. We exchanged a few words—he was part owner of that smelly farm.

The road passed by the Tekapo Church, considered one of the most beautiful in New Zealand. A small structure of rough-hewn stones and heavy beams stands as a memorial to local pioneers. A panoramic window behind the pulpit frames the blue lake and snowy mountains, offering a more serene and uplifting view than any stained glass. Before entering, I waited for a busload of loud tourists to vacate the church—incessant picture-taking, loud calling out, totally divorced from the serenity of the local scene. I talked to the woman who looked after the church, read the memorial plaques, and left a small donation. There was no time to linger because another loud bus was disgorging its load at the door. Being on a bus tour under the authority of a tour guide tends to infantilize people and bring out the brat in them. This is one of the reasons why bus tourists are usually much louder than private travelers.

The peaks were covered in snow, but the valley was sunny, warm, and windless, and I took my lunch of fish and chips to an outdoor table. Breaded fish fillets and French fries were brought to New Zealand by Scottish immigrants, becoming the most popular fast food in the country. The quality could range from the pedestrian to the sublime. Another busload of tourists spilled out of a nearby restaurant. Having them was good for the economy, but those organized groups looked totally disconnected from the peaceful experience of this country. Strange birds circled my table, casting covetous glances at my plate. As a precaution I carried it with me when I stepped inside to buy another dark Monteith beer. The fish was cooked just right, moist and glistening in the sun. I spread a local newspaper on the table and read it while eating.

A news item caught my eye—the parasail operator in Queenstown who dropped that teenage girl from the harness a year earlier had been ordered to pay her NZ$10,000 (under 5,000 U.S. dollars). I remembered when my oldest daughter as a little girl joined a nationwide charitable group. Among many other things, on Christmas mornings, instead of sleeping late, she used to deliver fruit baskets to patients in a nearby hospital. After a couple of years of service, the group flew her to a convention where they put her into a physically unsuitable room, where she had two of her fingers broken in the door. Instead of taking her to a doctor, those charitable organizers gave her two aspirins and yelled at her. A few days later they dropped her off in front of the house with a swollen hand and a high fever, and drove away before I came out. I became viciously angry. I hated the hypocrites who loved the world as a whole but did not care about one hurt human being. I took Miriam to a doctor and then retained a killer of a lawyer and sued the group. The settlement came to over $6,000—an American girl received more for two broken fingers than a New Zealand kid for a broken spine and torn intestines more than ten years later. The New Zealand attitude of self-reliance is attractive, but I prefer our American ability to lay a claim against someone who wrongs you.

Finishing my late lunch, I got back in the car and followed the road around Lake Tekapo up into the hills. The road narrowed going through a forest, then turned in front of a little Anglican church at the edge of the family compound. Charles and Daphne, to whom I had been introduced by a friend, had invited me to stay at their high country sheep station. Their manor was surrounded by enormous thick trees, and I couldn't figure out which of the ancient iron handles outside the door was connected to the bell. I tentatively pulled a few and, failing in my research, walked on the terrace surrounding the house and knocked on the living room window.

A gentleman in old baggy clothes with a face straight out of a medieval English painting opened the door and led me into a two-story hall, filled with ancient family portraits, medieval weapons, and a wall of books. Charles helped carry my flight bag to a room on the second floor, the first in a long row of empty children's rooms, with portraits of the couple's children as youngsters in a long corridor. He hurried back to the TV, and a few minutes later I joined him there, in front of a substantial old brick fireplace near which he and Daphne watched the news, drank whiskey with water, and discussed politics.

When upper-class New Zealanders say that their country was settled by the second sons, they mean that the first sons of nobility inherited land in Great Britain, and the younger children had to seek their fortunes elsewhere, with some coming to New Zealand. Charles said, "Our family history goes back many centuries, but the bloke who came here from England, my great-grandfather, got no land but great education, became a lawyer. People had to doff their hats to him in the streets, but he hated it. In the 1850s liberal-minded people at Oxford wanted to create a more equal society. Christchurch was planned on that idealistic thinking. That bloke teamed up with a son of a minister, and in their thirties they both left England and came to New Zealand. When my great-grandfather set up this station here in 1855, there had not been a single European living in this area. The Maori used to travel across this land but never settled here."

"Here in New Zealand all immigrants speak to each other as equals. In England rivers are privately owned, but here they are accessible to all. Anyone who can pay NZ$30 can fish anywhere. The man who changes the oil in my car in town can come on this land to fish in the river—it is his legal right." All the while Charles was speaking, Daphne had been gliding in and out of the kitchen and finally called us to the table. I have seen good cooks and I have seen fast cooks, but Daphne was one of a kind—she was a great fast cook. After we sat down she said grace, thanking the Lord for having sent me to join them for the meal. She served as an unpaid social worker in a local high school, working with kids at risk.

I had not told them I did not eat meat, and Charles grinned—"Should have told us"—as he speared the second pan-fried lamb chop. Daphne cooked me some delicious vegetables, brought out local cheeses, and topped off the dinner with fresh fruit and whipped cream. We continued to talk politics. In this country of only three million, people "stand"—not "run"—for Parliament out of deeply felt convictions. It often costs them money to be in politics, even though campaigns tend to be short and inexpensive. A Member of Parliament (MP) earns only NZ$80,000 a year—about US$40,000—plus a pension after two terms if reelected. There is no subculture of lobbying like in the United States and after leaving Parliament people have to rebuild their businesses or careers.

"New Zealand is the most efficient agricultural producer in the world, capable of feeding much of the globe, but governments keep erecting tariff barriers. Even the United States, while beating the free market drum, keeps raising tariffs on imports from New Zealand. The U.S. agricultural lobby makes American consumers pay more and New Zealand farmers earn less." Charles used to fly to Washington to promote free trade, and while a plane takes five hours to fly across the United States, it can cross New Zealand in 15 minutes. The small country has to export in order to survive.

Charles spoke of New Zealand as a clean and green land surrounded by pristine waters. Its fierce agricultural controls ensure that the country remains clean. I told Charles that whenever I arrived in New Zealand, I was struck by the toughness of the agricultural inspection, much more serious than customs or passport control. New Zealand calls itself an Agrodome, as if the entire country were under a giant protective bubble. A few years earlier I had stopped over in Auckland for half a day with my son on the way home from Fiji. Danny carried with him a souvenir, a totokia, a Fijian war club. It was a tourist item, produced and packed by the main shop on the island, but the young agriculture control officers who gathered around it solemnly announced that since it was made from untreated wood they would have to drill it to test for bugs. I could see tears welling up in the eyes of the little guy with a war club—his totokia was going to be drilled. Then one of the officers asked how long we planned to stay in New Zealand, and hearing that we were going to leave within 12 hours said that he could impound the totokia and Danny could reclaim it before boarding the flight home.

Charles sighed and said that owning a station was no guarantee of easy life. The family had 45,000 sheep in the 1890s, but lost 19,000 of them in the great snows of 1895, after which the business remained depressed for half a century until the Korean War broke out in the 1950s. Korea was very cold, the U.S. military demanded wool, and the station made serious money selling it to them. "Do you know how we survive in New Zealand?" asked Charles. "We grow grass better and cheaper than any country in the world and our farmers are probably the best educated." I told him that whenever I drove past grazing sheep, I saw white gold—little nuggets eating grass and growing bigger.

A year earlier, when I came to New Zealand with my daughter, she pointed out several cars with stickers that read: "GE free NZ." She thought they referred to the company in which her girlfriend's father was an executive, but no—those stickers referred to genetically engineered foods. I asked Charles and Daphne what they thought of it. They told me that at the request of the Green Party the government had convened a Royal Commission of respected experts, ranging from scientists who looked at the health risks to Anglican bishops who considered the ethical implications. The Commission's conclusion was to go ahead with genetically modified and engineered foods, but to do it slowly and with many safeguards. The Greens, who pushed for that commission, rejected its findings and forced the Labor Party to declare a moratorium on GE foods until 2003. In the last election they made a permanent moratorium their non-negotiable demand for entering any coalition. Several weeks after my visit with Charles, the Greens found themselves out of the government, as Labor found another coalition partner.

I asked Charles about the Maori, and he said that many Europeans preferred to settle on the South Island because there were no Maori in most areas, and no conflicts over the land. Twenty years after settlement began on South Island, the Maori were still eating each other on North Island. Charles stressed that the history of New Zealand's relationship with its native population was unique, not repeated anywhere in the world. In all other countries colonized by

Europeans, the native peoples were exterminated, pushed out to reservations, or enslaved. New Zealand is the only country that signed a treaty with its natives, and has by and large abided by it. The Treaty of Waitangi, concluded in 1840, protected native land rights and the tribal structure in perpetuity. There was no such treaty in South Africa. There was no such treaty in Australia—white settlers just grabbed the land and killed the Aborigines or pushed them off into the deserts. Until quite recently the Aborigines were treated like wildlife. Here, on Charles' station, they killed three sheep each Friday for farm hands and three for dog food. On a station in Australia his relative saw an old sign—"Aborigines will no longer be killed for dog tucker."[2]

New Zealand has not been entirely free from conflict, however. There have been wars with the Maori and the Europeans did confiscate some Maori lands. But then in 1974, New Zealand established the Waitangi tribunal to review past injustices and give out compensation. There were big differences in what Maori tribes did with their settlements. The Ngaitahu on South Island set up a commercial operation that may throw off income in perpetuity. The Tainui in Waikato on the North Island bought a rugby league and have already lost money on it.

16 A Flying Shepherd

In the dark I tiptoed down the corridor, past the long row of empty children's bedrooms, into the warmest room of the wing. It was the bathroom, the size of a small Manhattan studio apartment with a large window and an armchair, where a heater had been going full blast all night. I was engrossed in writing when about an hour later I heard knocking down the hallway. Charles was standing outside the bedroom door, trying to wake me up. He said he had a great day planned for me, but I had to be down in 10 minutes and out the door in 20.

I threw on my clothes, had a quick breakfast, and hopped into Charles' jeep, which he drove to a nearby field where four prize stud bulls grazed on green grass. Just as we pulled up, a small plane landed in the paddock, with the bulls hugging the wire fence. A young woman jumped out and helped me into

[2]Tucker is Australian slang for food.

the back seat. Her father, Colin, who owned the neighboring station, was at the controls. Next to me sat a French agricultural exchange student, whom the pair in front good-naturedly but constantly razzed for being French. "When I told my kids a Frog was coming to stay with us," laughed Donnie, "they asked whether he'd be making frog sounds." A pack of farm dogs in an open compartment behind the back seat kept circling and rubbing against my head. It was cold, but Colin roared, "Those are farting dogs, hoo-hoo-hoo!" and told me to open the air vents.

He flew over a river, banking his small plane to show us a rafting operation run by one of Charles and Daphne's children. Landing on a grass strip he taxied towards a hangar where Trev, his huge hulk of a son, puttered around a helicopter. It sat on a small square trailer attached to a tractor. The dogs leaped from the plane. Colin and Trev started fueling the chopper, sending Donnie to make coffee with an admonition not to let the Frenchie near it, lest he do some awful thing to it. "Ever run out of gas in a plane?" Colin asked. I told him I once had run out of gas in a car on the Queensborough Bridge between Queens and Manhattan, but fortunately past the midpoint, and rolled downhill through two lights and into a Manhattan gas station. "You know how to tell when a plane runs out of gas?" asked Colin. "Suddenly everything goes very quiet, including the pilot, hoo-hoo-hoo." He gave me and the French kid two boxes made of heavy wire, each big enough to hold two or three dogs, and told us to attach them to the helicopter. "Put them safety pins into bolts, or else those dogs will go flying in more ways than one, hoo-hoo-hoo." The box on the right went over the exhaust pipe—good for the warmth in winter, not so good in summer, and the box on the left just the opposite. Those dogs really got around.

Drinking coffee with sugary brownies in the flight shack, I noticed a wall plastered with photos of ice fields. Colin had flown a helicopter from a ship in the Antarctic. He pointed to a photo of a white ship in blue water. "Half an hour later we were surrounded by pack ice—things change so quickly there." It was impossible to make out the white ship amidst the ice floes. Once Colin returned from a flight with thirty minutes' worth of fuel in reserve, but the ship was gone because the ice had shifted. "What did you do?" "Shit in my pants, hoo-hoo-hoo," he roared. In fact, he used his head: he radioed the ship and asked the operator to step out and listen for the sound of his rotor. When the operator could not hear him, Colin told him to watch the horizon, turned on his search lights, gained altitude, and started rotating slowly. When the radio man saw the light, he could tell Colin which way to fly.

I strapped myself into the middle seat, with the father and the son on either side, and we flew over low hills, fields of dry yellow tussock grass, the wide river delta broken into hundreds of streams and rivulets. Colin controlled his chopper effortlessly like a bicycle, pointing out what looked like black commas on beige paper—his cattle. The cattle in New Zealand live semi-wild in wide open spaces and see humans only a few times a year. Colin touched down at the edge of a valley and Trev jumped out, carrying a long mean stick and releasing his dogs. Donnie had already driven herself to the other edge of the valley with her dogs. Having taken care of the flanks, Colin spent several minutes buzzing the cattle in the center of the valley, swinging his machine right and left just above their horns until he packed them into a tight herd. I enjoyed the views and took photos. Suddenly Colin touched down softly, as if stepping down from a curb, and turned to me—"Can you do me a favor?" He leaned across and opened my door. "Can you move those cattle down the valley?" The valley was several miles wide with low ridges on both sides, and Colin waved in the direction where those ridges converged—"Move them that way. You'll meet up with Trev." I hopped out, Colin leaned across the seat to close the door and stuck out his hand—"If I don't see you again, have a nice vacation, hoo-hoo-hoo." Then he disappeared like a puff of smoke.

I stood, surrounded by the sudden silence, in my hiking boots and a ski jacket from which a lift ticket still dangled. The sandy ground, crisscrossed by streams and overgrown by knee-high rough grass was so broken it was unsuitable for ploughing. The grass, the water, and the absence of any predators must have made this area heaven for the cattle. A herd of several dozen stood staring at me—big black hulks with mean horns. It felt surreal. I had faced my share of situations, but never a herd of semi-wild cattle.

I picked up a dry stick and advanced, looking them in the eye and telling them in extremely explicit Russian what I was going to do after I closed in. The cattle must have been bilingual because once I was within earshot they turned and started trotting away. I picked up speed and trotted behind. They crossed several rivulets, and I hopped from rock to rock. Then they forded a stream that was about knee-deep and 10 or 15 feet wide. I stopped. To run across would have meant spending the rest of the day in wet boots, not an appealing prospect in winter. I could have set down and waited for Colin to come looking for me in his helicopter, but that would not have been too sporting. I took off my boots and socks, pulled up my jeans and ran through ice water, then stood on my jacket and put my socks and boots back on, feeling fresh and full of energy.

As the sun rose in the cloudless sky, I took off my ski jacket and then the sweater, tying them around my waist and trotting behind the cattle. Colin had the right idea, as usual. He had sent his grown children, who knew what they were doing, down the sides of the valley with their dogs, to flush out any cattle from the groves, and he sent the city slicker—good for nothing more complicated than waving his arms—down the middle. Whenever a small group of cows tried to break right or left, I chased them, but their herd instinct worked for me—when stressed, the cattle stuck together. I yelled and waved my stick, at times wishing I had another pair of legs and a tail, just like one of Colin's dogs. After a couple of hours my herd connected with Trev's who whistled at his dogs to turn the combined herd towards the enclosure, moving them so fast that I dropped behind. The streams grew wider and deeper. A hunter on a cross-country motorbike suddenly appeared and gave me a ride across several streams. I caught up with Trev near the fence where he sat on a tiny mound, surrounded by his dogs lying in the dirt.

Trev was a big young man with a heavy lower jaw and a ski cap that said Tekapo Curling Team. He told me that the purpose of today's muster was pregnancy testing. With ultrasound? "Nah, too late for that. We just stick an arm up to the shoulder into the cow's rectum and feel for the fetus. We now have gloves that go up to the shoulder. If a cow's dry, we pull its head off."

I asked Trev whether he skied, with Mt. Hutt just a few hours away. "When you work with it, you do not play with it" he growled cryptically. He loved New Zealand. "We got no history here, so we can f**k with anything." The worst people are the French, he said. I asked whether he referred to their nuclear testing in the Pacific. I remembered when restaurants publicly poured French wine into gutters during the nuclear tests several years ago. "No, man, it's the Rainbow Warrior." Several years earlier two French secret service agents blew up a Greenpeace ship in Auckland's harbor, killing a photographer. "That's the worst thing one could do to a nation." I could not resist asking him what he thought of 9/11. It was too far from him to affect him much.

Donnie, with her dogs, brought her cattle to our paddock. Like all farmers in New Zealand, she used two breeds—the bigger hunt-away dog loudly brought up the rear, while the quiet strong-eye dogs controlled the sides and the front. Surrounded by barking dogs, the cattle huddled and moved together, which was exactly what Donnie needed. Livestock farmers in New Zealand could not operate without their dogs. The production of meat in the United States is an industrial process. The animals are artificially inseminated, kept in tight pens, fed formulas with meat byproducts and shot up with antibiotics. In New Zealand animals procreate naturally and live in the open fields, eating grass. They have so much space that a farmer needs several dogs to move them.

Watching farm dogs at work is one of the most fascinating sights in nature, offering a view of smoothly controlled aggression, like a game of professional tennis. Their relationship with farm animals is essentially that of the wolf and its prey, but they have been civilized over generations, bringing their aggression under control and using it to serve man. I have seen farm dogs, rushing to the far end of a flock of sheep and unable to get through while unwilling to waste time by going around, take the high road—they jump up and run on the backs of the sheep, hopping from one to the other. I have watched a strong-eye dog bring down three sheep from a rocky, almost vertical slope. The sheep backed up against the rock and put their horns forward, keeping the dog at bay. The farmer whistled, and suddenly one of the sheep got a bloody nose after the dog nipped at it. A moment later all three sheep were running downhill towards the farmer with a silent dog hugging the ground behind them.

Colin and Charles came in a pickup truck, drove us back to the station, and opened lunch boxes at the edge of the truck's flat bed. A pack of dogs lying at the other end of the flat bed did not even look at our food. I was used to dogs begging at tables and said that they seemed exceptionally well behaved. "They understand pain, hoo-hoo-hoo," growled Trev. The working dogs could not be more different from house dogs. They slept on the dirt in unheated cubicles. They stank because they never got a bath, and they seldom got petted. They did not get too much to eat because farmers did not want them to get fat and slow down. When not working they were kept on a chain, and if a farmer saw an unfamiliar dog on his land, he was likely to shoot it.

Before we left his neighbor's station, Charles drove me to a paddock with a flock of ghar—long-haired, long-horned mountain goats. These animals, slightly larger than farm goats, came from the snow-covered peaks of the Himalayas and were introduced into New Zealand for sport. Hunters from abroad, mostly from the United States and Germany, spent up to NZ$20,000 a week trying to track down and shoot a ghar, taking home its mounted head. Charles, turning down the corners of his mouth, explained that a hunter who failed in the mountains could pay a farmer to shoot one up close and take home "a sporting trophy." These wild animals are difficult to track but surprisingly easy to domesticate. When we walked through the gate, Charles tossed out a few handfuls of grain and a flock of ghar came within 10 feet of us. They were gentle even though their horns were very sharp—a few months before my visit some joker had tried to sit on a ghar and it took off his testicle.

Driving back to Charles' station, we passed a hillside where three men were running a crop-dusting operation. A pilot took off downhill and landed uphill every few minutes, while a driver in a fertilizer truck pulled up after each landing and dumped a ton of chemicals into the plane through a hole in its back. The third man's job was loading the truck. Charles explained that the fertilizer was a relatively cheap superphosphate, which helped grow clover. Clover grew well in New Zealand because of its very sunny weather and did not require expensive nitrogen fertilizer.

The value of farmland is measured in livestock units, which shows how many animals it can support. A sheep is one livestock unit, cattle five or six, deer two. A paddock big enough for 100 sheep can be used for 20 cows or 50 deer. There had been no native deer in New Zealand until they were brought from Europe in the 1880s and released into the wild for hunting. By the 1930s they multiplied and became pests, destroying vegetation and carrying illnesses. Hunters were paid bounties for every deer tail, but in the 1970s some people figured they could capture wild deer and farm them. They shot nets from helicopters to catch the wild deer, airlifted them out, and put them behind six-foot fences. They were bred in captivity, first for their meat and later for their horns. Those were called velvet and were highly prized in Asia for their alleged ability to enhance sexual performance, especially before Viagra became available, but farmers insisted they had many other health benefits.

The harder, rockier ground can support heavier male deer, bred for their velvet. The softer ground can be used for the lighter does, bred for their meat. When the deer reach 18 months, Charles measures the circumference of the males' horns, selecting the biggest 10 to 15 percent to keep for their horns, which are harvested annually under local anesthesia. The rest of the males and all the females are slaughtered and shipped to Germany as venison. The quality of land also drives sheep farming decisions. Charles explained that Colin's rough, hilly, dry land was good for the merino sheep—he probably derives 90 percent of his sheep income from wool, the rest from meat. For Charles, whose land is softer and wetter, the ratio is reversed—most of his sheep income comes from meat, with only rough wool sold to the carpet industry.

Early European settlers introduced many animals to New Zealand, which until then had only dogs, rats, a few bats, and no other mammals. Rabbits were introduced for hunting, but multiplied until they ate the grass intended for the sheep. Slopes were soon overrun by the whirling, moving masses of rabbits. The settlers tried introducing cats, ferrets, stoats, and weasels to help control the rabbits, but that created other problems, as many native birds, such as the tomtito and fantail, had evolved not knowing any predatory animals. The birds were naturally inquisitive and fearless, falling easy prey to introduced predators. Eventually, in the 1930s all the farmers in the valley united, elected a "rabbit board" and taxed themselves to hire a "rabbiter." This person came to live in the valley and poison its rabbits with strychnine, making the valley essentially rabbit-free.

Charles stopped to talk with scattered groups of workers. Mechanization and automation have driven down the demand for farm labor. The elementary school at the far end of the valley had closed because there were not enough children. It used to have one teacher who lived at the opposite end of the valley and drove a bus to school every morning, collecting his students along the way and driving them home in the afternoon. All the kids went to the same elementary school, but in high school their educational paths diverged. Charles' kids went to an Anglican boarding school in Christchurch, while his workers' kids went to a state-run local school, even though all the kids played and worked together during school holidays.

All structures on Charles' station, such as sheds and paddocks, were named after long-term employees. Once he sold a piece of land with MacGaffy paddock, named for an old livestock manager, but later bought it back. Mr. MacGaffy was already dead, but Charles ran into his widow in a nearby town. "Good boy, Charlie," she patted him on the shoulder. "Bought that paddock back, but it wasn't yours to sell in the first place." A crew was repairing a wool-shed where sheep were brought to be shorn. A shearer earned NZ$1.25 to $1.50 a sheep (a little over 50 U.S. cents), but could shear more than 300 sheep a day. Many of the best shearers were Maori who liked working in groups and enjoyed the competitiveness of piece work.

Charles took me to meet some of his neighbors. A German named Dieter wasn't home, but Charles pointed out his deer, bigger and fatter than the rest. "He did something better than us. After he bought this farm, he went to Yugoslavia, bought their deer, and crossed them with local breeds." The sun was setting down when we went home. We showered and changed after a day on the farm, then sat in the armchairs near the fire, drinking whiskey with water. The New Zealand custom of having a drink before dinner was starting to grow on me. Daphne went into her kitchen for a few minutes and returned with a tray of freshly baked oysters—moist, sweet, and succulent. It was like eating candy and soon Charles and I were eyeing the last remaining piece on the tray.

In the evening I invited Charles, Daphne, and several of their friends to a restaurant. The service was friendly but slow. There is no tipping in New Zealand—you pay your bill and that is that. Waiters get real salaries instead of depending on tips, but I prefer the American system, which gives the customer more control over the process. That night I taught my New Zealand friends the Russian custom of putting empty bottles on the floor. They were quick learners, and by the end of our dinner several bottles had migrated downward. On the way home we stopped at Dieter's house again and helped him and his friends, who had gathered after a game of tennis, kill a bottle of Drambuie along with two boxes of chocolate.

17 *Poverty, Chastity, and Obedience*

Charles returned for a cup of coffee after I came down for breakfast—he had already been up for hours, running his station. An old farmhand who worked there for 27 years stepped up to the terrace, glanced into the kitchen window, took off his boots, and came in for a cup of tea. Whatever we discussed, he linked every topic of conversation to the patterns of animal behavior "because we are all animals." Charles took me into the formal dining room to see his family portraits, and then we went outside, where he and Daphne led me through an alley of tall trees from several continents, including an American redwood. We made our way to a small Anglican church. Charles and Daphne had walked their children down this alley to their weddings. In a tiny unfenced cemetery next to the church heavy family crosses were rising above the valley, surrounded by low headstones of family friends. A poignant thought crossed my mind—some day they too will lie there, in their land to which they were so intensely attached. Daphne showed me the stained-glass windows and the bell rope they used on New Year's Eve to ring in the new year. She began each day by feeding her hens, then coming here alone. She never locked the church, even though a pair of candlesticks was stolen. She hoped some day they would be returned.

We shook hands, with the last round of invitations to visit and revisit. I got in the car and drove north, past Mt. Hutt gleaming in the distance. The road was signposted "Inland Scenic Route," running between breathtaking snow-capped mountains and green meadows teeming with sheep, deer, cattle, and occasionally llamas. I stepped on the gas, slowing down only in tiny villages, some of which had a single gas station, a fish and chip shop, and a pub with a sign reading "Pint and Pie for $5.95." My destination for that day was Blenheim, a major wine growing center on the South Island. I shot across the Rakaia Gorge, picking up speed as the road straightened, when a pebble from the wheel of an oncoming car cracked my windshield. Damn, there went my deductible! The glass probably would not have cracked at a lower speed, but the regret faded fast.

In Christchurch I left the car in a municipal parking lot and went to look for an Internet café to check my emails. I walked amidst substantial stone buildings and rich monuments, streets filled with good-looking people, quite a few formally dressed men in dark suits and ties, women in short black skirts and black stockings. They had attractive English faces, but fresher and healthier than those you see in London—we were in the Pacific. Outdoor cafés lined sunlit avenues where locals lunched in the unexpectedly warm winter sun. I found a table and sat with my back against the brick wall, watching the sidewalk and the park. After ordering a pint of dark draft with a smoked mackerel salad I dialed my daughter's number in New York. She almost screamed with joy—did I get her email? I had not yet checked my emails. Only a few minutes earlier she had emailed me after receiving a call from the place where she was dying to get a job. She got it! Did I believe in telepathy? Why did I call that minute, on a whim? I know there is no scientific proof of telepathy, but incidents like this make me wonder. The waitress set down a large yellow plate with a blue rim, on which perfectly grilled slabs of smoked mackerel were served on a bouncy bed of green salad, with dark drops of balsamic vinegar on the leaves. It was heaven.

Christchurch is the third largest city in New Zealand, after Auckland and Wellington, and the largest on the South Island, but until this visit I had only driven through it at night. On my previous trip I had flown in late with my son, and we stayed in a motel near the airport. Opening the door to our room, I heard loud snoring, closed it, gave the key to Danny, and asked him to scoot back to the front desk and ask with a straight face for a room without anyone snoring in it. In the morning we stopped by the Antarctic Center near the airport. Several countries with bases in the Antarctic, including Italy, New Zealand, and the United States, have supply stations near Christchurch Airport. The well-designed center has a room that imitates Antarctic weather—

cold, windy, and dark—with a pile of warm clothes near the entrance. I liked it so much that in buying a souvenir I broke my rule against wearing legible clothing and to this day occasionally wear an Antarctic Center polo shirt.

It was tempting to stay in Christchurch that night, but I already had plans for exploring the upper part of the South Island. Christchurch would have to go on the list of places to visit on the next trip. By the time I pulled out, around 3 PM, the schools must have just closed. There were kids everywhere, on sidewalks, at bus stations, on bicycles, with and without backpacks. The boys wore dark jackets and ties, the girls long dark skirts. I thought New Zealand was a wonderful place to educate adolescents. Anyone who wants to send their children to study in an English-speaking country would do well to consider Christchurch. The educational standards are as high as anywhere in the world and the living conditions very pleasant. The country is safe and is a great place to come visit your kids.

I pulled off the road and leafed through a few guidebooks before using my cell phone to reserve a room for the night. I missed not having my kids on this trip. They were very good at taking care of travel logistics. They began doing it when my oldest daughter was ten and my youngest son five. We traveled through the United States together and the kids chose places from AAA travel books while I drove. Money was a bit tight, and they had to choose places that were both attractive and inexpensive, a challenging task that taught them well. I called the lodge that my guests at dinner the night before had described as top luxury and left a message. The owner called back half an hour later, while I was steering through hairpin turns. They were closed for renovations, but he suggested another lodge, run by his friends in a converted convent, and recommended the suite in the sanctuary. "Will I have to take the vows of poverty, chastity, and obedience?" "Not at all, quite the contrary," he laughed and gave me the number, which I wrote down while holding the steering wheel with my knee. Swinging the car on the mountain road, working the gas and the brakes, I liked that idea less and less. I grew up in a country where we were taught, religious or not, to take your hat off when stepping into a church and to speak in whispers once inside. Old habits die hard, and I pulled off the road, consulted my books, and dialed another place. The owner sounded happy, told me I could have either a room or a private cottage and volunteered to light up the fireplace before I arrived.

The road ran on the ridges of the foothills, swinging right and left, diving sharply down, then rearing up. Holding the steering wheel felt like being on the back of an animal trying to shake me off, twisting from under me. The road was well-built and smooth, but there were no guardrails over the abysses, only waist-high wire fences. They were designed to stop a 100-pound sheep traveling at two miles per hour from escaping, not a 3,000-pound car doing 50 from tumbling down the hill. I felt New Zealand could have done better than that—controlling the sheep was no more important than saving people from crashes.

The road swung onto the Pacific coast near Kaikoura, the whale-watching capital of New Zealand. I stepped out and looked at the big slow Pacific rollers crashing on the rocks. In the dusk, I passed a lodge on the beach side of the road whose name I recognized from one of my guidebooks. I pulled in, but no one was home, and I walked around the house to the dock. I would love to spend the night here, I thought, fall asleep, and wake up to the surf. A brown cat came out, curved its back, and gave me an evil eye. I looked up the phone number in the book and called the owners. They answered from a car near Christchurch. I asked whether their neighbors had the key, but they were not too friendly, and I drove off into the dark.

Near Blenheim, I called Gino, who guided me to his house by cell phone. All my doubts were dispelled—the cottage was magic, a warm small ship of stone and wood sailing into the dark night. The fireplace growled softly in the living room, the heaters stood in the hallway and the bedroom; the bathroom had heated tile floors. I asked for a bottle of wine, listened to Gino's Italian CDs, ate grapes, cracked walnuts and soon drifted off to sleep.

18   Bad Girls' Guide to Wine

In the soft morning sunshine I drank in the quiet privacy of my cottage. The previous four nights I had stayed with friends, and even though I liked them very much, it felt good to be silent for a change, not to have to talk. I caught up on my notes and took a long bath. As I stepped out and reached for the towel, the cell phone rang—a Russian reporter wanted to know my opinion on the likelihood of a crash of the Russian ruble. Ever since it crashed in 1998, pundits have been expecting a repeat, but in my opinion such lightning was unlikely to strike twice. I pleaded ignorance, but the man would not take no for an answer. Modern technology never ceases to amaze me—there I stood, naked, in rural

New Zealand, tracked down from around the globe using a handheld piece of electronics.

The night before Gino had recommended I hire a driver for touring the wineries and concentrate on drinking rather than driving. His friend Barry came to pick me up in his minivan—I was his only customer on that winter day. He was a happy driver who wore shorts in any weather because long pants, according to him, were much too formal. Barry came to Blenheim from much colder Invercargill 22 years ago after doctors recommended a change of climate for his daughter. He drove a taxi and ran a bus service to Greymouth, then retired but could not stand the boredom and started a wine tour business. When he came to this area, the Montana vineyards, the country's biggest commercial wine operation, was only a shed by the side of the road, but now the area had 46 vineyards, many of them internationally known.

Barry was a sober driver, but no connoisseur. He pointed out a local museum and when I asked what was there, he answered in all seriousness, "Oh, bits and pieces." I asked how he chose which of the 46 vineyards to visit, and he said he drove to those that his most knowledgeable passengers asked about. That seemed like a reasonable plan, and after quizzing Barry on his business arrangements I was satisfied that he received no kickbacks from wineries other than such trifles as a free lunch or a case of wine for Christmas. In winter he averaged one customer a week, in summer he could get work seven days a week, but limited himself to five in order to have enough time for more important things, such as fishing.

The Blenheim area is famous for its white wines. Red grapes grow better on the warmer North Island. Smooth, silky, oaky whites—I kept sampling and buying them at different wineries throughout the morning. After several tastings Barry drove me to a restaurant at a winery. The tour books said it was built like an Italian palazzo but to me its pink boxy cement towers looked more like a medium-security prison in upstate New York. It was the second day of August, the equivalent of February 2 in the northern hemisphere, but the first buds were already on the vines. The earlier they came out, the hotter the summer was going to be and the better the wine—the vines knew the weather in advance. I sampled more wines, then chose a table on the terrace. It was so warm that I had to take off my sweater; I saw a stack of straw hats by the door for those who wanted to protect themselves from the sun. Rows of well-tended vines ran from north to south, catching the prevailing westerly winds and changing from green to blue in the distance, like a picture on a wine label. A hawk slowly circled above the vineyard, looking for mice for his lunch.

Barry chatted with a waitress, then leaned towards me and said in his confidential soft growl that she had told him the salmon was divine that day. We ordered, and I drank the first full glass of Sauvignon—fresh and green, its chill a pleasant contrast with the warmth of the vineyard. We faced a pétanque court—a strip of soft ground with metal balls slightly larger than billiard balls. It seemed like an obligatory feature of any restaurant in a vineyard, and the people waiting for a table often played a friendly round. The previous year, tasting wine and having lunch with my daughter in the Bay of Islands, I had become so enamored of pétanque that I bought a set and carried it to New York in my hand luggage. We flew home two days before 9/11, and that was probably the last time anyone flew with eight solid metal balls in their hand luggage without a single question from security. The pétanque set has been sitting on my bookshelf ever since, with Nika teasing me about the dangers of impulse shopping in a state of mild inebriation.

The fish arrived—reddish-brown from the grill, firm on the outside but separating into pink soft layers under the slightest pressure of the fork. I ordered a glass of Chardonnay and soaked up the sauce with a slab of freshly baked sourdough bread. Afterwards we leaned back in our chairs and drank espresso, basking in the sun, taking in the view. I bought a few more bottles of wine and the steps of Barry's van seemed higher than they had been in the morning. We drove on and he showed me a farm that raised ostriches and alpacas. It had a beautiful house on a hill, facing the vineyards, with the wind whistling through the gallery that connected two halves of the house. There was a B&B vacancy sign, but I was perfectly happy at Gino's. We drove past an Air Force base and golf course—typical of New Zealand, there was no fence between the two. Then I asked Barry to drive me to the Cloudy Bay vineyard.

Six months earlier, at a financial trading conference in the Bay of Islands, the hotel had given me a double suite, a sprawling space with two terraces. Each evening after classes and before dinner a group of women traders gathered there to drink wine. I called them the "bad girls club"; the definition of a bad girl being someone who used bad language, drank good wine, and made independent decisions. My friend Phyllis was the original bad girl. Another was an Australian who was a serious wine connoisseur and often brought Cloudy Bay to our get-togethers.

Afterwards Barry took me to a liqueur tasting and then hinted that at that point all wines tasted pretty much the same. He was right; it was time to go home. I was glad to have hired him instead of driving. I sat on the tiled terrace outside my cottage, with Italian songs wafting through the open doors, watched the sunset, smoked a cigar, and read a book, then went into the main house for a cup of espresso with Gino and his friends. He showed me two charming guest rooms in front of the house, one with a sitting area above the swimming pool, which was closed for the winter.

Gino invited me for dinner—he had gone fishing that day in Kaikoura and had caught a lot of fish and crayfish. His brother was due to fly to Italy several days later and he was going to give him some crays to take there, but he had caught too many. He fried a mound of fresh fish and served it with cold fresh crays, salad, and green peas. I went back to my cottage and brought out some of the bottles I had accumulated during the day. Heather, Gino's wife, kept stepping into the garden and bringing fresh lemons from the tree to squeeze on our fish and crays. Luca, their beautiful collie, hovered in the room. He was a serial crotch sniffer, but otherwise an extremely friendly creature.

Gino was born on the Adriatic coast of Italy that now belonged to Yugoslavia, where he had met Heather, a Kiwi, who had traveled there as a young woman. They had a grown son and daughter who moved away and had good careers. Heather taught high school math, while Gino looked after the house, fished, and ran a small import business. Whenever the phone rang Gino launched into a fast-paced Italian dialect, sounding much more emotional than when he spoke English. There was a palpable feeling of hospitality and generosity in this impromptu invitation to a family dinner. Just like at Villa Sorgenfrei I thought that a traveler might find a house in a more breathtaking location, but one could never find greater warmth or generosity. Heather started yawning as I made arrangements with Gino to buy a kilo of excellent coffee he had imported from Italy. I went back to the cottage with its welcoming fireplace, hot bath, and large, soft bed. It would have been nice to have some company here, I thought, drifting off to sleep.

19 Meeting Captain Cook

I woke up early, packed my bag, and rang Gino's doorbell. A mail boat was leaving from nearby Picton, which one of the "bad girls," had recommended for touring Marlboro Sounds—a tangle of land and bays at the northern end of the island. The bell rang, but there was no answer. I put my luggage and a case of wine in the car, then went back to leave Gino a note with my credit card number. By now I was used to the New Zealand custom of no check-ins, no

forms to fill out, and no credit card imprints in advance. Gino opened the door—
he had been on the phone with the boat company, making a booking for me.
He brought out a kilo of coffee, took an imprint of my card, and as we shook
hands I repeated an invitation to him and Heather for a dinner in New York.

I raced across the mountain to catch the early morning boat, but the girl
at the counter told me about a longer ride which would leave at 1:30 PM. Picton
was a picturesque little town, splattered on a narrow coastal strip that zigzagged
between the bay and the mountains. I found a café and had a leisurely breakfast
of a tomato frittata with fresh orange juice while I read a local newspaper, then
found an Internet café. They were ubiquitous and inexpensive, used by all
young travelers and some old ones, too. The advancing technology can
improve our lives, and the Internet helps me maintain a closer connection with
my children, office, and friends.

Picton was named after a British general—a scoundrel who, as a governor
in the Caribbean, had authorized the torture of mulatto women, but sailed into
history by leading a decisive charge against Napoleon at Waterloo. He had
walked in front of his troops, carrying only a furled umbrella to show his dis-
dain for the enemy and took a bullet to the forehead. The sidewalks of Picton's
tiny downtown were tiled in a gentle wavelike pattern, so that by following the
lines you meandered rather than walked straight. The sun came out from
behind the morning clouds, and I walked to the waterfront park, finding a
bench under a palm tree. In that impromptu office I spread out my travel
guides, opened an electronic organizer, and made so many calls that Phyllis'
prepaid cell phone ran out of money and I had to recharge it.

I made a reservation for that night with a couple in Nelson whom
Heather had recommended. I bought a ticket for a ferry crossing from the
South to the North Island three days later. Several months earlier, after I had
already bought my ticket to New Zealand, an invitation came for several speaking engagements and a book tour in Australia, a five-hour flight away. It would
be exactly in the middle of my eight-week trip through New Zealand, and even
though I did not like losing a week, that invitation would pay for the entire
trip—it was an offer I did not refuse. Wellington, the capital of New Zealand,
sits at the southern tip of the North Island, almost in the middle of the country.
I was going to spend three days there, then fly to Australia for a week and return
to continue my journey.

I called a lodge in Wellington that had been highly recommended by several people and told the woman artist who owned it I was looking for a place
where I would not see a single cow and needed no car. After three weeks on the

road I was ready for a break from livestock and driving. I wanted to be back in a city and walk to museums and concerts. The woman laughed and said that while she had no livestock, her house was too far from downtown to walk there. She recommended her friend's homestay in the center of the city. Logan said he had only one room and it would not be available on my first night in Wellington. He offered to put me up elsewhere and bring me into his house for the second and third nights, but I did not feel like moving and found another homestay in the center, where a woman enthusiastically took my reservation.

The mail boats run a different route each day in Marlboro Sounds, a fringe of spits and bays at the northern end of the South Island. The patchwork of channels between forested ridges had been formed after huge glaciers slid down the mountains during the Ice Age. Their enormous weight pressed soft valley floors about 100 feet below sea level. When the climate warmed up and the glaciers melted, the sea came in and flooded the valleys, with only the ridges remaining above the water. They protected the flooded valleys from storms, creating a perfect breeding environment for fish and other sea life. Gino loved fishing in the Sounds. Most of the area was DOC land, with just a few isolated houses on the roadless seashore, accessible only by water. The post office put out a contract for mail deliveries by boat, and the boat company also carried tourists.

After putting a salmon sandwich and two small bottles of local beer into my day pack I hurried to the harbor. The catamaran was bobbing in green water so clean you could see the bottom. A young Maori was teaching his two very young sons to fish by dropping a line from the pier. The cat could carry nearly 100 passengers, but on this wintry day, with the sun hiding again, we had only a couple from Auckland, two young women from Scotland, and an Indian family. The captain, as usual in New Zealand, was the only crew member, taking tickets, tying up the boat, driving, acting as a tour guide, and delivering sacks of mail. I asked about his bandaged left hand. He had banged it against a sharp corner four months earlier and tried to tough it out. It got worse, he went to one doctor, then another, took antibiotics, but nothing helped, and now they were saying he had nerve damage. We talked about how a man does not heal so well past 50; he does not bounce back like a young kid. I told him we had medical centers in New York that specialized in hands—he should look for something like that in Christchurch. The captain had the grim air of a man in his 50s who suddenly faced the possible end of his working career.

The twin-engine cat buzzed amidst low mountain ridges. The day turned overcast and chilly, too cold to stand on the open deck while the boat moved. Inside, the captain used his public address system to comment on the areas we passed, but without too much zing. I volunteered to hoist boxes of groceries and stood looking over his shoulder. We pulled up to about 20 docks on our four-hour run. Each owner stood with a small post office sack, which the captain exchanged for his mail sack through the side window. I handed about a dozen heavy boxes of groceries and supplies from the Picton supermarket through the window. We picked up two passengers at a fishing lodge. Most residents were retirees, a few farmers, a few commuters from Wellington, enjoying their solitude. Almost all had dogs, and the captain carried a bag of dog biscuits, which earned him an enthusiastic reception with much barking and tail-wagging. A year earlier I had gone on a mail boat cruise with Nika in the Bay of Islands, on the North Island, and that captain had also carried a bag of dog biscuits, making him very popular with the local four-legged population.

Long lines of big black buoys bobbed gently in a remote bay. Getting closer, we could see two fields of buoys, each with ten long parallel lines. The captain told us they were mussel farms. A rope hung from each buoy, seeded with mussels that grew well in the clean, gently lapping sea water. Each line of buoys held about 30 tons of mussels, worth at least $1,000 a ton. Since there were ten lines to a farm and two farms in the bay, I did quick arithmetic and asked the captain whether there really was half a million dollars bobbing below the water. Granted, those were New Zealand dollars, but still, it was almost a quarter million dollars in American money. Did anyone look after that property? "You're not in Manhattan, mate," growled the captain, wincing as he moved his hand. Of course, who would steal them? You'd need a big boat, and the people who lived along the shore saw everything and knew every local boat.

The last sack of mail was for a couple so isolated they did not even have a dock and rowed out to exchange mailbags. We crossed open water and passed the rocks where the Soviet cruise ship Lermontov had sunk in the waning days of the empire. Then we reached Ship's Cove, tied up the boat, and hiked to the Captain Cook memorial. Cook is an iconic figure in New Zealand, the man who opened the country to Europeans. The Maori, after migrating here centuries ago from the Pacific islands, lived in a state of total isolation. They were Stone Age hunters, fishermen, and gatherers, with extremely primitive agriculture, living in tribal groups, many of which practiced cannibalism.

James Cook, born in 1728, was the son of an English farm laborer, but he did not allow that huge social disadvantage to stop him. The man had enormous drive and charm, which helped him acquire important patrons. The first of those was a local ship owner who gave the boy a job, and to whom Cook remained loyal for the rest of his life. Refusing an advancement to be the master of a coastal coal-hauling ship, he took a pay cut to volunteer for the Navy, where his dedication and continued learning were noticed by several important commanders. He saw action in the 1758 war against the French in Québec, but attracted more notice by compiling the first accurate coastal maps of eastern Canada and Newfoundland. He earned a reputation as the Navy's finest cartographer and was promoted to the rank of lieutenant (his maps remained in use until the twentieth century, when satellite technology offered a higher degree of precision).

An extremely rare astronomical event was anticipated in 1769—the passage of Venus across the Sun, visible only in the Southern Hemisphere. It offered the opportunity to measure the distance from the Earth to the Sun more precisely than ever before—a valuable addition to navigation. In the continuing rivalry between the British and French Empires, the Royal Society, a London scientific club sponsored by wealthy and influential men, prevailed upon the Navy to send a ship to the South Pacific to take the measurements. When the Navy agreed and appointed Lieutenant Cook to command the ship, it added its own instructions. Cook was ordered to conduct a journey of discovery and look for Terra Australis, a mythical continent in the Southern Ocean that was thought to counterbalance the weight of Eurasia in the Northern Hemisphere. That myth lived on because when Cook embarked on his first voyage in 1768, almost half of the Earth's surface had not yet been mapped by the Europeans (by the time Cook was killed on his third journey in 1779, the map of the world was essentially complete).

Cook sailed around the world aboard the Endeavour, a slow but stable converted collier, armed with several cannons, a crew of 80, and several paying passengers—scientists and artists (photography had not yet been invented). For several months prior to his sailing he practically lived in the boatyard where the Endeavour was being outfitted, supervising every detail. In those days it was common for up to half the crew to die from scurvy on an ocean crossing. More than a century later that disease, which greatly impeded ocean voyages, was traced to the lack of vitamin C in preserved foods. The observant lieutenant knew from experience that men who drank extracts of fresh branches and ate sauerkraut, both sources of vitamin C, remained healthy. When the tradition-bound crew refused to follow his diet and insisted on salted meat, bread, and rum, he had several offenders tied up and whipped to make the rest eat what was good for them. After that convincing argument, Cook did not lose a single man to scurvy on any of his voyages.

Cook crossed the Atlantic, bought provisions in Brazil, rounded Cape Horn, and reached Tahiti, where he successfully performed the measurements during the passage of Venus. From there he headed southwest—he had seen Abel Tasman's ancient maps and announced a reward to the first man to see the land. On October 5, 1769, his cabin boy Nick Young screamed "Land!" from the top of the mast. Cook named the promontory near today's Gisborne on the North Island Young Nick's Head. He circumnavigated the new land and drew remarkably accurate maps, then headed south where the Admiralty wanted him to look for the mythical Southern Continent. Cook sailed amidst the icebergs, hauling up chunks of ice for drinking water and landing on ice floes to kill penguins for food. After reaching a solid wall of ice he turned north, hugged the stormy West Coast of New Zealand, passed Murderers' Bay and pulled into Marlboro Sounds, where he proved that New Zealand consisted of two large islands.

Here, in Ship's Cove, Cook found plentiful wood and running water, and ordered his crew to haul the wooden ship ashore for much-needed repairs. There was not a single European outpost within thousands of miles. Cook got along with the natives, who responded well to his combination of firmness and kindness. When he gave them nails as presents, it was the first time the Maori encountered metal, which they greatly valued. Cook kept returning to Ship's Cove, using it as his repair station and a provisioning base; he spent a total of 100 days there during his three great voyages of discovery. Standing there I realized that the sailing ship in which Captain Cook crossed the oceans (with no radio or navigational tools other than a sextant and a chronometer) was not much bigger than the little cat in which we zoomed up from Picton that afternoon. I asked one of the Scottish girls to snap my picture while touching the monument. It stood on a narrow strip of land between the water and the mountain, and nearby, discreetly tucked away behind some trees, stood a working toilet with running water and three spare rolls of toilet paper in a dispenser. This was New Zealand, and the DOC did not want tourists to foul the bushes.

It began to drizzle, and we headed back to Picton. Travel by boat is one of the most pleasant ways to see a country, and I was thinking of some of my favorite rides. A dinner with my son on a boat floating down the Seine in Paris. Sailing up the Moskva River from the Kremlin to Moscow State University, working on a bottle of cabernet on a sunny deck with two friends. Taking my kids from the Westminster down to Greenwich, past Shakespeare's Globe theater. Going through Amsterdam's canals in a pedal boat. The woman with me had pushed the pedals, while I stretched in the sun, and locals pointed from the low bridges and smiled. I wanted to take this mail boat again, but only when it was sunny enough to sit outside.

After the evening became too dark to see the shores, the captain gave me a folder with an article from the New Zealand Geographic about the sinking of the Mikhail Lermontov in these waters in 1986. The Soviet cruise ship ferried Australian pensioners on cheap package tours using a local pilot who was experienced but extremely overworked. In a burst of bad judgment, he first took the ship so close to the shore that the huge ocean liner almost touched the trees, then veered off its charted course into a narrow passage with three underwater peaks. An investigator had said it was like playing Russian roulette with three bullets loaded into a six-shooter. One of those peaks sliced open the ship's belly, filling it with water. The captain panicked and missed his chance to beach the ship, which drifted offshore and sank. Amazingly, only one person out of more than a thousand crew and passengers was lost. The hero of the rescue was a Kiwi grandmother who worked a ham radio from her house on a hill overlooking the disaster. She coordinated the rescue in what was called a Dunkirk-like operation, bringing in a flotilla of small vessels to save the passengers and crew.

Back at shore, I got into my car and drove through the dark on an incredibly twisty mountain road from Picton to Nelson. At one stretch it took me an hour to cover 20 miles—up, down, brakes, gas, ravine on one side, water on the other. I stopped in Havelock, the self-proclaimed mussel capital of the world, and had a pot of steamed mussels with French fries and a local Chardonnay for dinner. The mussels came from the fresh waters of Marlboro Sounds, harvested from the ropes suspended from the buoys. They were very fresh, but to my great surprise not any better than those served in my favorite bistro three blocks from my home in New York. At home they cost twice as much as here, but the sauce was better and I could look forward to returning.

The homestay recommended by Heather was run by a friendly English couple with three dogs. They were hospitable, and invited me to nip from the two carafes of sherry in the guest parlor, a red and a tawny. My room on the second floor was comfortable and had windows overlooking the bay, but I could not avoid noticing a few hairs in the bathtub and thought those dogs could really use a bath—I had to wash my hands to get rid of dog smell after petting one of them. I missed Heather's spotless cottage.

20 *Above Murderers' Bay*

Jan and Stan joined me for a leisurely breakfast in their dining room facing the bay. Tall rose bushes bloomed outside the windows, and my hosts kept saying how this early August in New Zealand was equivalent to early February back home in England, but what a difference in the climate! We ate yogurt with mounds of fresh fruits and fluffy croissants with homemade jams; we drank freshly squeezed juice and dark pungent tea. In brilliant sunshine I drove a few miles up to Nelson and walked into the Bishop Suter Gallery, a large building with a pagoda-like roof. Suter was an early missionary who collected art and bequeathed his collection to the public. Not only was his museum going strong, but Nelson has become an important handicrafts center, with many artists and craftspeople settling in the area and showing their work in local galleries. I began my tour in one of my favorite parts of any museum—the gift shop. Museum shops in New Zealand tend to carry authentic works by local craftsmen rather than tourist kitsch. I saw several attractive wood pieces but resisted the urge to buy because I still had a long road ahead.

More than once in art museums I had played a bit of a tug-of-war with my younger daughter; she was drawn to modern art works in textile, while I always wanted to go to other rooms and see paintings or sculptures. This day, to my great surprise, I was swept away by a textile show. The walls of a large hall were hung with framed squares of textiles, interspersed with black and white photographs and a row of mannequins in the middle. "Joie de vivre celebrates the work of Avis Higgs" read the sign. The energy of colorful designs spilled into the room and I started reading notes and looking at photographs.

Avis Higgs was born in 1918 in Wellington, the daughter of a prominent artist. The photos showed a stylish, dashing, strong woman, slender and dark-haired, always well dressed, accompanied by other well-dressed women and men. Between 1941 and 1946 she worked in Australia as head designer for STP, the most innovative fabric house in the country. Its owners, two Italian brothers, were interned during the war as "enemy aliens," and the young woman had a free hand with her designs. They shimmered, danced, leaped from the walls—surfing themes, tropical and underwater themes, New Zealand themes (paddock flowers!), Maori, Aboriginal, and Polynesian motifs. Other designs, bursting with energy, drew upon her experiences as a single young woman living in an exciting metropolis. The fabric squares showed her waterskiing, promenading, swimming with friends in a risqué bikini. In a wartime country with a clothing shortage, wearing dresses made from her own fabrics, Avis must have turned heads in the nightspots of Sydney. She returned home, put together a portfolio, and in 1950 went to conquer England, stopping on the way in Ceylon (Sri Lanka) to design tropical fabrics. Soon her work was being taken up by some of the best fabric houses in London, but a severe auto accident near Rome in 1951 put an end to her career. She returned to Wellington and never designed again.

I walked from the gallery to a park that must have felt like hallowed ground to most Kiwis—the field where the country's first rugby game was played in 1870. A billboard had a copy of the first ever rugby team photo—young men with strong open faces, standing and sitting shoulder to shoulder, looking into the camera. Rugby is the closest thing New Zealand has to a national religion. It is a pity that I am not the best person to write about it. I'll gladly run, lift weights, row, or do any number of other sports, but I get bored watching other people perform. All I know is that New Zealand is rugby-mad, especially when it comes to its rivalry with Australia. New Zealand is a mild country, but when the Australian rugby team flew in, the front-page headline in the local newspaper read: "They may be descendants of criminals, but we will not let them steal our Cup." Pretty strong stuff.

The trail led up the hill signposted "the Center of New Zealand." I was starting to feel sentimental—my journey was nearing its midpoint. But New Zealanders are down-to-earth people who never let you feel sentimental for very long. The next sign read: "It is suggested that the actual geocentric is about 55 km South West in the Spooner Range, but the first trig station [a pyramidal mast from which land measurements were taken] stood on top of this hill and all the surveys radiated from here." So I was not at the center after all, just very near it.

The trail zigzagged uphill, and even though the sign said "Roundtrip 40 minutes," I sweated up to the top in only 12. This was no Disney ride, there was nothing ready-made or passive about it. There was no moving sidewalk, no happy music, no announcements to keep your hands inside. This was real—

you sweated and you enjoyed it. I stood on a hill under the needle marking the near-center of New Zealand and looked around. The sun was bright and hot, I took off my sweater and shielded my eyes from the sun. Green fields and forests spread in all directions, the little crossword of a city lay below, and low flat waves rolled in from the Tasman Sea, with ships in the harbor and a few clouds overhead.

What a piece of heaven, I thought—I must come back here. I will return to the South Island, but follow a different route the next time. Of course, I would begin near Queenstown, on Villa Sorgenfrei, relax for a few days with Micha and Klaus after the flight across the ocean. Then stop for a couple of days with Evan and Heather at the Abisko Lodge to ski Mt. Hutt. Several days at Christchurch to take in its museums and nightlife, meet people at the University, eat in the outdoor restaurants. Take the Tranz-Scenic to the West Coast and spend a couple of days looking around Hokitika. Soak in hot pools at Hanmer Springs, amidst the Alpine scenery. Stay for a night in Kaikoura on the water, then to Blenheim to stay with Gino and Heather and ask Gino to take me fishing if the water is smooth. Drive to Nelson and, if the weather is warm, spend a few days in a lodge on the beach in the Abel Tasman National Park.

An English girl walked up the hill and took a photo of me near the center of the country. The sun grew hot. I should have left my sweater with the people who were gardening at the foot of the hill with whom I chatted on the way up. I kept meeting people on my way down—families and friends enjoying a fine winter weekend. Thick palm trees with huge bushy crowns basked in the sunlight, children and dogs ran on freshly cut lawns. It was Sunday, August 4— the equivalent of February 4 in New York, London, Moscow, and all other cities in the Northern Hemisphere whose seasons are shifted six months relative to the Southern Hemisphere. If this was the local winter, I thought, what will summer be like? What will it be like on February 4? Probably full of tourists crowding the beaches.

I had to hurry—a pilot was waiting for me at the local airport. The night before I told Stan and Jan that I wanted to drive to Murderers' Bay, where the Dutch captain Abel Tasman first approached New Zealand, the site of first contact between the Europeans and the Maori. My hosts explained that the road was every bit as twisty as the one I had traveled the night before. Driving to Murderers' Bay—long ago rechristened Golden Bay—would take at least two hours each way and it would be better to charter a small plane. Stan called the company in the morning, and they said that a roundtrip flight, with a landing if need be, would take an hour and a half. The company had a Cessna for NZ$350/hr or I could go in a small two-person Cub for NZ$180/hr (less than 90 U.S. dollars). I asked Stan to book the little plane for me.

My pilot Paul, who was also a flying instructor, locked the hangar and led me to the grass field. The plane weighed less than my car, had fewer horsepower, and cruised at about 90 mph. Paul warned me to place my hands and feet only on the appropriate markings while climbing into the plane so as not to bend or break anything—the Cub Tomahawk was very light. There was just enough room behind our seats to throw a sweater and a camera. The Cub had dual controls and Paul asked whether I would like to fly it. I had no prior experience, but this was New Zealand—very informal.

After a preflight check and a brief dialog with the control tower—an Air New Zealand jet took off right before us and another followed—Paul took off. After rising to 1,500 feet, he told me to fly. I took over and the little Cub, which until then had flown straight as an arrow, began swaying and porpoising. I flew in the direction Paul indicated, holding more or less above the road and gradually climbing to 3,000 feet, while Paul kept reassuring me with a running commentary on the restaurants we flew over. The sky was clear, with just a few clouds above the mountains. As we climbed, distant snow-covered peaks appeared above the green valleys. Paul said we would fly over the foothills on our way to Golden Bay and return along the beach.

Crossing the foothills, the plane began to pitch and yawl because of the air currents from the mountains and Paul took over the controls. I turned air vents into my face and stared at the horizon to prevent airsickness, just as I had done two and a half weeks earlier on the boat off Stewart Island. We crossed the mountain range and flew above a green coastal valley. Paul banked to show me his friend's farm and green mineral pools where blue spots marked underwater fresh springs. There was a yellow strip of beach and in a few minutes we were suspended above Golden Bay.

The Dutch East India Company that had sent Captain Tasman on his expedition was the most powerful commercial enterprise of his century. It used armed sailing ships and a network of fortresses to assert its near-monopoly on the import of spices and silk from Asia to Europe and the export of European goods to the area. During a brief truce in its incessant armed struggle with the Portuguese it freed up two ships—the Heemskerk and the Zeehaven—and sent them to explore the South Pacific. The ships were loaded with trade goods, armed with cannon, and carried marines whose main role was to prevent mutiny rather than make war. Tasman, a naturally cautious man, was given written instructions to avoid trouble with the natives with whom the company hoped to trade.

When Tasman sailed into this bay, he had no way of knowing that the Maori society was extremely warlike, and fighting skills were the main measure of a man's worth. Those skills were kept sharp by constant tribal warfare for territory, women, and slaves. The losers were often eaten, providing a great incentive to maintain one's fighting skills. When people saw a group of strangers, they did not expect a social visit; they expected an assault and responded accordingly. Tasman stumbled into one of the richest bays in the area, whose local tribe had seen many invaders and repelled them all. His ships arrived at the tail end of a mini–Ice Age, and in cold weather people were hungrier than usual, with especially intense competition for fishing and hunting grounds.

The Dutch described the attack on their ships as a savage act, but the Maori had a different view. They saw two huge ships enter the bay and head for their *pa*, a fortified settlement. Tasman wanted to get fresh water and explore trading opportunities, but the Maori did not know that. They had seen too many intruders. Their chiefs sent two *waka*—war canoes—to row around the ships. The ships were bigger than anything the Maori had ever seen, but the weak spots were the rowboats, no bigger than their own *waka* that shuttled between the two vessels. The next morning the tribe launched about 20 *waka*, and when one of them noticed a rowboat carrying seven men from the Heemskerk to the Zeehaven, they rammed it and killed three sailors with their war clubs, injuring the fourth so badly that he died soon after being pulled out of the water. Tasman shot at their *pa* from his cannon, but there was no point lingering. They had enough fresh water to get by, and the trading opportunities did not look promising. He sailed away without having set foot on the beach.

I was just about to repeat Tasman's experience—minus the war clubs—and leave without stepping ashore. Paul advised against landing because of a strong wind over an airstrip that was soft and soggy from recent rains. He flew low over the area where the fight took place, then turned and flew above the site of the *pa* by the beach. You had to admire the courage of Tasman's men who crossed an unknown ocean. You also had to admire the courage of a Stone Age people who set out in their canoes to attack two ships the likes of which they had never seen.

Paul asked whether I wanted to fly the plane back, but I was too busy fighting airsickness by keeping my eyes on the beach and the horizon. I had a friend in New York who was a flying instructor and kept offering to teach me to fly, but I always refused. Paul easily landed the plane in Nelson despite a strong crosswind. He tied it up and I helped him cover it with a tarpaulin which was lighter than those Suzie had used to cover her horses at Franz Joseph. I invited my pilot for a drink and he led the way to The Honest Lawyer, where we shared two dark rich drafts in the garden, while basking in the winter sunshine.

Back at Stan and Jan's house I soaked in a hot tub in the garden. Just as I was getting out, their teenage daughter hopped in, wearing a tiny little bikini. Her boyfriend, who was staying over for the weekend, pulled her out of the hot tub and tossed her into a cold pool. She screamed, scrambled out, dived back into the hot tub, and they started wrestling. This was neither the first nor the last time I encountered a teenager in New Zealand whose parents did not object to an overnight visitor. This was no longer a Puritan country.

Jan had prepared an appetizer of local chili mussels—spicy and succulent, they made us all thirsty and hungry for more. For the main course we had the freshest trout, pink as a sunrise. I ran upstairs and brought back the camera to photograph it. We drank a bottle of Sauvignon I brought from Blenheim. When we could eat no more and there was still trout left on the table, Jan brought out an almond peach pudding. It was a poem and a dream, and afterwards I floated to my second-floor bedroom after the tiniest sip of red sherry.

21 The Emperor of New Zealand

I jumped out of bed at five, startled, awakened by the roar and clatter of traffic. In New York my apartment faces a busy avenue, and I have learned to sleep through the noise, unless it's a nightclub letting out screaming kids at four in the morning. After several weeks in New Zealand I had grown used to peace and quiet. Pulling the curtain aside I noticed a detail I had overlooked on previous days. Between the house and the bay, behind blooming rose bushes, ran a major highway. It had been quiet when I arrived on Saturday and sleepy on Sunday, but on Monday morning the wheels of commerce started rolling. The room grew quiet for a moment, but as soon as I turned towards the bed a sports car, swinging through a curve, screamed like a jet in a wind tunnel. I turned on the light and opened a book to read until breakfast. I had one more night on the South Island, but this was definitely not the house in which to spend it.

After another delicious breakfast I told my hosts that my plans had changed and I had to leave a day early. I paid the bill, loaded the car, and drove back to Nelson. The morning was cloudy, but for a while it felt like the sky wanted to clear up. Back at the Suter gallery the director was in her office, and she told me I had missed Avis Higgs by just a few days. She lived in Wellington, very chipper at 84, and had visited Nelson to give a talk at the gallery. I was eager to meet the woman behind the designs and asked for her number in Wellington. The director promised to call me once she got the artist's permission.

Nelson was chock-a-block with galleries, art house movies, open air eateries, and crafts shops. The weather kept worsening and I decided to put off exploring the town until my next visit. Instead of galleries I went to several hardware stores in search of an essential device that I knew existed on this planet, that I craved to own, but never found in New Zealand—an adjustable tube for connecting hot and cold water faucets. New Zealand was a technologically advanced country, on par with the United States, and by some measures ahead of it, but to this day half its houses held a relic of medievalism—separate faucets for hot and cold water, with no connection between them. You could boil your left hand while the right was freezing, or you could attempt a complicated dance, trying to catch a bit from this and a bit from that faucet into your cupped hands. If the people of New Zealand ever decided to institute monarchy and elected me their emperor, I would let them run their country pretty much how it is today, but give them two major new laws—put a guardrail over every ravine and a fixed spout water mixer in every bathroom.

I felt a tinge of sadness leaving Nelson—this was the farthest point on my latest drive west, not counting the flight the day before. The vortex of my roadtrip was tightening; I was headed for the ferry, the exit from the South Island. I dialed Gino's number on my cell phone and asked whether I could come back for one more night before sailing to the North Island. Heather was already gone and Gino was on his way to fish, but I caught him near the door. I noticed a hitchhiker, a big tall guy in a ski cap carrying a large backpack, whom I had first seen standing in the same spot a couple of hours earlier on my drive into Nelson. The day was becoming colder, my windshield wipers were on intermittent and the guy looked thoroughly miserable. I used to hitchhike as a student, and to this day I like picking up hitchhikers, after slowing down for what I call a quick psychodiagnostic. I look them over and either stop or drive by, depending on my judgment.

The big fellow neatly put his backpack on my back seat, buckled up in front and visibly enjoyed the dry warmth of the car. He told me he was a software engineer from Ireland and had saved up money while working on a project in California to take a few months off to see the world. He introduced himself but I kept asking him to repeat his name until he finally spelled it for me. I should have written it down because I had never heard that name before and can no longer remember it, except that it started with a D. He told me it was the Irish equivalent of David. We compared notes on our journeys as the road climbed into the mountains, becoming dry again. I told David that in my experience, a hitchhiker should never wear a hat. People tend to be suspicious, and a ski hat, especially on a big guy, looks menacing. I always took my hat off when I hitchhiked. I also told him he needed a sign giving his destination. I used to carry a piece of cardboard and a marker in my backpack. People slowed down to read the sign and then it was easier for them to connect with you. I could see that my advice was taking the usual route—in one ear and out the other.

David said he planned to take a ferry to the North Island, only he was going to stay the night in a backpackers' hostel in Picton, near the harbor. New Zealand was full of backpackers' hostels where a person could get a bunk bed in a shared room for a few dollars. Neither of us was in a hurry and we stopped several times for short hikes on roadside trails. I told David I had never been to Ireland but thought of visiting it with my son around Thanksgiving, when he would be free from school. David thought that was a terrible idea. He could not say enough bad things about the weather in Ireland in late November—most of the year, in fact. He kept ranting about the Irish weather when I asked whether he had ever considered moving to New Zealand. He could easily get a permanent visa and a job in this prosperous English-speaking country with a gorgeous climate. "I couldn't do that," he said. "Ireland's my country."

The laws of New Zealand are absolutely transparent even in the area where most countries find themselves in a hopeless muddle—immigration. With only three million people, the country is underpopulated and its laws encourage immigration, as long as it is orderly and beneficial for society. A prospective immigrant has to fill out a questionnaire, with answers rated on a scale. Anyone can download this form from the government's Web site and see whether he or she has scored enough points to get in. A person earns points for being educated and young, speaking English and having money, although it is not necessary to score high on all of the above. A person in his or her twenties, fluent in English, and with a good degree could come in with very little money;

people who are over 40 and do not have a degree, however, have to bring in money to invest in the country. If you score low on the English test, you are told how much schooling you have to pay for before retaking the exam. There are also several preferential groups—Pacific islanders, humanitarian cases, and family reunifications, for example.

On my drive through New Zealand I exchanged several emails with my friend Bettina in Germany who had decided to immigrate to New Zealand with her husband. They were in their thirties and both spoke good English. Bettina was a photographer, Tim a mechanical engineer. After filling out the form, Bettina got a six-month conditional visa to enter the country and look for a job in her field. If she found a job as a photographer, she would be granted a permanent visa and then Tim could join her as her husband. I told Bettina I could email all my friends in New Zealand to help her look for a job.

David and I stopped in Havelock—I was headed east to Gino's house in Blenheim, while he needed to turn north to Picton. I dropped him off in front of the mussel restaurant where I had dined two days earlier and saw huge green shells arranged in a whimsical design above the roof. We shook hands and I saw David in my rearview mirror, standing on the corner, pulling his ski cap down low, and sticking out his thumb.

The road meandered downhill between wet pastures, entering the wine country. The day turned grey, cold, and miserable, a real taste of winter. I passed the restaurant in the vineyard where Fred had driven me for lunch a few days earlier, but the vines looked like wet cats in the rain and I did not feel like getting out of my car. In the middle of the day I pulled into Gino's driveway and rang his bell, but no one answered. The last thing I wanted to do on this dreary day was drive downtown and look for a café, read, and wait. I walked up to the cottage and tried the door handle. It was open! I walked in—the fireplace radiated warmth. Gino had left that door unlocked for me, with the fire going. There was a bowl of fruit on the coffee table and a tray of walnuts. The refrigerator was stocked with orange juice and the cupboard with bread and a pot for making tea or coffee. Gino even left me his favorite Italian CDs. I felt like Robinson Crusoe, finding an island of comfort and warmth in a grey, wet sea.

I improvised some lunch, cracked a few walnuts which went well with the grapes, sipped some single malt whiskey, caught up on my computer notes, and then napped on the couch by the fireplace. I drank in the warmth and the friendliness of the place. It did not have the greatest location—just a nice piece of land on the outskirts of the town, extremely comfortable but no magnificent views, but I did not care. I could drive to magnificent views in ten minutes, but who knows how many hours I would have to drive to find this kind of hospitality. I awoke from a gentle knock on the door—Gino had returned from his fishing trip and came to invite me for dinner.

When I entered the kitchen carrying two wine bottles, Gino was presiding over the stove, skillfully frying mounds of fish. We settled around the kitchen table and opened the first bottle. Gino, Heather, and I were joined by Hamish—Gino's tall and eccentric Scottish mate, actually a friend of his kids whom he had pretty much adopted. The fellow had never been outside New Zealand, but was very well read and informed. Gino and Hamish had gone fishing together in Cook Straight earlier that day, but the waves were so big that the refrigerator door on the boat swung open, spilling all the drinks. Hamish got seasick, could no longer fish, and just held on. I thought he still looked a little greenish. Gino fished in any weather, but he had trouble finding his crawfish pots. He caught three crays, which he sliced and served cold, squeezing fresh lemons on them. The fish which we ate at 7 PM had been caught at 4:30— it did not come much fresher than that. We refilled our plates with more slices of golden perfection and opened the second bottle when Gino asked whether anyone wanted fish heads. He was the only one who ate them, crunching like a big, comfortable tomcat. Heather told me that Gino taught Italian cooking at a local college. She began to yawn, said good night and went up to bed—the only person among us with a real job and an alarm clock. Gino brewed a pot of rich coffee whose aroma filled the kitchen and brought out a bottle of grappa. Gino, Hamish, and I sat late into the night drinking, discussing the problems of the world and solving most of them, if only we could have rememberd those solutions in the morning.

22 The Cat across Cook Strait

This was my last morning on the South Island, and I walked over to Gino's house for my last cup of espresso. Heather was long gone to teach school, but Hamish was still there, along with Gino's two Italian mates—the guy who had sold him the house 12 years ago and a fellow visiting from Venice who spoke a little English. Sitting around a well-worn round table and drinking coffee it felt like we had been neighbors for years. Luca, the collie, hovered at the edge of the kitchen in his shiny spotless coat of white, black, and red, sniffing politely and waiting to be petted.

I drove back to Cloudy Bay and bought a six-bottle case of their best Sauvignon Blanc and another of Chardonnay. The case I had bought a few days earlier was going to fly with me to New York, but these were for friends on the North Island. I drove across the mountain to the ferry, checked my luggage and returned the car. Rental cars never went on that ferry—you returned your car near the pier and picked up a replacement on the other side if you needed one. There was still enough time to walk over to the museum of the *Edwin Fox*, the only surviving sailing ship that carried convicts to Australia and settlers to New Zealand, and the only surviving transport ship from the Crimean War.

An old wooden hulk without masts stood under a roof at the edge of a small harbor, filled with pleasure craft, dwarfed by the interisland ferry. The *Edwin Fox* was built in Calcutta, India, in 1853 under British colonial rule. It was built from teak, whose quality was so high that when the ballast was cleared away almost 150 years later, the inner timbers looked like new. On the pier sleek electric cranes were loading the ferry, but elephants had done the heavy lifting when the *Edwin Fox* was built. The top handle of its steering wheel had been made of brass instead of wood to help steersmen feel the top in the dark because there was no electricity.

The *Edwin Fox* sailed on its maiden voyage with a load of tea to London, where it was bought by a war profiteer to carry troops and supplies to the Crimean peninsula where Britain and France joined Turkey in its 1854–56 war against Russia. After the war the *Edwin Fox* was sold and modified to carry convicts from Britain to Australia. Under England's draconian laws of the time, stealing a sheep or breaking a shop window were hanging offenses. British prisons were overcrowded by people awaiting execution, while the government did not have the stomach for mass hangings and commuted most death sentences to "transportation"—exile to Australia.

It took several months to sail from Britain to Australia in the late nineteenth century. Prisoners were kept below the deck, with a single exit so small that a man had to get on all fours to come out. Two cannons loaded with grapeshot were pointed at that door from the quarter deck and the officers, soldiers, and crew were armed. Once in Australia, convicts had to work to support themselves, but were not incarcerated, unless convicted of new crimes, in which case punishment was brutal. The ships that carried prisoners also brought "pensioner guards"—retired soldiers who got free passage with their wives and children plus a housing allowance for coming to live and help keep order in Australia. Guards and prisoners, Australia's original European population, inflicted major atrocities on the Aborigines. Voluntary settlers came later, and as their political power grew, they ended prison transports, telling Britain to keep its problems at home instead of shipping them abroad.

As the era of "transportation" drew to a close in the nineteenth century, the *Edwin Fox* was modified again to carry voluntary settlers to New Zealand. Some paid for their passage and came in cabins in relative comfort, like flying first class on an airplane. Others were "assisted settlers" whose passage was paid in full or in part by churches and charitable organizations. They traveled below the deck in a spartan environment, with married couples housed in the middle, single women segregated in front, and single men in the back, to reduce mingling. Their one advantage over modern airplane travel was the luggage allowance—600 pounds for a single person and twice that per couple in steerage, twice that again on the upper deck.

New Zealand's agricultural economy received a strong boost after coal-fired freezers were put on sailing ships, enabling farmers to export meat and butter to England. The *Edwin Fox* was converted into a freezer ship, whose machinery could freeze 400 sheep a day, while storing 14,000 frozen sheep carcasses. When bigger and newer ships edged the *Edwin Fox* out of that niche, it was converted into a floating dormitory for meat workers. When a dormitory was no longer needed, the dismasted ship was used for coal storage and then abandoned. It drifted to the far end of Picton's harbor, rolled on its side, and sunk into the mud, where it was rediscovered in 1967 by local historians who have been working to restore it ever since. Walking through its hulk was like walking through a century and a half of history, and I thought of the soldiers, prisoners, and settlers who had walked those planks before me.

Back at the ferry terminal I had my first and only run-in with a security guard in New Zealand. When I had mentioned to the woman at the vineyard that I was going to the ferry, she laughed and said she would never check her wine as luggage because too many workers handled the cases. I was rolling my liquid treasure on a folding cart when a stern guard said no alcohol could be brought on board. He sounded officious and crude just like many security guards back in the United States, but I overcame the nostalgic feeling, got hold of a stewardess, and told her I wanted to upgrade to first class. She instructed me to pay NZ$15 (about seven U.S. dollars) for the upgrade and told the guard, who listened like a big child, that my cart was OK. First class boarded first, so I settled in a deep armchair by the window in the lounge and ordered lunch from the menu.

The huge catamaran crawled through the Marlboro Sounds at 18 knots—a slow speed demanded by local environmentalists to reduce its wake in sheltered waters. We overtook a mail boat, passed a few isolated houses and mussel farms, and I pointed out to the Englishman sitting in the armchair next to me that each field of buoys had a quarter million dollars bobbing underneath. With the South Island astern, the cat roared up to 40 knots in the open water. I sipped beer and looked through the panoramic window at the slowly rolling waves, their color changing from green to dark grey. Suddenly the waves were pierced by several sleek, brown-black bodies—a pod of dolphins raced the cat at 40 knots. They played in the water before disappearing under the grayish green waves. I put on my ski jacket and walked to the open deck in the rear, protected from the wind, where I marked my departure from the South Island by lighting a cigar. I kept looking back until the mountains turned into a string of mossy bumps on the horizon and disappeared. The Cook Strait, the channel between the North and South Islands, could be a dangerous place because the wind sometimes picked up great speed on its run from the Antarctic before slamming into the funnel between the islands, but this day was reasonably quiet.

My English neighbor came out for a cigarette and told me he was an electrical engineer and had been on the road in Asia for the past several months. He complained how all hotels were the same, whether in New Zealand, India, or the Philippines, with the same international programs on TV and similar food in the restaurants. Some dishes had a bit of local color, but not much—the idea was to provide a uniform experience for a business traveler. I told him about my farmstays and homestays and how, when I traveled with my children, I had two rules—no TV and no fast food. I wanted them to be open to the countries in which they traveled. The cat passed by the rocks on which several years ago I saw penguins during my crossing with Danny, but there were none this time. Soon high-rises with neon signs came into view along with rows of smaller houses running up into the hills—we pulled into Wellington, the capital of New Zealand.

A slender woman in her early thirties waited for me with a cart near the luggage carousel. We loaded my luggage into her jeep—two suitcases, two cases of wine, a flight bag with another case, a computer bag, and a folding cart. Elizabeth apologized that her jeep was strewn with children's toys, but I liked that. It seemed odd that she was dressed like a corporate employee, wearing a black business suit, a white blouse, and black pumps. The only non-corporate detail was a bijouterie-encrusted cross dangling in her cleavage. She used to work for Tyco and often came from New Zealand to their office in Connecticut. We chatted about the sad state of her former company—its CEO arrested for tax fraud, and the firm itself on the brink of bankruptcy after a decade of creative accounting.

Pulling out of the parking lot, Elizabeth told me there was a slight problem. She had three guest rooms, but had miscalculated her reservations. On my third night she had no room for me, but would move me to her girlfriend's homestay and give me a $15 discount. I felt livid—not because of the mistake, since all of us who live by complex schedules occasionally make errors. What burned me was that she had been calling or emailing me every single day to confirm my arrival and had never once mentioned this problem. She waited until my luggage was loaded in her jeep and we were driving to her place where she was going to collect rent without giving me a chance to decide. Apparently the woman had stayed at Tyco for a little too long and learned one shady practice too many. If I had a car, I would have turned and left immediately, but it was getting dark and I had a ton of luggage.

The house hugged a steep hill near the botanical gardens, with a charming cable car clattering downtown every few minutes. I put my suitcases and boxes in the room, found a local newspaper, called several theaters, and went to soak up some city life after weeks of country living. I saw Harold Pinter's *The Birthday Party* in an attractive theater on the waterfront, where the stage was no higher than a foot. Sitting in the front row you were practically next to the actors. The complicated play told the story of a group of people staying in a shabby seaside boarding home and it fanned my determination to get out of Elizabeth's home the first chance I got. I took the cable car back uphill, returned before ten, found Logan's number, and called to ask whether he still had a vacancy for the next two nights. He did, although he sounded a little miffed that I did not book the first time. This time he wanted a credit card in advance. Fair enough. Could he come tomorrow at ten to pick me up? He could do it at nine. "Fine, see you then," I said, sweeping two dozen tiny embroidered pillows off the bed and falling asleep.

23 Once-in-2,000-Years Earthquake

Early in the morning I brought my luggage downstairs and sat in the living room, reading a newspaper and drinking tea, giving a pass to industrial croissants waiting to be heated in a microwave. Elizabeth lived next door with her family and used this house purely for the income. An Australian couple came down for breakfast—they were looking for a house, planning to move to New Zealand. Both Australia and New Zealand made it very easy for their citizens to move between the two countries and work without losing any benefits. At half past eight I called Elizabeth and requested the bill. When she arrived I did not want to say anything unpleasant in front of her Australian guests and only treated her very coldly. She took my credit card but was not smart enough to leave well enough alone and kept asking questions.

Have you found another place? Yes. Where are you going? Some place where I will leave when I am good and ready, not when someone tells me. Have you called a taxi? A car is coming. I told her it was not the scheduling error that turned me off but her dishonesty. She continued to chirp. Did you go to the theater yesterday? Yes. What did you see? A play. What play? In the theater.

Logan pulled into the driveway at 9 AM sharp. I could have hugged this crusty, retired banker as my liberator. When I told him what happened with Elizabeth, he growled that she should be reported. To whom? Well, she is in the book, isn't she? He meant the B&B listing. That was an excellent idea!

Logan lived in the lower reaches of Mount Victoria, a charming lively neighborhood full of small restaurants and low buildings running up a hill. The house was old and quaint, with a single guest room overlooking downtown. I asked Logan's wife whether I could join them for dinner, which accord-

NOTE: Wellington is on the North Island, but is described in The South Island section of the book for continuity reasons.

ing to their listing was available for a fee. Annette told me she would be delighted. And yes, she would do my laundry and iron the shirts. Logan stored my wine in his cool cellar. I asked him and Annette about local plays and they enthusiastically recommended *The Pickle King*, written and performed by a local troupe in a theater just a few blocks from the house. Delighted with their hospitality, especially in contrast with what I had received the previous day, I invited them to be my guests at that night's performance.

I bundled up against the wind—Wellington, on the northern shore of the Cook Straight, was the Windy City of New Zealand—took my computer, and strolled to Te Papa, the new national museum. The museum of history, ethnography, and natural history opened in 1998, incorporating the latest in museum technology. It was young, just like the country itself, housed in a modern, structure, harmonious with the city and harbor near which it stood. Outside its walls was a natural habitat, with a forest, river and lake, fish, ducks, and other birds. It felt just like a DOC trail, only with tall buildings peeking out behind the treetops.

The first exhibit was outside the front door, where a stairway led to an underground space that showed how the huge museum was protected from earthquakes. New Zealand is in a seismically active area of the Earth, and earthquakes are a constant risk. The bigger the building, the more protection it needs. Buildings collapse when the land shifts from under them, so this museum stood on rows of enormous pillows, made from steel, rubber, and lead that dampened any fluctuations. On a video screen a project engineer was saying this building was designed to withstand a once-in-500-years earthquake, and even though it would fall in a once-in-2,000-years earthquake, the pillows would hold it long enough for the people to escape. I pushed the button that lit up the pillows and admired their bulky grid, before returning to the surface and strolling through the glass doors.

The first person I met in the lobby was an American wearing a museum uniform, greeting visitors, and offering directions. Bruce told me he had been a zookeeper in Arkansas for 20 years, but married a local woman and moved to New Zealand two years ago. He normally worked in the mammals collection, but this day had been deputized to the lobby to meet and greet. I asked how a good ol' boy from Arkansas found himself a Kiwi wife. On the Internet, grinned Bruce, in a chat room on jokes. She always liked his jokes, so they started emailing each other outside the chat room. Bruce called her, then came to visit, and one thing led to another.

His colleague, a New Zealander whose parents had immigrated from China, led a small group on a "get acquainted" tour of the enormous museum. His amazing politeness stood out even in overwhelmingly polite New Zealand. Listening to him was good for my vocabulary because I never knew that so many pleasantries could be said during the simple act of opening a door or leaving a room. Throughout the day I kept returning to the exhibits he pointed out that morning.

A wooden platform across the treetops. A blue whale—the real thing, not fiberglass. The creature had been hurt by killer whales and was floating injured on the water's surface when it was fatally struck by a refrigerator ship. Instead of abandoning the dead whale, the ship towed it to port and donated it to the museum. A huge irregularly shaped greenstone weighing more than a ton, an object of great value, lying on a bed of sand amidst running water. Nature had encased the gem in brown rock, which the visitors rubbed with wet sand—years from now the entire rock will be rubbed down to green. A room with two clusters of poles standing at opposite ends. Voices emanated from each pole—Maori from one group, European from the other. They threw accusations at each other before giving way to conciliatory voices. On the wall hung the Treaty of Waitangi which in 1840 set the principles that are still central to modern New Zealand—laws, civil rights, race relations, land, government. An art object—a car built from corrugated metal, the material of farm country. Australians went gaga over it and made an offer to the artist but he donated it to the museum. More exhibits on immigrants. A man named Babich had come from Croatia in 1904 to dig for kauri gum, local amber. He sent tickets to his brothers, started making wine, now a famous label. A tribal exhibit—each tribe held the space for two years. Each European country also got a space for two years. It was the Netherlands' turn, its exhibit focusing on the influx of ex-soldiers to New Zealand in the 1950s after they lost Indonesia. Tasman's problem in 1642 was described as an unfortunate accident based on misunderstanding.

New Zealand's understated humor was evident even in the national museum. The countryside teemed with possums, cat-sized herbivores that damaged fields and forests, and their remains littered country roads. One exhibit contained a slab of asphalt the size of a small coffee table with fossilized remains of a possum, dated 1992. The critter had been pressed into soft asphalt by a truck, and the sign explained "The chemical process that preserves possums killed on our roads is very similar to the one that naturally occurs at the famous tar pits of La Brea in Los Angeles with saber-toothed tigers." It was nice to know that possums were to New Zealand what saber-toothed tigers were to the United States.

At noon the theater box office opened and I ran out to buy tickets. The show had sold out, but a woman in the box office scrounged up three tickets, looking extremely unhappy for some reason—two in front and one up in the gallery. Returning to Te Papa, I saw Bruce in the lobby and invited him for lunch. Waiting for his break, I browsed in the museum shop with its superlative collection of books about New Zealand. I picked up a book on Captain Cook, one about Abel Tasman, another on New Zealand folk vocabulary and an illustrated history of New Zealand, as well as the autobiography of a writer I was going to meet a few days later. Asking a clerk to hold my stack, I headed to the museum restaurant, rated as one of the best in Wellington.

The sun was beginning to break through low grey clouds, warming up the terrace just enough to eat outdoors. Our table overlooked a little nature preserve with a river and multicolored ducks. Beyond the park was a broad waterfront promenade, surrounding a harbor teeming with ships. Mountains rose from the harbor and the streets ran uphill. Bruce had changed out of his museum jacket into a windbreaker, but he could drink no wine on his lunch break. I studied the wine list and recognized the cabernet Bob had ordered on Mt. Cook. Holding a ruby glass against the light, sniffing its rich and musky aroma, savoring nuts and berries in its aftertaste, I felt like a New Zealander with his geographically connected wine.

We studied the menu and ordered. I started with a pear and endive salad with Kikorangi cheese, honey walnuts, and fig wine dressing. Both of us had fish for the main course—I asked for Akaroa salmon with pink peppercorns, and Bruce waxed poetic about local fishing. There were rivers where you could catch freshwater and saltwater fish from the same bridge, depending on the tide. Bruce liked fishing with locals since he still did not recognize many fish. He also loved hunting, going after wild pigs with dogs and a knife. You had to know what you were doing, he said, because those critters could bite. There are no native mammals in New Zealand—they were all introduced by settlers, and since they hurt the habitat, hunting them is like doing a public service. There is no "Bambi complex." Possums, for example, eat two million tons of grass and leaves per night, and everybody is trying to figure out how to put them to commercial use.

Bruce admired New Zealanders' honesty. They return found wallets and he had seen billfolds with a thousand dollars turned in at the museum. "In the U.S. if you ever get your billfold back, it would only have the pictures of your ugly relatives—they would have stolen the good-looking ones." People pay their bills, and because of that, if you are a little late, nobody gets excited.

Bruce's wife had once overlooked a medical bill and three months later received a phone call. When she started apologizing, the secretary said, "Oh, it's OK. It was only three months, pay when you can." When Bruce's visa was delayed, he asked both his mother and his bride's mother to write to the Department of Immigration. Letters from two moms were seen as proof that the relationship was real and the visa arrived in return mail.

The police patrols in New Zealand are unarmed—they have to call for someone to bring a gun. But they are fit and can run you down. "In the U.S., some of those big fat cops have to shoot you because they cannot run after you to the end of the block." New Zealand is not a prejudiced society, its neighborhoods not harshly segregated. There are no problems for biracial couples. Bruce's wife, originally from Samoa, is dark-skinned. Back in Arkansas he once had a relationship with an African-American woman and they heard bigoted remarks every day, but here in New Zealand no more than once every few months.

Bruce loved the variety of local eating choices. Two days ago he had Nepalese food for lunch in a local food court. He had never eaten Nepalese before, certainly not in Little Rock, even though its population was the same as Wellington's, about half a million. Here, if you were poor, you ate lamb and seafood, rich people bought pork and chicken. Bruce smacked his lips, as if kissing those words—roast mutton and green-lipped oysters. Yesterday he had eel for lunch, having bought a tin for a few dollars at an Asian store. There was no tipping in restaurants—some waiters thought a tip was a bribe and could get offended, although not in an international restaurant like this.

Bruce spoke of New Zealanders' love of the language and wordplay. A computer rental store was called Hire Intelligence. A restaurant in his neighborhood was called The G Spot, and a waitress told him the clientele was largely female because most men did not know how to find it. In the United States such a place would have been shouted down for political incorrectness. We ordered coffee and picked our way through chocolate fantasy desserts when Bruce's lunch break ended and he hoisted himself from the table. He tried to connect the flaps of his windbreaker, but it seemed to have shrunk a little while we ate. Bruce glanced at the notebook where I kept scribbling notes while he spoke. "Don't write too much," he said, shaking my hand. "We don't want everyone to move in here and overrun the place."

I stepped out of the restaurant without paying the bill, went down to the coat check, and retrieved my computer from a Maori who teased me about having dropped it. Back on the terrace I lit a cigar, ordered a single malt whiskey and updated my notes. I then paid the bill and returned my computer to the Maori, who was in the midst of a teasing match with Bruce, both men convulsing with laughter. I bought a ticket to the Explorers' Hall to see an exhibit about Pacific explorers—medieval Polynesians and Europeans, as well as modern sportsmen who retraced their steps, sometimes without a compass or radio. Two people could follow exactly the same path in that hall, yet have completely different experiences by choosing what buttons to push on video displays and computer terminals.

My cell phone vibrated—it was the director of the Bishop Suter Gallery in Nelson, calling with Avis Higgs' phone number. I dialed, and she laughed— "I don't know why they made such a fuss about my number!"—and invited me to come over the next afternoon. The museum was closing for the day, and I walked to the lobby, past Captain Cook's cannon. On his first journey of discovery, charting the unmapped east coast of Australia, Cook had run aground in the Great Barrier Reef, and he threw much ballast, cannons, and even fresh water overboard to free up his ship. Several years earlier the Australians had recovered the treasure and donated one of the cannons to Te Papa, which responded by positioning it facing Australia. Very cute. I paid for my books, said goodbye to Bruce and to the funny young Maori at the package check and walked to my homestay.

Logan, ever the banker, said Te Papa was good for business. Tourists used to fly to Auckland, drive down to Rotorua, then fly to Christchurch. Now they come to Wellington and go to Te Papa. The city hoped for 350,000 visitors the first year the museum was open, but got 800,000. I told him it was a smart business to offer free admission—they made it easy to walk in, and once inside, they made it very easy to spend money. I left NZ$90 in the restaurant, over NZ$150 in the bookshop, and another NZ$20 for the optional tour and exhibit.

My laundry and shirts were done—many homestays in New Zealand offer this service for a small fee, making life easier for travelers. Annette served us dinner—pleasant but very ordinary. Logan pontificated throughout the meal—this retired banker was very right-wing, proud of his volunteer work for an extremist political party in the recent election. He would start his sentences with "I'm not a Maori basher, but…" I have heard enough of "I'm not a racist, but…" in the United States to know what was coming next. Dinner mercifully over, we walked a few blocks to the theater. A memorial board in the lobby displayed a lack of political correctness, praising the founder, "...fondly remembered as a connoisseur of commerce, wine, women, and the Arts," and also a framed photo of the theater's cat, whose name was Evil.

The Pickle King was, to use my kids' most damning word, lame. A mechanical mouse kept running across the stage as actors mouthed stale jokes. The public laughed in mirth. I normally walk out of bad performances—I had already wasted my money, no point also wasting my time—but I could not leave because of Logan and Annette. They adored the show. The people in the theater were much more patient than in New York. Logan and Annette ran into some friends and stopped to chat, blocking a passageway through which people returned to their seats. 40 to 50 people stood right behind them, but nobody pushed, tried to squeeze by them, or even say "excuse me." They quietly stood and waited.

24   *Sherry with a Painter*

I woke up in a small, cozy room that felt like it belonged to middle-class older people, with fussy, old-fashioned decor. Like all homes in which I stayed in New Zealand, it had no central heating—with temperatures almost never falling below freezing, people used space heaters and electric mattress pads covered in wool. I stayed home for most of the morning, using the Internet and the cell phone to make arrangements for two fishing trips. My friend Tony was coming in from Sydney in a few weeks to join me on the road for a while. Since he was a mad crazy fisherman, I decided to take him fishing in some of the best places in New Zealand.

My hair had to be trimmed before flying on my business trip the following day, and Logan gave me a ride to his haircutting place. It was in the back of a candy store and a post office, typical for New Zealand, where small unrelated businesses often share space. In the back room of the candy store two very flamboyant gay guys cut hair, while a show about men's love played on the radio. At first I thought that perhaps Logan was not a total right-winger after all, but then maybe he was just blind to such things. The blond guy who worked his magic on the remains of my hair told me he was coming to visit the United States, but had no interest in national parks, wanting instead to see big cities like Los Angeles and New York. I suggested adding San Francisco to the itinerary—fly to LA, drive up the scenic route to San Francisco, hop up to Vancouver and take the Trans-Canadian railway to Toronto, then down to New York, and use the Web site of *The Village Voice* to look for accommodations.

I walked downtown, where a profusion of banks and upscale shops on Lambton Quay made it look like a cross between Wall Street and Fifth Avenue. I felt like having Asian food for lunch and dived into a shopping mall in whose food court a small crowd of office workers lined up at several take-out restaurants. I chowed down a plate of three colorful Chinese dishes and walked to the waterfront. The sun played on blue water, but sharp gusts of wind cut through my jacket and drove me into the Museum of the City and the Sea. At the ticket counter I chatted with a girl from New Orleans who had come to Wellington on a one-year work visa after college and was about to leave when she fell in love with a Scotsman who was in the process of immigrating to New Zealand. I listened to her and thought, with a tinge of worry, of my own daughters' worldwide travels.

Just as I reached to pay for the ticket, my cell phone rang—it was Elizabeth from my previous homestay. I had had enough of her. Now what do you want? "Look, I am sorry," she said. "I realized you were angry and upset. I should not have done what I did. I wanted to let you know I will not charge your card for that one night." I thanked her and told her I considered the incident closed. "I'll tell you what I'll do," I said. "I was going to send a letter about you to every B&B rating agency in New Zealand, but now I won't." I could hear her jaw drop. She had just saved herself more trouble than she knew.

Wellington is a major seaport, but the narrow entrance to its harbor could be dangerous. I saw an exhibit on the 1968 Wahine disaster—an old interisland ferry had been driven on the rocks by a hurricane. Despite a heroic rescue operation, 51 people died that day, most of them smashed against the rocks while trying to swim ashore. Modern ferries were much better equipped, but they still canceled sailings once or twice a year because of violent storms. Another exhibit allowed visitors to interview various members of a harbor piloting company. An exhibit on whaling showed how an old family used to maintain lookouts on a hill, and whenever they spotted a whale near the entrance to the harbor chased it in speedboats with harpoons. Since New Zealand joined the moratorium on whaling in the 1960s, local companies were earning twice as much each year taking tourists to see the whales than they did from killing them.

The girl from New Orleans walked through the exhibit hall, making the rounds of a nearly empty museum. She said she liked it better than Te Papa, which she found "playgroundish." She talked about how nice New Zealanders are, with people at work taking time to talk. If there is a problem with a job, the boss does not descend from on high to blast the peons, but walks up and says; "No worries, mate, it'll work itself out"—and it usually does. People from many countries and of many colors live in proximity. The quality of life was probably higher than in the United States for most people except for the upper crust. They are not quite as high above the rest and have fewer grand options, but for the great majority life is better. Food is better. In Louisiana, which has great agricultural land, farmers still put crap in the ground. In New Zealand the government does not allow it, and supermarkets are full of healthy organic food.

I went to the top floor to see the exhibit on the city's social life. Wellington had always been a progressive city—the eight-hour work day started here—but it was also very businesslike, with the country's first Chamber of Commerce. An exhibit showed how New Zealand became the first country in the British Commonwealth to offer a universal old-age pension. An exhibit on local customs had models of hillside houses with private cable cars but no roads. I thought it would be fun to stay in one of those on my next visit here.

Back on Lambton Quay I found a flower shop and bought a single imported rose for Avis Higgs, exquisite like a work of art, which they wrapped in several layers of elegant paper. Because I was a little early, I took a bus uphill instead of a taxi. I feel at ease riding on subways anywhere in the world, walking, and, of course, taking taxis, but buses always leave me puzzled. Sure enough, I got off at the wrong stop, got lost, and rung the bell of the wrong house. Avis lived above the harbor in a substantial stone house with a door on each of its four sides. What followed was like a scene from a silent comedy, with the two of us going to different doors again and again. I would hear a door open and run, but by the time I got there it was locked, and then I would hear another door. Finally I stood firm by one of the doors until Ms. Higgs came out, looking much younger than her 84 years, and let me in.

She led me into her living room, whose bay window had a grand view of the harbor. Low clouds ran above the water, skimming the hilltops and changing the colors of the seascape from minute to minute. Avis said she had to have an ocean view because she had grown up on the water. I asked about her work in Australia and she laughed. She had gone there to visit her aunt on a roundtrip ticket, but was unable to return when the war broke out: All civilian shipping stopped because the ships were requisitioned as troop carriers. She was still trying to get back when she found a design job at a textile factory. The owners were interned, but the manager kept the business going and needed a designer. There were wartime limitations. For example, the manager wanted simple designs in order to save on pigments. She ran a design shop where five or six other girls copied her small-size designs onto large sheets, a job that today would be done by a single computer.

Avis had shared an apartment with another girl and recounted a startling memory of waking up one morning to see the harbor, which had been empty the night before, filled with troop ships. Trains were backed up to the waterfront, troops taken off the ships and loaded onto trains. It was 1942, the Japanese were about to invade Australia and local troops were returned from the Middle East and rushed across the country to defend Queensland. The boys were not even given a day's leave. Several months later, the U.S. Navy rolled back the Japanese in the Battle of the Coral Sea. The invasion was off and the troops went on to fight in the Pacific.

After the war, Avis returned to Wellington where her father was a well-known painter. There she assembled a portfolio and went to London. Major manufacturers started accepting her designs. She told me of the excitement she felt from seeing people wearing her designs in the streets and seeing her fabrics sold in stores. She visited Paris, skied in Switzerland, and then an Australian girl invited her on a car trip to Rome. Shortly before reaching that city, the girl flipped the car and was killed, with Avis seriously injured. To this day Avis has four pieces of metal in her leg, but they do not prevent her from getting around very briskly. On her way home to recover, still on crutches, she had met a young man whom she later married. A letter awaited her when she got back to Wellington—a job offer from one of the best London fabric houses. Avis spoke of that with a tinge of sadness—a major road not taken.

She showed me a few snatches of her fabrics, but did not have many left since the exhibition had taken the best. After the exhibit ended in Nelson, her work would go to a permanent collection in Napier, an art center on the North Island. Avis poured two glasses of sherry and invited me upstairs to her studio. The walls were hung with her works, as well as those by her father, sister, and other relatives. She showed me a book put together by a relative in Tasmania about a surprisingly large number of Higgs men and women who had been noted painters for generations. Her father was an aquarellist who had studied painting in London, where he lived after fighting in World War I. He also studied patent law, and on returning to Wellington became a patent attorney. Painting was something he did on weekends. New Zealand had very few full-time professional artists—some of the best in the country were weekend painters. It was a practical country; a living had to be earned. As I got up to leave, Avis pointed towards downtown at the bottom of the hill and said she preferred to walk down and take the bus up the hill because parking in the center was too tight. It was wonderful to have such choices at 84.

On my way back to Logan's house a bar sign stopped me dead in my tracks. It combined New Zealand's love of language and its understated humor. While many pubs in the United Kingdom had the word "arms" in them—King's Arms, Knight's Arms, and so on, a sign above this bar in Wellington proclaimed: "Fat Lady's Arms." I walked in, stopping at another sign on the door that warned" "Beware of pickpockets and loose women." Inside, the manager concentrated on tossing a rubber chicken into a net under the ceiling. The chicken was not cooperating. I had a pint of dark beer and went for dinner at a Thai restaurant, taking a design magazine from the rack and reading it while waiting for my prawns.

SECTION
3

Australia

25 Swim in an Anti-Shark Cage

Wellington was still completely dark when Logan drove me to the airport. I carried only a flight bag and a computer, having left my suitcases and wine with Logan, who was charging me for their storage. That did not feel too generous, especially considering our theater excursion, but he had his rules.

I was interrupting my journey for a week of conference presentations, newspaper and TV interviews, and book signings in three Australian cities. At the last moment I had to rush and buy an Australian visa because that country, unlike New Zealand, requires them from Americans. Getting on the plane, I sprawled in a comfortable seat, moved my watch two hours behind to match Brisbane time, pulled up a blanket, and went to sleep.

The flight across the Tasman Sea was similar to flying from New York to Los Angeles, and when I woke up the sun was shining and it was time for a light breakfast. Trying to catch a glimpse of the shore through a break in the clouds I kept thinking about the differences between the country I left and the one I was approaching. Their histories, landscapes, and people were very different in many ways, even though they spoke the same language and had a special political relationship.

New Zealand is one of the most remote countries in the world, far in the ocean above the Antarctic, safely isolated from any potential enemies. Australia is closer to the equator, with only 100 miles separating it at the narrowest spot from Indonesia, with which it has an uneasy relationship. New Zealand is relatively compact, its long and narrow shape good for coastal navigation and almost the entire country easily accessible. Australia is much larger, and the huge desert at its center is poorly suited for living, forcing most people to huddle along the

117

coasts. The landscape of New Zealand is extremely diverse, and driving for an hour could put you into a different environment, a different climate. Australia is by and large very monotonous. Whenever friends drove me to see sights in Australia or even flew somewhere in a helicopter, I felt I could have seen more interesting views from roadside rest areas in Utah or Wyoming.

Australia is full of dangerous wildlife, deadly snakes, and insects. The community swimming area in Sydney where I lived for a few months in 1996 was inside an anti-shark cage, and once there was a guy who dived from the walkway above the cage in the wrong direction. He jumped into the harbor instead of the pool and straight into the teeth of a shark. When I stayed in the tropical North, two girls got killed in knee-deep water, stung by a Portuguese Man-o-War as they ran from the boat to the shore. People came to the beaches, but during the poisonous jellyfish season no one who feared for their lives would dare go into the water. The lakes and rivers teem with crocodiles. New Zealand has no predators, not even snakes, which provides a comfortable feeling of safety for its people. Tony told me of an Australian fisherman who began his visits to New Zealand by rolling in the grass in his camp; he could never have had that pleasure at home because of the snakes. The feeling of safety helps turn New Zealanders into great travelers and explorers, while for Australians wide open spaces represent danger. One of the great books on Australian psychology is called *The Tyranny of the Distance;* for Americans the frontier symbolizes promise and freedom, to Australians it represents a threat.

After American colonies declared independence, the British government needed a new place to dump its condemned prisoners. It dusted off Captain Cook's maps and sent the first of many prison convoys to the land about which it knew next to nothing. After sailing halfway around the world, the prison transports arrived in Botany Bay, which is where planes land today flying into Sydney. The guards opened the hatches, issued the prisoners of both genders a double ration of rum, and disembarked them to an orgy on the beach that Robert Hughes, in his witty *The Fatal Shore: The Epic of Australia's Founding,* called the first beach party in Australia. The first European settlers in New Zealand, by contrast, were not prisoners or guards but merchants, whalers, and sealers. If some of them were a pretty rough lot, they were soon followed by a more civilized crowd, first by missionaries and then by church-sponsored groups of farmers and craftsmen. Since then, different waves of immigrants have come to both countries, but the early patterns have left their imprints. There is a harsher, louder edge to Australia and a softer, kinder style in New Zealand.

The natives of the two countries could not have been more different. Both the Maori and the Aborigines were Stone Age people without a written language, but that is where their similarities ended and the differences began. The Maori, living in a colder climate, built villages with elaborate fortifications and had a well-developed tribal system, with chiefs and high chiefs. They planted kumara (sweet potato) and ate fish, moa birds and even human flesh. They tended to be tall and strong, with a great sense of tribal identity and loyalty. The Aborigines, in contrast, lived in an extremely inhospitable climate, and were primarily gatherers. Dispersed family groups moved across barren landscapes, following "songlines"—the tracks of ancestor worship that followed the shifting availability of scarce food and water. They had an extremely weak tribal structure. All Maori in New Zealand spoke the same language, while the Aborigines had hundreds of language groups, did not understand each other, and had no sense of a common identity. Where the Maori had clothes, weapons, and farming implements, the Aborigines were likely to travel naked, carrying all their meager possessions except for the grinding stones which they hid at campsites along their songlines. The Maori built huge war canoes in which a hundred men could sail to make war on their neighbors, while coastal Aborigines had only small fishing boats. Observers noted the overall listlessness and passivity of the Aborigines. Where the Maori could attack, trade, or negotiate, the Aborigines would lie down and go to sleep just as a European landing party was hitting their shore for the first time.

These differences had important and tragic consequences for the two peoples. Cook, charged with acquiring the lands for the Crown with the consent of the natives, left New Zealand for later, but took possession of Australia through the simple expedient of declaring its Aboriginal inhabitants inhuman. The warlike Maori were not to be pushed around and thanks to their remarkable toughness and tribal loyalty have to this day preserved their tribal structure, language, and even much of their land. The passive and unorganized Aborigines, on the other hand, were subject to two centuries of genocide. Tasmania, the large island the size of Ireland off the southern coast of Australia, was subject to an early ethnic cleansing. Its Aborigines were poisoned, hunted, and killed like wild animals, with only a few survivors shipped away to the mainland. In Australia, land was allocated to settlers without any respect for native rights. If a settler's sheep needed a water hole and the Aborigines were slow to vacate their traditional land, the settler could kill them with impunity. In the middle of the twentieth century Aborigines were shot at from the aircraft, and as recently as the 1960s Aboriginal children were taken away and placed with white families. These children have become known as the Stolen Generation. The only area where some native life was preserved was in the North, where Aborigines proved useful for working with livestock. What goes around comes around, and I thought this history helped explain the greater sense of harshness felt in Australia.

When the British began to colonize Australia the main currency in the colony was rum, as money was of little use on the frontier. The colony was effectively run by a "Rum Corps" of corrupt military officers who at one point mutinied and threw out their Governor, Captain Bligh. Years earlier Captain Bligh, who used to be a midshipman for Captain Cook, became the unwilling hero of the world's most famous mutiny, "Mutiny on the Bounty." The man had a life-long problem with personnel. New Zealand was originally governed out of Sydney but received its own government when John Busby was appointed its first Resident (Governor) in 1832. He has been credited with introducing Shiraz vines to Australia, and established the first vineyard in New Zealand when he brought the grapes to the land. Today both Australia and New Zealand are democratic, English-speaking states. The event that brought them closer together was the First World War. Their military contingents, under overall British command, were combined into ANZAC—Australia and New Zealand Army Corps—and thrown into a mindless and hopeless attack against fortified clifftop Turkish positions at Gallipoli in 1915. Pinned down on the beach by Turkish troops shooting from high ridges, they held their ground despite massive casualties. Having their troops thrown into a useless bloodbath did more than anything for the development of a sense of national identity in both countries and promoted a republican feeling among the people who used to see themselves as loyal colonial subjects.

Australia's landmass is almost 30 times bigger than New Zealand's, and its population at the time of this writing was almost 20 million against New Zealand's three million plus. The bigger country has a more vibrant economy and a bigger stock market; quite a few young New Zealanders move to Australia to take advantage of broader opportunities. The sense of rivalry between the two countries is very strong. Barbara Drury, a perceptive Australian journalist, told me that New Zealanders were more preoccupied with this rivalry than Australians because their country was smaller, while Australians were more likely to focus on their rivalry with the United States. A visible, or rather audible, reflection of this sibling rivalry is the flow of jokes across the Tasman Sea.

"A New Zealander who emigrates to Australia," a rancher on the South Island told me, tightly pursing his lips, "raises the IQ of both countries." Australians respond with an incessant flow of jokes referring to New Zealanders' alleged sexual practices with the sheep. One asked me whether I knew why New Zealanders wore gum boots. Gum was the local word for rubber, and high rubber boots are popular among farmers. "To stabilize their sheep's hind legs," he roared. Another told me the three biggest lies in New Zealand: "I am married to a Maori princess," "My brother's an All-Black (a member of the national rugby team)" and "Officer, I was just helping this sheep over the fence." On the other side of the Tasman Sea, a New Zealander asked me whether I knew where to hide my money if I was ever invited into an Australian home: "Under the soap." Another asked whether I knew what to call ten Aussies standing in an open field: "A vacant lot."

The plane banked, and the captain announced that Surfers' Paradise was below. In Brisbane airport a broken luggage carousel clattered around a mockup of a casino pit, and I read a book while waiting in a long line to have my passport stamped. An hour later I walked out, met by a man from the publishing house that was selling my books in Australia. He wore a suit and tie, and I felt underdressed. It was the beginning of a week during which I would keep running into the types of workers I had not seen in a month, like marketing assistants and valet parking operators; I had grown used to seeing farmers, wilderness guides, and boat captains. Checking into a hotel for the first time in a month, I took the elevator to the seventh floor, fumbled with an electronic lock, and tried to open a window, but it was sealed. The winter was hot in Brisbane, but to turn on the air conditioning you had to insert your room card into a slot. To simplify life, I put my frequent flyer card in it, changed into a jacket and a tie, and went to the conference.

In 1993 I wrote *Trading for a Living*, which gradually became the most popular book in the world on trading in the financial markets, translated into nine languages. It felt strange because I was a psychiatrist by training, not an economist, an immigrant from a communist country, and still spoke English with an accent. I took both trading and writing very seriously, worked hard for many years and hit the ball just right. Writing a popular book is like getting a college degree—it certifies you as being intelligent, and people start paying to hear you speak. Nine years later, I wrote a new book *Come into My*

Trading Room that beat the first one out of the number one spot. You have to compete with yourself or someone else will. The new bestseller got me invited to Brisbane.

I gave my audience the definition of an expert—someone who wears a jacket and tie and is more than 100 miles away from home. Since I qualified on both scores, I could take my jacket and tie off and get to work. I hooked my computer up to a projection screen and spent the evening looking at Australian stocks and analyzing them for several dozen people in the audience. The market was not doing well and I wanted to show them how to stay out of trouble and trade the next upswing.

26 *Parfume Downwind*

The man from the publishing house drove me to a bookstore in downtown Brisbane. They had a sign with my name in the window and a table in the middle with a stack of my books. I was signing books and chatting with the staff when a tall, slender, broad-shouldered man walked in, his white mane flying behind him. He put out his hand, grinned and looked familiar, but I did not recognize him until he said, "Singapore." Ivan, of course! We had met in Singapore in 1996, where I taught a course, while he consulted in a bank.

I loved his book, published only in Australia, with a short masculine title, *Listen to the Market*. I had given it a great review that must have caught his eye because I used to be a prolific reviewer of trading books but was known as a sarcastic critic, so my positive reviews were few and far between. We had stayed in touch on and off for a couple of years, then lost contact. That day, driving downtown, Ivan recognized my name on a poster.

He went back to park his jeep and returned with his wife—an attractive, dark-haired woman with a warm laugh. He had been very single when we met in Singapore. We started catching up on our news, blocking traffic in the center aisle, when Ivan asked about my plans for tomorrow. That was my only free day in Australia. He cut our conversation short—"I'll pick you up at 11, you spend the day and the night with us, and the next morning I'll drive you to the airport." He disappeared as suddenly as he had walked in, and the marketing guy drove me back to the hotel. My work was finished for the day.

A year earlier an Australian woman had flown to the United States to see me, but I ended the relationship, believing it was not good for either of us. She heard I was coming to Brisbane and emailed me: Let's be civilized, meet for a cup of coffee. She came into the city and took a room in a local hotel. Our cup of coffee turned into lunch, then a walk, then a visit to a local museum and then a boat ride. By the time we began traipsing through the museum, I felt trapped. On the deck of the riverboat I tried to stay upwind so as not to be over-powered by her perfume mixed with cigarettes. When you love a woman, you want to smell her, inhale her breath, but here I was trying to inch away. It was getting dark, dinnertime was approaching, and she told me she was hungry. Who knew what was coming next? I did something I hated doing and told her I had to go back and speak at the conference again. I kissed her on the cheek and walked across the city back to my hotel. They had a seafood buffet that night and I dug into sushi and lobsters, listening to a huge Aboriginal guy play jazz while I ate alone.

27 *An Esky Party*

Ivan picked me up in a van with a roo guard—a set of staggered horizontal bars across the front of a vehicle, an entirely Australian invention. The uppermost bar protrudes the most, killing any kangaroo that runs in front, with the lower bars pushing its body under the wheels where it cannot damage the hood and windshield. Roo bars had been outlawed in England after some stylish people started putting them on their jeeps. There aren't too many kangaroos on English roads, but a roo bar is just as efficient at killing hapless pedestrians.

A water bag hung from the roo bar, partially obscuring the license plate and providing a measure of innocent-looking protection against speed cameras. We zoomed through a Florida-like landscape of flat scrubland. The eight-lane highway between Brisbane and Gold Coast was built for growth. I caught a glimpse of Gold Coast from a hill—the tallest residential building in the world rose incongruously on the beach. We turned on a country road and passed several herds of cattle, then a small flock of sheep. "Do you know how a New Zealander finds his sheep in tall grass?"—asked Ivan. He paused and whispered, "Delightful!"

He lived at the far end of a steep, narrow driveway that twisted around a hill. "Must be a bitch to drive here in the snow," I said and we laughed. It was August, the height of the Southern Hemisphere's winter, but the temperature was in the high 70s and there was not a cloud in the sky. The warm dry air had a wonderful smell of eucalyptus—the sprawling hilltop house stood in the middle of a grove. A spaniel ran out to greet us, trying to lick us while wagging the stump of its tail. His name was Atlas, after Ayn Rand's *Atlas Shrugged,* Ivan's favorite book.

Ivan had always been single, moving from one country to another—Singapore, Indonesia, the United States, Vanuatu—but three years ago he married Anne and settled down with her on this remote mountaintop. Anne's teenage children came out to shake hands. Greg wore a mortarboard that said Doctor of Mischief, and when I took a picture of him wearing it, Beth put on her mortarboard that said Doctor of Dreams, and I took a picture of them together. The kids were polite, intelligent, and attentive—fun to be with. Ivan doted on them and they were close to him. He had stayed single forever, but once he got married, he got himself an entire attractive family.

It turned out that day was Anne's birthday and they were having a picnic with friends. We loaded the van with hampers and the ubiquitous Australian "eskies"—Styrofoam coolers. When Atlas was put on a leash and realized he was coming along for the ride, he leapt into the air with joy and appeared to hover, flapping his paws like in a cartoon. On the way we passed several calves grazing on the side of the road. As Ivan slowed down, Atlas stuck his head out of the window and barked. The calves, who until then had totally ignored the van, started running and cleared the road.

We stopped at a wine shop and then at a fish shop with a sign "Fresh from the trawler." The variety and freshness were amazing and I could not stop photographing the fish, lobsters, crabs, and shrimp piled on rows of crushed ice. After loading more eskies into the groaning van we drove to the beach and in a few minutes were parked at the water's edge.

The sun shone brilliantly on the water as the boats kept passing by—jet skis, sailboats, floating homes. More friends of Anne kept arriving as Ivan set up folding tables and chairs, put out cotton napkins, unwrapped champagne glasses, and commanded me to open the first bottle of champagne. The cork popped and flew, we drank to Anne's health. Greg and Beth played football with the dog, who seemed to be floating through the air after the flying ball.

The fresh seafood was heavenly. We switched to red Australian wines which tasted so rich and strong on this hot Australian winter day.

Time seemed to stand still and fly at the same time. It seemed like only 15 minutes had passed since we had arrived at midday when a huge red disk of the sun touched the horizon. We started to pack up, and as soon as the sun disappeared the air felt cold. I nodded off on the way home, but there the table was set again and another friend had arrived for a dinner of sushi and rolling conversation—about music, about New York, about the kids' school. He was also invited to stay overnight but had to leave. Anne and the kids went to sleep, while Ivan and I went to his office and played pool on a full-size table in the midst of seven computer screens, talking politics late into the night.

28 The Stolen Generation

On the previous day I saw a eucalyptus grove under my window with rows of hills running down to the distant sea. In the morning the huge valley was flooded by pastel-colored fog, with only a few reddish mountain peaks protruding above it, like strawberries floating in a deep dish of cream. I had a quick breakfast with the family; the kids were already dressed for school. After the last round of invitations to visit and stay longer, Ivan drove me to the airport. A two-hour flight south took me into a cold and grey Melbourne. The overcast sky pressed down on tall buildings, breaking out into a drizzle. People were bundled up in warm coats and I pulled out a sweater, a windbreaker, and a baseball cap from my flight bag.

Two marketing reps drove me to sign books in two stores, and in the afternoon brought me to Lindrum, a new boutique hotel that proclaimed itself the best in the city. I recognized it from the article in the design magazine I had read on my last day in Wellington while waiting for my meal at the Thai restaurant. The hotel was full of beautiful people—a fashion shoot was going on in the lobby. The door key did not work and the elevator did not run, but the exquisitely stylish staff only arched their eyebrows at such trifles. They could not be rushed and kept slowing down in front of the tall mirrors in the lobby.

I walked down Flinders Street to the Immigration Museum. Two young, beefy drunks stumbled out of a McDonald's, one with a bloody face, fresh from a fistfight. A fat policeman was running after a guy down the street, a big black pistol flapping up and down on his butt. Melbourne was a busy place.

The museum of immigration became more interesting once I started asking questions about its exhibits rather than taking them at face value. Clearly, it was better to be an immigrant in Australia than a native, especially an immigrant from the right country. A 1901 law consigned Aborigines to reservations, but even there the government would not leave them alone and forcibly took away their babies and placed them with white families to "civilize" them. The Aborigines were considered subhuman, had no Australian citizenship and were not included in any population census until 1965. Many countries have marred histories, but I found those dates depressingly recent.

Australia is almost as large as the United States, but its population is less than one-tenth of the United States. It knew it was underpopulated and always tried to attract immigrants, as long as they came from England, but there were not enough takers, even with free ticket offers. The government then opened the doors to northern Europeans, but there were not enough of them either and most of the country remained empty, creating a security risk that was brought into sharp focus after the Japanese near-invasion in 1942. After the war the government demonstrated its generosity by taking in some refugees—as indentured laborers. Then it held its nose and admitted southern Europeans—Italians and Greeks—but the commitment to a "White Australia" remained on the books and party platforms. An Australian Immigration Minister, addressing a press club in Hong Kong in the 1950s, imitating a Chinese accent, quipped, "Two Wongs do not make a White" (two wrongs do not make a right). When several weeks later a fiery prime minister of an Asian country was asked to comment while making a speech at the same club, he called Australia "the white trash of the Pacific." That was the level of Australia's relationship with its neighbors. Only in recent decades, following spectacular economic growth in Asia—much of which Australia has missed out on—did the country scrap its official racist policy.

I hurried back because the conference organizers who put me into Lindrum had invited me for dinner at its restaurant. Our menus were printed on brown paper in a fine faint script—very stylish, but I couldn't read them and asked for a flashlight. Our waitress messed up every single order, and after she failed to bring us cutlery, I switched to self-service and fetched it myself. After that the head waitress took over, finally bringing us the right wine, but spilling it around two out of three glasses. The food was edible. On my way to the elevator, which had been fixed, I passed our waitress and noticed how strikingly tall and willowy she was. She was preening in front of a high mirror with her back to the restaurant.

29 Directions for a Hanging

The next morning was brighter in Melbourne, and since my speech was not until six, I looked forward to exploring Australia's second-largest city. I walked down Flinders Street, turning right at McDonald's, which was peaceful that early morning, and stopped at an Internet café. In New Zealand people sit down in front of the screens and afterwards pay for whatever time they used, a simple and a straightforward practice. In Australia, you have to prepay your usage in 15-minute blocks, and if you use less, that is your loss. The rates differ depending on whether it is a simple cafe or an upscale hotel, but the edgy harshness of the Australian system is the same in every place.

On the way to the museum I passed through Greektown, several blocks of Greek businesses, shops, and restaurants. A display in a bakery window pulled me in like a magnet—an open pastry shell tightly packed with green pistachios under a gold honey glaze. Across the river from my apartment in Manhattan is Astoria, with one of the largest Greek communities in the world, but I had never seen such a pastry there. It was too rich for breakfast and I tried to resist, but then inhaled, walked in, and ordered.

The plaza in front of the massive, modern museum was tightly packed with school buses, but whoever spent a fortune giving money to local construction firms to build that pile never followed it up by funding attractive and educational exhibits. A huge hall, as big as anything in the National Air and Space Museum in Washington, D.C., had a table with several dozen dead parakeets under a glass. It was an awfully long run for a very short slide. The enormous mound of concrete reminded me of the restaurant from the day before with its triumph of style over substance. The admission fee was already lost, but the time could still be saved, and I walked out.

Several blocks away a small yellow and red plaque on a building proclaimed that its inhabitants recognized the Aboriginal ownership of the land on which it stood. A sign above the door read "Melbourne's Radical Bookstore." Inside they sold those plaques and I thought one would make a nice souvenir for my office, but the price of a plastic rectangle the size of a sheet of paper was $40. I wanted to buy a souvenir, not pay party dues for a year! Browsing, I saw a PLO flag and large sign that admonished visitors not to steal because the books belonged to their friends. I thought the comrades had some unresolved property issues and walked out empty-handed.

It began to rain, and I stepped into Melbourne's old City Gaol (jail). The structure was being demolished in the 1950s when preservationists realized it was a major landmark, saved a three-story wing, and turned it into a museum. Each room in the long row of solitary cells hosted an exhibit about a person hanged in that prison, complete with case details, newspaper clippings, at times a final letter, and a death mask. The cells were tiny, the doors thick, the details sickening. Needless to say, the first to be hanged were Aborigines who, after being "cleansed" from the area, gave way on the gallows mostly to immigrants who spoke little English and had few friends.

The building was shaped like an oblong donut, with an empty space in the middle, and on every floor you could hear the rain beating on the roof. Metal walkways ran along the inner perimeter of the three-story building, and on the third floor stood a holding cell for condemned prisoners. In front of it a rope hung from a bar above and a trapdoor opened to the floor below. One of the executioners had worked out a formula, based on massive experience, for calculating the proper length of rope for each condemned prisoner. A professional hanging resulted in an instant death with no signs of external damage. If the rope was too short, the prisoner would hang convulsing and die slowly, but if it was too long he could pick up enough speed on the way down to tear the head from the body. The formula depended on the person's weight because a heavier prisoner needed a shorter rope, a lighter one a longer rope to pick up more speed.

I returned to the hotel, changed into a jacket and a tie and caught a streetcar to the Convention Center. While I waited for the organizers in the lobby, an attendee came up to me, asked whether I was Dr. Elder and shook my hand. To my amazement, he wore thin leather gloves. I would not oblige until he took them off. A few minutes later he ran back, full of enthusiasm, and wanted to shake hands again. The conference went extremely well. We stayed up late into the evening, and the woman who owned an investment bookstore had set up a book display in the lobby, where she sold so many books that my every free minute was taken up by signing them.

30 *I'll be Buggered*

A marketing assistant from the publishing house drove me to Melbourne airport where I sat half-asleep by the gate, waiting for an early morning flight to Sydney. A man in a flashy business suit opened his laptop computer with flourish and made a big show of pounding on it. As passengers disembarked from another plane, a young fellow rushed towards him, crying out cheerfully, "Hello, Mr. Reed!" The gentleman lifted his butt a few inches from the seat, extended his hand, beamed, and drawled "I'll be buggered." I had almost forgotten this charming Australian expression of surprise, which sounded so anatomically quaint to an American ear. My Aussie vocabulary was starting to return: "Right on, mate." "Be stuffed." "Fair dinkum."

A publishing house manager was waiting for me in Sydney. He certainly knew how to sell books, but navigating an Alfa Romeo was not high on his list of skills. I had to call my friend Tony to get directions to my hotel. After I checked in and paid for an upgrade to a harborfront room, the manager got lost again driving us to a downtown bookstore. I took over the navigation and led him to a Chinese restaurant where we enjoyed a lunch of ginger scallops, washing them down with Tsingtao beer. We returned to the bookstore in the best of spirits, if a few minutes late, and had another book signing. Afterwards I walked back to the hotel through an extremely crowded downtown, missing the peace and quiet of New Zealand.

In the evening two managers from the publishing house drove me for a guest appearance on Australia's most popular business TV show. We crossed downtown, the nearby suburbs, drove across a dam, through a nature preserve, the road snaking in the dark. This was no case of driving dyslexia, since the woman driver knew her way around Sydney. After a dark stretch alongside a golf course, we pulled into an industrial-looking row of low buildings where the famous business show had its studio. A fellow who saved on rent could better concentrate on profits. The small staff appeared busy and happy, and their pleasant mood stayed with me through the corporate dinner which followed the interview.

31 The Best Brains of All Fish

In the morning my phone rang and a woman's voice poured over the line like honey. "Are your nipples warm?" she asked, before breaking into peals of laughter. It was Karen, one of the "bad girls" from our conference six months ago. She had seen me on TV the night before and tracked me down at the hotel. Her joke reminded me of the day when half a dozen people at our conference piled into my minivan and we drove to a nearby town, where I had seen an object in a gift shop that amazed me. Two circles of soft brown possum fur, each about twice the size of a quarter, were attached to a piece of cardboard with a label. I never knew such an object existed. The label read "nipple warmers."

I thought it was a gag, but Karen, a grown-up woman of boundless self-confidence, explained that in a country devoid of central heating this was a very useful object that a woman could use in one of two ways—either to line her bra or wear in bed directly attached to her anatomy, with no other garments. I stood there speechless. My education had just taken an enormous leap forward, while my self-image as someone who was reasonably well-informed about the intricacies of feminine garments was shattered by this exposure of ignorance.

But Karen was not finished with me. At dinner that night, with 30 or so people around the table, she got up and tapped her wine glass with a spoon, demanding attention. As people turned to her, she said, "Alex, it is time for you to learn how these are worn," and flung open her jacket. There, attached to her white turtleneck in two strategic spots were her own nipple warmers. She produced a fresh pack from her purse and gave it to me as a gift. The group applauded, but I thought the joke had gone a little too far at my expense. When the laughter subsided, I tapped my own wine glass and answered, "Thanks, but I usually orient myself by remembering that the fur side is down, and these might get me disoriented." The group roared again, and now it was Karen's turn to be speechless. I carried her gift home and hung it on my bedroom wall next to a grass skirt from the Pacific islands of Vanuatu.

I walked to my friend Tony's law office to check my emails. He was away at a business meeting, but his wife Julie was holding down the fort, with everything under the coolest of control. Larry, their friend who was subletting a room in the suite, was online and invited me to use his computer. I enjoyed their friendly reception after feeling infuriated by the hotel's charging an exorbitant rate for a connection so slow that I played Solitaire waiting for pages to refresh. Tony returned from his meeting, Julie hovered, waiting for a report, but I had to rush back for another interview, and we agreed to meet for lunch. The man from the newspaper seemed shocked to see me in jeans and a polo shirt rather than a business suit like everyone else in the lobby. Halfway through the interview a photographer arrived, clicking away with his camera. The interviewer told me he was one of the most famous photographers in Australia whose greatest coup had been to snap a picture of the prime minister in his underwear while he was sick at home. Instead of being greatly impressed, I said I hoped mine didn't show. The joke landed flat, and while they promised to email me a copy of the article, I am still waiting for it.

Tony arrived to pick me up after the interview—tall, with movie-star good looks, immaculately dressed in an expensive business suit with a handkerchief in his breast pocket. People around us took notice that there walked a man of substance. Now in his forties, Tony had been a senior partner at a law firm but went into semiretirement a few years ago to look after his business interests. He looked so upper class that it came as a surprise when he told me when we first met years ago that he had been born to a family of very modest means in England, brought to Australia as a child, and went to work at 18 as a clerk at the firm in which he eventually became a senior partner. Tony was so mild that I told him he would fit in well in New Zealand, but professionally he was extremely tough. He had won what was at the time the highest personal injury award in Australia. Another time he had been retained by a man who owned a large plot of waterfront land and wanted to remove his commercial tenants in order to sell out to developers. Tony's job was to get rid of those who did not move voluntarily. He studied their leases, evicted everyone who was in violation and after that his real work began. For example, one of the largest Asian importers of electronic goods kept his warehouse on the property, with huge trucks bringing containers from the pier. Coming to work one Monday morning the importers discovered that over the weekend the landlord had pounded a crisscross pattern of metal poles in the garden area in which the trucks used to maneuver because the driveways were too narrow for them to turn around. When they screamed, Tony explained that their lease allowed them to use driveways but not the garden areas, and soon the landlord had one fewer tenant to worry about. Before the importers left he made them pay a fee for being let out of their lease.

Tony led me to a delightful dim sum (they call it yum cha in Australia) with a stylish clientele, half Chinese and half Western. A dozen smiling Chinese women rolled carts with tiny trays of freshly prepared delicacies between the tables. They kept slowing down and inviting you to pick anything you liked, stamping a little slip of paper on your table in Chinese. Tony had done a great deal of legal work in Hong Kong and gave me a fascinating lecture on the differences between the Chinese and Western ways of doing business. It was not that one or the other was better, as outsiders often thought, but both had different sets of well-established rules, and you had to be comfortable with both in order to succeed.

In all his worldwide travels Tony never visited New Zealand, and I invited him to join me there. He had always been extremely hospitable to me in Australia, and I wanted to reciprocate and enjoy his company. Because of his business and family commitments, he could only hop over for five days, Monday through Friday. Since he loved fishing, I decided to take him to two of the best fishing areas of the North Island. Unfortunately, I could not take him fly-fishing for trout, which was his favorite, because for that one had to go to the mountain streams of the South Island. Since Tony was joining me on the North Island, I made arrangements to charter a boat on Lake Taupo and then fly north for some saltwater fishing in the Bay of Islands.

Lake Taupo, the largest lake in New Zealand, teemed with silver and rainbow trout, originally brought from California and introduced to the country in the 1880s. None of the restaurants on the lakeshore had trout on the menu because commercial fishing was prohibited. If you caught your own trout and brought it to a restaurant along with your fishing license, they cooked it for you. In March 2000 I took a group of six on a half-day boat trip on the lake. Phyllis had recommended a captain who was like a one-man band—driving the boat, baiting the hooks, opening beer and wine, and cleaning the fish, all at a fast but seemingly effortless pace. Between the six of us we bought four licenses and within half an hour caught three trout, each weighing four to five pounds—we did not even use the fourth license because we had more than enough to eat. We took our fish to a waterfront restaurant, showed our licenses, and were told to return in half an hour. Walking through Taupo, I bought a copy of *A Girl's Guide to Fishing and Hunting* by Melissa Banks from a remainder bin at a bookstore—a piece of New York fiction that I enjoyed tremendously— and we returned to a feast. They did not charge for cooking the fish, but of course we ordered all the trimmings and wine.

A year later I returned to Lake Taupo with another small group, but that time, even though the weather was delightful and the Chardonnay delicious, we did not catch a single fish. They simply did not bite. Suzanne, one of the "bad girls" and the most expert fisher among us, hooked one on her last cast, but it got away. Suzanne was the president of a fly-fishing club in New York and I once gave her a gift of three framed lures, writing on the back of the frame, "To Suzanne, my favorite hooker—from Alex." She was a serious woman who took nonsense from no one, and when she saw people eating freshly caught trout at another table, she got angry. "If that captain was a real professional, he'd know where the fish were and take us there. You hired the wrong guy."

I told Tony about it, but he disagreed. Trout are smart, he said, they have the best brains of all fish and they use them. Fly-fishing is the hardest sport. You have to select the lure that looks just like what the fish are eating at that moment. If you tie a number eight fly while the fish in that stream are eating flies that look like a number six lure, they will not bite. The trout, unlike other fish, do not bite at once. They come up to the lure and take it in their mouth, and if they do not like it, they can suck in water through their gills and blow the lure out. They spend their lives above some underwater ridge where the current is the fastest, head upstream, and stay in place by swimming against the current, eating what the current brings down to them. You have to cast your lure, which is at the end of a three-pound line, and if they rise to it you have to move fast to hook them before they spit it out. And once you hook them, they begin to fight.

Trout spend their lives swimming against the current and become very strong. The current can be so fast that sometimes you have to struggle to keep your balance in one-foot-deep water. Once hooked, the trout dive and go behind the rocks, while your line will hold only three pounds. It is a miracle when you outfight the fish and your line doesn't break. And then, almost always, you end up releasing the fish. Tony even had special tweezers for taking out the hook without killing the fish. You may have hiked a couple of hours to get to the stream and if you catch the fish in the morning, they will smell by the time you get home and you're not going to want to eat them. If you cook your catch on the spot it is heavenly, but how often are you going to do that? A couple of times Tony caught trout just a kilometer away from the car, on his way home, and then he would bring his catch home. But of course every time you release a trout, it gets smarter and all the more difficult to catch the next time.

Tony had gone game fishing off Fiji, but that was not the same as fly-fishing. He caught a six-foot barracuda, which was a fighting fish, but the line was essentially unbreakable and the reel had a clutch. If you reeled too hard and risked breaking the line, the clutch released and compensated for you. Equipment has become so good that this type of fishing is no longer a sport. If you stay out long enough some fish is going to bite, and then it is no contest—you reel it in and land it. Trout, by contrast, are so smart and the line only three pounds, that landing them is almost a miracle.

The restaurant was nearly empty when Tony lunged across the table and grabbed our check. I thought of the trout hitting a fly and didn't struggle. He walked me to Karen's office, where a small group of friends had gathered for a drink at her massive bar. Soon it was time to leave and speak at the conference. The attendees were very pleased, the woman who owned the bookstore flew in from Melbourne and sold another ton of books, which I kept signing, but I was glad when it was over. I was looking forward to returning to New Zealand and continuing my journey on the North Island.

SECTION
4

The
North Island

32 Prawn Sambal from KL

At the Sydney airport I headed for the duty-free shop because Phyllis had emailed me from Auckland, asking for a bottle of blue Sapphire gin for her daughter. It cost $24.95 (Australian) a bottle, and I picked up two. I fished in my pockets and found $49.50 of Australian money, which I wanted to spend before leaving that country. I was short 40 Australian cents—about 20 American cents—and the salespeople sneered at me. I asked a manager who growled to pay in full or put one bottle back. Niceness and accommodation were definitely not on the menu. I handed them my American Express and told them to charge 40 cents, but they got really angry, telling me there was a $10 minimum, and so I left Australia with $9.50 of its currency still in my pocket, promising never again, as long as I live, to spend another dollar in Sydney duty-free.

I was glad to leave the hotels, the schedules, the duty-free behind me. As the plane approached New Zealand, I drank in its chiseled shoreline, waves rolling in from the Tasman Sea, breaking in long white strips in front of a neat patchwork of pastures. Above the North Island the plane flew into low clouds, and a few minutes later, breaking through and coming in low and slow to land in Wellington, I saw houses with their own cable cars. Very substantial houses were cut into hillsides with no roads, but with private cable cars connecting them to the roads below, where owners parked their cars. I wanted to stay in one of those on my next visit, and imagined it must feel like staying on an island.

It was afternoon in New Zealand when I drove a rental car to Logan and Annette's house on Mt. Victoria. It made sense to stay there for the night and hit

137

the road the next morning. Logan was uncharacteristically quiet after having undergone some cardiac procedure earlier that day. I told him of my duty-free experience, and he growled, "Those Australians are a pretty hard-bitten lot." I dropped off my laundry with Annette, took the cell phone and called Emily and Anders.

Charles and Daphne on the South Island spoke with great fondness of an American woman who bought a station north of Wellington and ranched there with her husband. When I got her number and called before flying to Australia a week before, she said that on the evening of my return from Australia she and her husband were taking their entire staff to a rugby game in Wellington and invited me to join them. I did not relish the idea of sitting on a bench under an open sky on a cold evening amidst a roaring crowd watching a game I didn't understand. When several friends heard of it, they told me I could not write a book without going to a rugby game because it was a national obsession. Returning to Wellington, I called Emily to see whether she still had an extra ticket, but the bus she chartered had already left. I would have to write my book without going to the church of rugby. I took a cigar, lighter, and my computer, and went to work in a nearby café.

It was dark when I brought the computer home and went for a walk in the small colorful neighborhood between the foot of Mt. Victoria and the Te Papa museum. The windows of a gallery blazed with light and behind them people mingled, holding wine glasses and plates of appetizers. The gallery owner told me it was a party to celebrate her second anniversary in business and poured me a glass of wine. I wished her happy anniversary and wandered through the gallery, looking at its Maori art and modern handicrafts. I was tempted to return the next morning to do some shopping, but remembered I still had a long journey ahead.

Every other building in the area had a gallery, restaurant, lounge, or bar, many with live music. I walked up the steps to a Malay restaurant, ordered a dish of fiery prawn sambal, and chatted with the owner about his native Kuala Lumpur, the capital of Malaysia. The way you pronounce certain names marks you as either an insider or a tourist. For example, in New York we have a major downtown street called Houston, pronounced "house-ton." When someone asks about "hews-ton," you know that person is not a local. Similarly, those of us who have lived in Asia no longer say Kuala Lumpur, only KL. After putting the fire of the main course out with Singha beer, I walked into a tiny neighborhood theater, paying NZ$16, about US$7, to see a play by a local playwright. Waiting for it to begin, I ordered a cappuccino and brought it to my seat. There was a café in the lobby and people brought drinks into the theater, sipping a glass of wine or a cup of coffee during the performance. As always in New Zealand, there was an atmosphere of quiet consideration, as people were expected not to make noise, spill, or disturb others.

33 *81 Sheep an Hour*

After paying Logan I packed my belongings into the trunk of my large rental car. Logan wanted to help, but I carried everything down myself since he still didn't look too good from the day before. I pulled out of Wellington, driving north along the waterfront but stopping again and again, overcome by the piercing beauty of the morning's landscape. The sunlight was breaking through the clouds, its wide beams stabbing the bay like knife blades. The water was every shade of dark green, covered with whitecaps and encircled by blue mountains. Several cargo ships, tiny as splinters, bobbed in the water, and airliners the size of toy planes glided overhead towards Wellington. From this distance the city looked like a dainty white fungus running up the side of a mountain.

I pulled over and parked facing the water to drink in the view, take a few photos, and make phone calls. My next destination was Castlepoint, Emily and Anders' station, which received its name from a distinctive rock, mapped and named by Captain Cook. As soon as I turned north, Wellington disappeared from view. There was no suburban sprawl, only a few tidy villages and an endless patchwork of farms. The powerful car kept overtaking others on short straight stretches, shooting up into the hills, so steep that railroads used to link several locomotives together to hoist ore from the valleys.

I passed Masterton—the site of the annual Golden Shears competition, the Super Bowl of sheep shearers. Last year's champion has shorn 647 adult sheep in eight hours—that's 81 sheep an hour, a little more than half a minute per sheep. The road swung towards the East Coast and climbed again. There were white sheep on mountainsides and sharp turns over the ravines, and then the road dropped towards the ocean. Soon an enormous rock on the beach came into view and turning at the sign for the annual Castlepoint beach horse race, I pulled into the station. Emily was in the driveway, unloading gear from the van after her daughter's game of field hockey.

Emily had grown up on the land her family farmed for six generations in Westchester, north of New York City. Farming so close to the city was becoming less economically viable, as taxes went up and services which farmers depended on began moving away. As a teenager, Emily discovered New Zealand and decided she wanted to study here, but at that time foreign college students were not accepted, and she worked three six-month stints on New Zealand farms. Anders, her future husband, went to Andover and Dartmouth, and rowed and competed as an ocean sailor. He worked as a financial analyst, but was drawn to farming and wanted to get away from the city. Four years ago the couple decided they had to move before their children became teenagers and grew attached to New York. After the family farm in New York was sold to real estate developers, Emily took her share of the money and came to New Zealand with Anders to shop for a station. They had a laundry list of requirements, having asked approximately a hundred ranchers what factors were important in choosing a farm. Two and a half weeks later they bought this station. A neighbor commented on their speed: "Twenty-five years of building the foundation and two-and-a-half weeks of putting up the roof."

Emily shooed her daughter away from the TV and popped in a cassette. A local TV station had filmed a show about them, as carriers of valuable skills who settled in local communities. Emily spoke of the trust with which the locals had treated them, signing a contract without a deposit. It was a small country, and what went around came around very fast. You were given the benefit of the doubt—once. Emily's share of the family farm in Westchester was 35 acres, and that had paid for a working farm on 7,000 acres of oceanfront land in New Zealand. Shortly before coming here the family vacationed in Nantucket, Massachusetts, where the same money could have bought an oceanfront lot, big enough for two houses. One of the amazing values in New Zealand is the price of its land, so much lower than in other developed countries. The so-called "lifestyle blocks" in Castlepoint area—10 to 20 acres of land for a country home, with good views—sold for about NZ$200,000 (less than 100,000 U.S. dollars).

We sat down at the kitchen table for a lunch of freshly baked bread with slabs of amazingly rich and flavorful local cheeses. I teased Emily and Anders that I had wanted to bring them a six-pack of Bud to uphold the American tradition but, failing to find it, had to settle for a case of Cloudy Bay. I played devil's advocate: "Why didn't you put your money into municipal bonds? The tax-free income would have been enough to live at ease without working." "It would have been boring," replied Anders. "We want to work and live in a place where we can educate our children. Land is life; you cannot buy that with muni bonds." Emily said that coming to New Zealand was a transfer of their heritage rather than an emigration. Farming was her life, and New Zealand was focused on farming.

Their kids went to a boarding school during the week and returned home on weekends. Instead of playing video games, they would say "Let's go build a hut! Let's go ride ponies on the beach!" Two preteen boys—their son and his friend—walked into the kitchen, shivering and stripping off wetsuits after a morning of surfing on a sunny winter day. Their son's blond hair looked like a tossed up bale of straw. The kids were sent into the hot tub, and returned dressed in jeans, no longer blue from the cold, and tucked into their lunch. Afterwards Emily put her son on a chair in the middle of the kitchen, wrapped a towel around him, brought out scissors and started cutting his hair. Anders lent me a pair of gumboots for a drive around the station. He drove on the roads soggy from recent rains, and each time I hopped out of his jeep to open or close a gate, I was glad for those boots.

Their narrow and long farm was shaped like Manhattan, approximately half its length and width. Over 1.5 million people live in Manhattan, but the farm, one quarter of its size, housed just Anders' family and a few of his workers. Housing for single workers was built at the farthest end from the village, as far away from the local bar as Anders could make it. Nobody locked their doors. There were several cottages where shepherds used to stay, but they were abandoned after four-wheel drives and all-terrain vehicles (ATVs) made getting around easier. An empty shack where Fijian migrant workers used to stay while helping build a road was called the Fijian embassy.

The farm raised cattle and sheep, and its efficient grid of electrified fences helped move the stock from one pasture to another while the fields regenerated. I thought again what a nonsentimental business farming was as I listened to Anders explain how they sold wool ewes to meatpackers after five years—once they ground down their teeth—but how other farmers sometimes bought them up to keep for one more year on easier, softer pastures. An extra year of life or death depended on nothing more than teeth. I asked him whether he ever felt sorry for his farm animals. Not really, he said. They were bred for meat and while living on the farm they had a pretty good life. As we spoke, his live-stock chewed fresh grass under a sunny sky, cooled off by an ocean breeze.

All the stations in the area raised livestock, and Anders sneered about "horticulturalists"—people who grew marijuana in the bush, some of them also collecting the dole (welfare). I asked him about possums, and he said that they carried tuberculosis. Whenever the cattle became infected, the animals were condemned by government inspectors, and he received a partial reim-bursement. Anders said sarcastically that possum-fighting agencies wanted to control possums, but to do away with them would mean losing their jobs. I asked him about the custom of docking—clipping short the tails of newborn lambs. This prevents their hind ends from becoming encrusted with fecal mat-ter (sheep do not wipe) and therefore a breeding ground for flies, which can lead to a dreaded flystrike—a deadly attack of maggots burrowing under the sheep's skin. Anders sneered that while a dead sheep would definitely have maggots, flystrike was a myth. He tried docking and not docking and saw no difference, but his farmhands believed in docking, and it did not cost him any-thing to humor them.

Anders drove along fantastic beaches, pointing out that the coastline was so jagged it provided three aspects for surfing. Beaches faced north, south, and east, so that you could always find the one where the waves were just right. When Anders and Emily bought this farmland, its oceanfront resort potential was not even considered by the sellers, but recently the station was revalued at twice the purchase price. Anders pointed to the fishing boats on trailers parked on the beach and explained that local commercial fishermen used to fish for crayfish all year round, and barely made a living until the government established a quota system for them, which has worked well. Now they catch their quota in three months and then ran charters for tourists, while the number of crays has rebounded.

We returned for dinner, washing our boots outdoors before entering the house. Anders opened a bottle of white and a bottle of red, then ran up to his office and returned with a book of computer printouts—his annual report. While Emily had an eagle eye for livestock, Anders ran the business side of their ranch like a modern corporation. They had an advisory board, on which they had first relied for operational advice, but now for strategic planning. His report for the last board meeting ran to 80 pages of charts and tables. The wealth of information helped make better farming decisions. The milk farms were the most scientific, but they had only one product, which was measured daily. A stock farm sheared twice a year, sold lambs once a year, and sold cattle once every few years. His records allowed him to discover that the two main swing factors of profitability were the percentage of ewes having lambs and their weaning weight. It would have been impossible to find that out without good records. The natural tendency was to pay more attention to cattle, because they were bigger, there were fewer of them, and they stayed on the farm longer—but that was not where the main money was. Anders' records clearly showed that their profit parameters were way ahead of comparable U.S. ranches. I was amazed that all of their products sold for approximately the same price—NZ\$3 per kilo (under one U.S. dollar per pound), whether lamb, beef, or wool. This confirmed what I heard from other farmers, that the business of New Zealand is to grow grass, with various agricultural products simply the vehicles for its use. The next big step, said Anders, would be to measure the cost of grass directly, in cents per megajoules of energy it provides.

With the kids sitting around the table, Emily said grace. I noticed a grand piano in the hall and Emily mentioned that she sometimes played the organ in local churches. Anders spoke about the Maori being very good traders and of the pleasure of their atonal music, but also of the danger of the claiming culture, with many Maori living off compensation payments. After dinner we piled into the van and drove to a community party. The manager of a vacation park (like a bungalow colony) was moving away to be closer to her daughter who was having a baby—she did not want to be "granny by post." Several dozen locals assembled along the tables in the community hall, eating and drinking, dancing and making speeches. As the wine levels in the bottles went down, the color of the speeches went up. The last thing I remembered was the manager taking false teeth out of her girlfriend's mouth to say a toast with four rows of teeth—two of her own and two borrowed from a friend. The party was picking up speed when Emily and Anders herded the kids into the van and drove home. I turned up the heater, crawled into bed, and immediately fell asleep.

34 Biblical High Tech

At breakfast Anders said most of the locals were at Sunday school that morning. Emily laughed and explained that those were their code words for sleeping late after partying on Saturday. They suggested a walk to the lighthouse, but I said, "I see you and raise you," and we hiked to the top of Castlepoint, a huge rise at water's edge that dominated the landscape. Emily had never been to the top, which is why, I said to her, it was good to have visitors—with them you go places and do things you would never do otherwise. I remembered having drinks for the last time at the top of the World Trade Center in July 2001 while showing New York to one of my Moscow friends.

The trail passed through a small forest, and Anders told me that the first time he went for a walk here, he felt a slight blow on the back of his head. He turned around, saw nothing and kept walking, but got hit again, this time harder. He still could not see anything or anyone and kept walking until the third blow, after which he said enough is enough and turned back. Later locals explained to him that it was the nesting season of the magpie, when the bird became very territorial and fearless and attacked anyone near its nest. Emily caught up with us and pointed out to Anders that the electric fence on a distant paddock had to be rewired. She noticed farming details as if she had an internal radar scanning her ranch.

A steep trail, muddy in places from last night's rain, led to the top. We zigzagged, but Anders' hyperactive Labrador kept scooting ahead, falling behind, then running ahead again, as if on perfectly flat ground. Finally we reached the rim—hundreds of feet above the ocean, and of course without a guard rail. It looked as if some giant had grabbed a pinch of the Earth's skin and pulled it up, ripping it, and leaving the huge flap in a near-vertical tear. We were high above the waves, a brisk wind kept pushing us away from the edge. There was no land between us and South America on the far side of the Pacific. This rock used to be a part of Castlepoint Station until a manager in the 1970s found there were valuable chemicals in the rock and prepared to mine them. The DOC got wind of his plan, came in, bought the rock, and opened it to the public.

We hiked back to the car along the beach, and Anders pointed out how native grasses held the dunes steady and low, while the introduced buffalo grass held sand better, allowing the dunes to build up higher until they collapsed. In the long run, native grasses are better for preventing erosion, but once the buffalo grass had been introduced, it was next to impossible to get rid of it. We walked to a little church in the dunes, built 30 years ago, whose panoramic windows used to overlook the ocean. The dunes with buffalo grass rose to the eaves, blocking the views. The Lab barked after finding an eight-inch-long pink body on the beach that looked like a dead piglet. Emily took one look and said it was a seal's fetus—the first and probably the last I was going to see in my life.

Emily loved the challenge of living in an isolated community. The nearest town of Masterton was an hour away and locals had to handle most emergencies themselves. She had an employee who had been with the station for 45 years, a walking human bank of expertise. He had taught them such essential skills as carrying a rope when going to look for a drowning victim and tying the body to a rock before going for help, otherwise the surf would carry it away. It usually takes seven men to carry such a victim because the bodies are so filled with water. Emily enjoyed the combination of high tech and low tech in the rural community. They use ultrasound to scan their sheep, but once they are color-coded, shepherds and dogs take over, using a technique that has not changed since biblical times. Their neighbor used wind power, one of the most ancient sources of energy, but when he had needed a spare part for his wind-mill, he ordered it using a cell phone.

Anders said that one thing he missed in this environment was the ability to order something from the Internet at 3 AM and have it delivered by 10 AM. He found most companies unprepared for the global economy. "They advertise themselves on TV as global firms, but try to fix something you bought in the U.S. here in New Zealand and you quickly discover how parochial they are." We drove home past the beach where their son was catching waves with a friend. Their cattle moved slowly across the pasture, converting grass into beef. We shook hands, I squeezed my computer into the trunk, and hit the mountain road.

I kept noticing white crosses, some with fresh flowers, next to sharp curves. I paid more attention to them now, since my incident on the South Island. Most fatal accidents were caused by drunk driving, often by youngsters, but Anders said that recently an American driver had killed two motorcyclists. He saw them coming through a tight turn on a narrow road, and having been in this country for only 24 hours, panicked and went right, as he would have done in the United States. The motorcyclists, of course, went left, as normal for New Zealand, and that was the end of them. I reminded myself to keep left at all times.

Reaching the main highway I turned north towards Hawke's Bay. The far-ther north, the more baby lambs tottered behind ewes in the paddocks. Lambs arrived later in the colder south, but here, in the warmer north, the lambing sea-son had already begun. The land became less mountainous, and more signs for wineries whizzed by as I approached Hawke's Bay. I had driven here several years ago with my son, but my memories of local landmarks had faded—only the memory of Bay and Shona's hospitality remained fresh. I called Bay on the cell phone, and he told me I had overshot his driveway and would hade to swing back. In 10 minutes I turned into Tukipo Terraces, slowing down for the ewes and lambs sauntering on both sides of the driveway. The baronial entrance, a gabled roof on heavy stone pillars, protected arriving guests from the elements.

Bay came out to help me with the luggage and to cheerfully demonstrate the effects of his recent knee replacement surgery by doing sit-ups and swinging his legs higher than I could. I gave him a case of wine from the South Island.

Before my first visit to New Zealand a friend had explained the concept of farmstays, popular in that country. Families in rural areas open one or two rooms in their homes to paying guests. The rate, about half that of a comparable hotel, includes a private room, dinner and breakfast, plus, if you work on the farm, a free lunch. I got in touch with a farmstay agency that faxed lists of available accommodations, and called them to discuss my interests. That's how I met Bay and Shona, and we became real friends in the ensuing years.

I had arrived with Danny in August, in the midst of New Zealand winter. It was dark, and a fire was raging in a huge fireplace. Shona and Bay warned Danny to stay away from their old dog Alice, who had had bad experiences with children and could bite, but the kid immediately connected with her and spent much of his time petting her and carrying her around. Since they doted on their dog, some of their liking for my son must have rubbed off on me. We had a gourmet dinner, and our conversation turned to history and crusaders. Estonia, the small Baltic country where I grew up, was old crusader territory. Armed young men who got beaten in the Holy Land went looking for softer targets, and some of them grabbed the area around the Baltic Sea—Estonia, Latvia, and Lithuania, and their descendants lorded over the locals for centuries. Bay showed me old papers, tracing his lineage to a French nobleman whom the crusaders in their winning days had elected the Emperor of Jerusalem. It felt amazing to be sipping wine in New Zealand with the descendant of a crusader Emperor.

At one point I had asked Bay why he took part in the farmstay program. A few days earlier, Danny and I had stayed on a farm whose young owners needed extra income, but that was clearly not the case with Bay. I never forgot his answer. "Well, our kids have grown and moved, and we have all these spare rooms. Shona loves to cook, and it is just as easy to cook for four as for two, so it is almost free money. But keep in mind that we live very far away from everywhere and you are more interesting than the TV." Later I was to find out that this answer applied to all the best farmstays. Their owners did not mind the money, but they ran their operations largely for their own amusement, enjoying a kaleidoscope of international visitors.

In the morning Bay issued Danny and me gumboots with coveralls and put us to work. Danny was given a wicker basket and sent to the edge of a grove to collect pine cones for the fireplace. Bay stationed me outside the paddock, where a farmhand was helping him shave spots on the necks of his deer in preparation for a vaccination visit from the vet. The paddock shook from the kicks of the terrified deer, who were not used to being shaved. The two guys handled the deer like pro wrestlers, while I held their instruments. After lunch Bay announced we could all knock off for the day and drove us to see his son's station, where we had tea with his daughter-in-law and watched a Maori worker shear sheep in a woolshed. In the evening Bay wanted to fly to a political meeting, but the wind was so strong that someone would have had to sit on the tail of his small plane while he maneuvered for takeoff. Since his new employee was afraid to do it and I had not thought of volunteering, Bay left early in his car. Our dinner wasn't quite the same without him.

We became friends on that visit and had stayed in touch ever since, emailing each other and exchanging family news. When I was planning this roadtrip, Bay and Shona were the only commercial operators who knew I was coming to write a book (I kept this information secret in order to get the same treatment as any other traveler, but I already knew what to expect from them). In a generous gift to me, they had opened a whole lot of doors, making useful introductions. It was hard to believe that everything had begun with me showing up on their doorstep one winter night with my son after making a booking through an agency.

Bay and Shona had teenage grandchildren but both moved like two teenagers themselves. Old Alice—Bay said she was 105 in human years—came out to sniff and do a little jig before returning to her pillow near the fire. That was the only big change—a gleaming glassfront fireplace Shona had ordered after becoming fed up with sweeping ashes. While Bay was getting himself a new knee, she replaced the original fireplace with a modern sealed version. Bay was irrepressible—while having his knee replaced, he increased his deer herd and started planting vines—now he was expanding into the wine business! The tail of his small plane could be seen from the window in the kitchen, which had a large comfortable sitting area, heavy leather couches, family photos, flowers, and books.

I followed Bay to his large garage where he pulled rolls of dog food out from the refrigerator, cut several thick slices, and went to the backyard to feed his working dogs. The oldest was off the leash, ambling between the doghouses. After it could no longer work for his son up in the hills Bay took it down into the valley and got five more years of work out of it. Now the dog was so old that even valley work was too much for it. It should have been put down, but Bay kept feeding it and I did not say a word about this deviation from the unsentimentality of farming.

Shona, as always stylishly dressed, worked her magic in the gourmet kitchen, while Bay drove me to the house of his daughter, a regal, tall blonde who lived a few minutes away. We drank beautiful Chardonnay and talked politics, while Bay's son-in-law looked a little down in the mouth because he had stood for parliament in last month's elections, when the National Party got trounced. His youngest son, a tall preteen boy, took on the role of wine steward, opening bottles and pouring with flourish. Imperceptibly, a family decision was made to deputize the oldest granddaughter, home on a break from boarding school, to be my vineyard driver the next day.

We returned home for dinner which started with oyster soup, its slightly smoky smell contrasting with the clean, green taste of young white wine. That was followed by pan-fried sole with red currant jelly. Shona heard about my dinner with David in Dunedin where we had a great time and drank much wine while Dorothea, who had been her roommate at the university, was in the hospital. I pleaded guilty to having been a corrupting influence on David. Shona and Bay wanted a report on my farmstays and homestays, but their own hospitality was unique. Recently, while they were having a visitor, one of their daughters delivered a baby in Gisborne, several hours away. Not wanting to leave their guest alone while they flew to Gisborne in Bay's airplane, they invited him to come along for a sightseeing flight and have a look around the town while they visited the hospital.

My large room at the far end of the house had windows on three sides and a huge bed. It was good to have it all to myself because on the previous visit I had shared it with my son. Even though the bed was the size of a small airfield, the juvenile had the habit of inching closer in his sleep, then turning 90 degrees and pushing with both feet. This time I read for ten seconds and fell asleep.

35 The Maori and the Mongrel Mob

When, after coffee and croissants with fresh fruit, I opened my laptop to update the diary, its screen had several ugly gashes. The day before, when I was putting my bag in the trunk after hiking to Castle Rock, I gave it a bit of a squeeze and the New Zealand converter—three prongs at an angle—must have pressed on the lid, cracking the screen. Several months earlier, when I had bought the laptop, Dell offered an optional warranty against accidental breakage, but I decided to save money because I had never broken a screen before. Now, halfway across the globe, I rummaged for Dell's New Zealand number.

My toll-free call was answered in Australia by a young man with a very heavy, non-English accent. He told me I had to transfer my warranty registration to the Pacific region before anything could be done, and that could take up to 45 days. I pleaded for a Dell address in Auckland where I could send the machine immediately and pay for the repairs with my credit card because the screen was not covered under my warranty. What was the point of paperwork if I was going to pay anyway? He was adamant—no paperwork, no repair. I asked to expedite the process, saying I was a loyal client who bought at least one or two Dells a year. I asked to speak to the manager but he would not take my call. Fortunately, I was at the house of friends who let me use their computer to go online and transfer my registration.

After completing the paperwork there was nothing left to do but wait. My day was brightened when Olivia, Bay and Shona's oldest granddaughter, came to drive me to the wineries. This very tall and serious 17-year-old girl got behind the wheel of my car—you don't want to see mine, she laughed—and proved to be a surprisingly competent and self-assured driver. Shona had given us a map marked with her favorite wineries. I sampled at each stop, but Liv, who had enjoyed wine the previous night at her parents' house, would not touch it on the road.

The day was sunny, the plains curled up to the distant mountains and the neatly groomed vineyards looked like orderly bluish crystals amidst the shapeless green of the pastures. Hawke's Bay is one of New Zealand's main winegrowing regions. The whites, as always, ranged from attractive to breathtaking, and I bought more bottles of Chardonnay and Sauvignon. There were also some surprisingly interesting roses, but most of the reds had the distinct flavor of saddle leather. On that day I had what psychiatrists call "an A-ha experience," a moment when a long process of thinking and feeling crystallizes into a sudden insight: New Zealand was a white wine country.

To get a good red in New Zealand, you have to know the local brands and be prepared to spend money, but even a high price does not guarantee quality. Good reds are few and far between, while good whites are everywhere. White wine in New Zealand goes from good to better and then, when you pay a little more, to superlative. The country's climate is a little cool for the reds but just perfect for the whites. From that day onward I only ordered white wine in New Zealand. The guesswork of the reds was no longer a part of my experience. I felt happier having adjusted to the country instead of trying to bend it to my taste.

The flyer at one winery explained that John Busby, the first English resident in New Zealand, had brought the vines from Australia in 1832. A resident was a Crown representative in a territory whose English population was too small to require a governor. While I swirled, inhaled, and tasted, Liv looked around the semi-dark cave, with its inclined rows of bottles gleaming in wooden bins along the walls. Bay had mentioned that he wanted me to stay with a Busby family on my next stop near Gisborne, and I wondered whether they were related to the first resident. Of course, said Liv, whose best friend at school was a Busby girl.

Liv was in the seventh form—the last year of high school—at a girls' boarding school. There were seven cottages in her form, each with six girls. They had private bedrooms but shared a kitchen in each cottage, a great setup for social life. The school was divided into several houses, like several tribes, and Liv was the head of her house. Many kids left school after the sixth form, and, if their grades were good enough, they could still get into the universities, but most of them went into trade schools, learning to be plumbers or beauticians. The seventh form was for those who were definitely headed to the universities, and they had to take "bursaries"—standardized national exams administered all across New Zealand on the same day. The school year ended in December, bursary results arrived in January and university started in February. Hostel (dorm) applications and deposits were due on the first of October, refundable if admission was denied.

Liv had already applied to a program for a dual degree in law and politics. She grew animated telling me how, after graduating, she wanted to enter the Foreign Service and travel the world. She had not been outside of New Zealand and wanted to get away—this country was too small. You go girl, I said—you get away. You go to countries that are dirty to see how clean New Zealand is. You go to countries that are corrupt to see how honest it is. Go by all means, so you can come back and appreciate it. In any event, when you come to New York, there is a guest room in my apartment, and it's yours anytime you want it. I only wonder who will get there first—you or your grandparents, because they were also planning to come.

It was mid-afternoon when Liv drove me from our last vineyard to a meeting with Alan Duff. Several weeks earlier, on the South Island, a friend had noticed my interest in Maori history and suggested I meet the author of *Once Were Warriors*, a New Zealand book made into a popular movie. She was friendly with the author's wife, while Shona, who lived nearby, participated in Alan's charitable foundation that supplied books to children. I had not seen the movie and went to a bookstore in Christchurch to look for the book but could not connect with its raw and violent style. Several days later, at Te Papa in Wellington, I chanced upon Alan's autobiography, *Out of the Mist and Steam*, which I bought and read from cover to cover on my trip to Australia. Alan's father came from a literary English family. He married a Maori woman, beautiful but explosive, who grew violent as she slid into alcoholism. While his father brought home books, his mother picked drunken fights outside the pub. As a teenager and young adult, Alan struggled to come to terms with both strains in his background. He oscillated between being a top student receiving national awards and a violent juvenile delinquent sent to a reformatory. In his twenties he ran from his own failing marriage to England, where he tended bar, fell in with a gang of thieves, discovered a gift for signing checks, and landed in jail for forgery. While in prison, he began to write. His writing and the support of his new wife turned his life around. In a bittersweet irony, this writer, a former inmate in Her Majesty's prisons, received an Order of the British Empire.

Liv parked in a cul-de-sac and we walked down a wooded hill to an architecturally interesting house—a large glass box with a fishpond outside continuing as a fish pool indoors and a massive fireplace in a two-story living room. Alan was in his forties, built like a professional rugby player, with a faint air of menace—you would not want to be on the wrong side of this guy. He showed us to a sofa and sat on the opposite side of the fireplace, as if at a diplomatic reception, facing the entrance, in control. I told Alan I had come to write a book about his country.

He began with a lecture on the virtue of self-reliance. It bothered him that a great many New Zealanders were on full government benefit. Welfare gave people money but took away their pride. A safety net became a trap. Only those too sick or too old to work should receive benefits. I asked Alan what he thought about single mothers—should they receive support?—but he said he had not thought about it. He talked about his program for distributing books to kids in the country's worst schools. Growing up he had seen many Maori homes without books. He wanted to teach those kids the habits of thinking, of using words, of reasoning rather than using their fists. His program had already handed out over two million books, backed by corporate and private sponsors, but Alan was bitter that he had not received a penny from Maori organizations. He said they only wanted to collect money, not hand it out.

The Maori, said Alan, becoming animated as he got into one of his favorite topics, are one of the toughest races in the world. Traditionally, the only measure of a man in society was how good a fighter he was. The Maori lived in the world of physicality, not planning for tomorrow. If a Maori worked for a millionaire who insulted him, the Maori would quit—or clock him. Modern society requires other skills—reasoning, planning for the future—but adjusting was not easy and led to conflict. Alan warmed up to me and announced he was going to take me where most white people would be afraid to go. He was going to show me the slums.

We got into his Lexus, and the girls took the back seat—Liv and Alan's preteen daughter who never said a word. We passed more vineyards—"the rubbish land turned out to be the best land for growing grapes"—and arrived in the Flaxmere area of Hastings. Alan told me he was buying small, single-family houses there at NZ$35,000 (about US$15,000), putting in another NZ$10,000 to fix them, then renting them out at NZ$190 week (the rents in New Zealand are quoted on a weekly basis). I did the math and said that grossing $9,000 a year on a $40,000 investment sounded like a terrific rate of return, as long as the rents got paid and the houses did not get trashed. Alan grinned—when one of his houses got trashed, he asked his connection in the Mongrel Mob to beat up the perpetrators.

He said Flaxmere is such a rough neighborhood that he would not walk there at night, but was disappointed that on that cold afternoon the streets were almost empty. When the weather was warm, you could see kids with hoods, people with facial tattoos. Many single story houses had fences so high that you could not see their windows. Alan said many people kept mean dogs. We drove past a house with a broken fence and I could see cargo netting draping the porch. It was the local headquarters of the Mongrel Mob, the meanest gang in New Zealand. I was surprised that most houses looked neat, with small lawns. By American standards the neighborhood looked like a pretty decent lower class area. A cluster of attractive school buildings sat on nicely landscaped grounds, with none of the fences or bars on ground floor windows that you see at schools in New York City. Alan pointed to a hole in the outer wall of one house, as if from a severe kick, but I still thought the neighborhood looked pretty good compared with New York's burned out slums. I mentioned the South Bronx and Alan said he had been there, but the place where he felt scared was Bushwick, a pretty rough area of Brooklyn. We engaged in a mild tug-of-war—whose slums were worse—and I said that his description of the punishment diet in prison sounded like a very decent meal compared with what my friends had received as political prisoners in the Soviet Union.

Alan said everything was relative and turned his Lexus back towards home. "I am proud of my Maori fighter genes. I hate softcocks (I worried about Liv in the back seat being exposed to bad language). I accept violence—but now only in self-defense. Don't let anyone rear-end my car." He grew sad saying there was virtually no Maori middle class. There were plenty of Maori in primary schools, but few in high school—and Liv nodded to that. Their warrior culture had no respect for education, no respect for the written word. It had respect for action, for violence, but not for words or vocabulary. As we got back to Alan's house, the place felt sad in the dark, perhaps because Alan's wife, whom he credited with being his main emotional support, was away. He offered me a drink, and we could have talked late into the night, but Bay and Shona had people coming for dinner, and Liv and I still had an hour's drive ahead of us. Alan went to the fridge and returned with two bottles of beer. Why two?—To save myself a second trip. He was headed to the United States in a few days, then to Europe, and we briefly talked about his hopes for a movie project.

On the drive home Liv told me her parents owned two rental homes side by side in a nearby town. Last year the Mongrel Mob moved into one of the houses, and the second became hard to rent. Then a single mother with two little children rented it because she felt no one would bother her under the wing of the Mongrel Mob and the children would be safe. The Maori were very warm and loyal to their families, she said, even though Alan was right when he said they could beat their children quite badly.

When we returned, Liv's parents were already there and her kid brother was serving as wine steward again, in a very efficient and important manner. We nibbled on curried walnuts and cheese crostini. Another guest, Donald, a prominent local rancher who was on the board at Emily and Anders' station, wanted to know about my visit there. The candles were lit and more wine bottles opened, as Shona's masterpieces continued to flow from the kitchen. Smoked salmon cakes. Fish with spicy rice. Sliced pumpkin and kumara rolled in olive oil and baked in the oven. A citrus tart with golden kiwi, splashed with peach schnapps. I sat next to Adrienne, whose rancher husband had been killed in an accident several years earlier when his ATV rolled down a slope. She ran her ranch, traveled the world, and held a wide range of strong opinions, which she forcefully expressed. As guests started to leave after coffee and liqueurs, the distance from the dining room to my bedroom in the far wing suddenly felt very large.

36 *A Knife for a Captain Cooker*

We had breakfast at a sunlit table in the large kitchen, my favorite spot in that house. Rose bushes grew under the window, and beyond them gentle downhill slopes teemed with sheep and deer. I could see a new vineyard being planted. On the other side of the road, behind the trees, more pastures stretched all the way to distant foothills that yesterday had been dusted with snow that had melted in today's sunshine. Shona poured grapefruit juice that she had squeezed from fruit picked just a few minutes earlier from the tree outside her door. The oranges we ate with our breakfast came from her son's farm. He had dropped by while I was sleeping to borrow Bay's airplane. I did not get a chance to visit his station this time, but Bay told me it was very cutting-edge. Each sheep had an electronic earring, readable by scanners. Everything about the sheep was recorded, and the chutes were controlled by a computer that could sort the sheep by gender, weight, or any other factor. The idea was to breed the smallest sheep that gave birth to the largest lambs, because that was the most efficient use of grass. The system took two persons to operate—one to work the computer and the other to make sure the sheep went forward through the chute.

It was time to ring up Dell, and my call was answered in Malaysia. A chipper young man said he would transfer me to the agent to whom I had spoken yesterday. Wasn't he in Australia? Nope, right here next to me, he said. My original agent told me in halting English that my paperwork had not yet cleared the system, but our poor communication went beyond the language barrier. I was approaching this problem as an American—take my money, fix the problem, then let's move on. I wanted results fast. For Malaysian tech support, proper paperwork came way ahead of the customer. I remembered Anders' remark just a few days earlier about how unprepared many major companies were for the global economy. Why did this man tell me yesterday he was in

Australia, while he was in fact in Malaysia? After I asked that, his comprehension of my English dropped to near zero and I demanded to speak to a supervisor. After holding for an eternity, with Dell paying for the free elevator music across the Pacific, I got a lecture on patience from another connoisseur of paperwork. Then I did what I hated doing. I told the supervisor I was in New Zealand to write a travel book, and my experience with Dell, good or bad, would be a part of it. He sneered—you can write anything you like.

Bay and Shona invited me to stay longer, but I wanted to get going. I still had a lot of ground to cover on the North Island. Tony was flying in to fish in less than a week and I figured if I kept moving at a good enough clip, I would be able to save a few days at the tail end of my journey to fly to a Pacific island and warm up before returning home. August was a winter month in New Zealand and even though the valleys were green and the sun was shining most of the time, it was a bit chilly and I looked forward to a few days on the beach. I had established this system years earlier with Danny—10 days sightseeing in New Zealand, 5 days skiing, 5 days on a Pacific island beach.

I was headed to Gisborne, the site of Captain Cook's first landing in New Zealand, but Shona would not let me leave without lunch. She served the freshest salad with olives and feta cheese, then a dish of grated carrots baked with breadcrumbs and raisins. Bay chewed and grinned—he got to eat like that every day, at every meal. He called to make arrangements for my next two stays. All of his Busby friends' rooms had been taken by visiting grandchildren, and Bay booked me in with a rancher he knew near Gisborne, who in turn recommended a place on the opposite end of the East Cape for my following stay. By now I had a rule not to follow referrals from one homestay to another because people invariably sent me to a place several notches down, which made their places look better. I made an exception for Bay—he was a friend. Later I realized that all three of them—Bay, Randy near Gisborne, and Natalie in Opotiki were all very active in the National Party (similar to the Republican Party in the United States). The three had never met, but knew each other well through their party work. That was fine with me because even after their disastrous loss in the recent election they remained the most hospitable hosts.

I counted dead possums as I drove towards Gisborne, noticing at least a dozen on my three-hour drive north, and probably missing many more. Those nasty herbivores the size of a cat destroyed huge amounts of vegetation, but when they crossed the road for a fresh meal they often had very unfortunate experiences with modern transportation. Some were flattened into asphalt, just like that exhibit in Te Papa, while some laid curled up in a ball. A few had bones sticking out and cleaning trucks went up and down scraping them off, but nobody could keep up with the possums. The New Zealand government had put the ascetic visage of Sir Edmund Hillary, the first man to climb Everest, on the $5 bill. I thought that the person who figured out how to rid New Zealand of its possums would probably get his or her face on the $10 bill.

My own contribution to solving this problem has been very minimal— one possum. Six months earlier I had driven a minivan south of Auckland with five friends, tired after a long and wet day. We were racing to a luxurious lodge where a hot bath and a gourmet dinner awaited us when, going through a tight turn in the rain, a possum appeared in the headlights, momentarily obsessional, trying to decide whether to run right or left. It's odd how fast one's mind operates in an emergency, as long as one does not obsess. I steadied my hands on the wheel, hit it, and kept going. "You killed it!" screamed one of the women. "I sure did, but would you have liked me to brake and skid on the wet road? I went straight because I liked you better than that possum, but please tell me if you'd like me to act differently next time." There was never a next time, making it unlikely you will ever see my less-than-ascetic visage on the $10 bill.

I sped through Napier. The town claimed to be the Art Deco capital of New Zealand, which is why years earlier I had wasted several hours there with Danny, only to discover we could see more Art Deco on one wall of Rockefeller Center in New York than in a week of touring Napier with a magnifying glass. Making such wild claims was very atypical of New Zealand. On the outskirts of Napier two very polite cops pulled me over to ask why my car did not have a proper registration sticker. I told them I was a foreigner who knew nothing about local stickers but offered to show them my rental contract. "Nah, that's OK, mate," they said. "You have a nice day."

A hitchhiker outside Napier looked like a local, in jeans and a light shirt, with a very large backpack. I slowed down—he was in his thirties, slender and muscular, with the face of a young Clint Eastwood—chiseled features, not an ounce of fat, and skin so tight that there was not enough left for a smile. He used to manage a farm, but had recently moved to Napier with his wife and kids. "My ol' lady couldn't stand the isolation. A pity." He was going pighunting with his mates who had dogs. "Do you use a gun or knife?" I asked. "Both," he said, without moving a muscle—very Clint Eastwood. "The biggest I took was 270 kilos [over 600 pounds], near Onga-Onga." That was only ten kilometers from Bay and Shona.

When Captain Cook came to New Zealand, the Maori had no pigs. They probably tried carrying them in their canoes during the great migration—there were pigs on the Pacific islands—but the porkers did not survive the journey. Captain Cook released several pigs into the wilderness, figuring that if they were fruitful and multiplied, he would have a supply of meat on his next visit. Now New Zealand has a good-sized population of feral pigs, called captain cookers, and hunting them is a big local sport. While foreign tourists paid tens of thousands of dollars to hunt the elusive ghar in the mountains, local blokes got together with their mates, whistled up their dogs, and went not far from their houses with mean long knives and occasionally a gun to hunt the wild pigs. When the dogs cornered an animal, a bloke dispatched it, trying to avoid its teeth. Rather than mount the head, they fried steaks and drank a lot of beer. The hitchhiker asked me to drop him off at a turn in the road, but since his backpack seemed enormous and I was in no hurry, I offered to give him a lift to his mates' house. "That's OK," he said. "It's less than a kilometer from here." He swung up his backpack and I watched him walk uphill with an effortless bounce.

The road climbed again. The views were stunning, but I missed having one of my kids or a friend in the passenger seat to read out loud from a guide book. The pastures gave way to tall pines on both sides when I pulled into a little flat spot in the forest and opened a guide book. A nearby sign said Morere Hot Springs. A tall, slender, light-skinned Maori came to the gate and drawled, "We're closing in 20 minutes, last chance to get in, mate." By New Zealand's low-key standards that was pretty heavy-duty marketing, and I could not resist. I paid NZ$10 for a towel and key to a private pool, unlocked a hillside cabin with a great view of the old forest, stripped, and was about to dive into a small, hot pool when a sign on the wall stopped me in my tracks. It warned of the risk of bacterial meningitis if that water got into your nose. I thought of dressing and leaving, but the steaming pool felt so inviting that I entered, cautiously keeping my head up. I remembered my grandfather's joke about two poor friends who met on the street. One asked why the other held his nose so high. "What makes you so proud?" "Not proud," the friend answered. "I went to a tailor to make a vest out of my old trousers, and he put the place that was here"—he patted his crotch—"up here," pointing to the top of his chest. That was the position in which I soaked in that hot pool.

In the dusk I missed Rodney's driveway and he grew a little impatient directing me on the cell phone. An old, comfortable house sprawled on a hilltop above the bay, surrounded by such a profusion of flowers that they grew even in the middle of a long driveway, between two strips of flat stones on which cars drove. A couple of medium-sized dogs ran out barking so viciously that I was certain they would tear me to pieces if only they would cross the six-foot distance from which they preferred to bark. Rodney carried my bag to a comfortable room overlooking the hills, offered a pair of gumboots, and told me to hurry and get into his truck for a look at the farm before it became dark. By now I knew the procedure—come to a gate controlling livestock, hop out and open it, let the truck pass, close the gate, hop back in. We briefly spoke about Bay, and when I mentioned his crusader history Rodney was unimpressed. "My forebear was also a Crusader. English. I think he went on the second Crusade. Got his head chopped off, so it wasn't a very good experience for him."

Even in the dusk I could see a multitude of horizontal grooves on the hills. Most hillsides in New Zealand had narrow ridges pounded into them by countless generations of sheep and cattle nibbling on the grass while moving across the face of a hill. The grass grew back, but the grooves got deeper, gently tattooing even the steepest and seemingly inaccessible slopes. The earth had a physical memory that faded very slowly. Rodney pointed out traces of Maori kumara fields on the hillsides, dating to pre-European times, well over a hundred years old. Historically, the Maori used to live near food sources—fishing from the beach or growing kumara on the hillsides. Now, he said, their main food source is the benefits office in town. This land was too poor for growing food and better suited for livestock, but there were very few Maori ranchers.

Near a gate a small group of workers was finishing their day's work, rebuilding wooden chutes for cattle. Wherever fences met at an angle, triangular enclosures held a few orange trees. Rodney planted them for his farmhands to refresh themselves while working with cattle on hot days. Those beautiful orange trees were like water coolers for the workers. We passed several piles of tree trunks where Rodney ran his small lumber operation. Since he had to wait 30 years to harvest good pines and 90 years for the eucalyptus, I joked, "You better be very young when you plant them." "I am harvesting trees planted by my grandfather and I am planting trees that maybe my grandchildren will harvest," he answered. We passed a paddock with a mob of lambs, and in the headlights I could see something unusual—they all had long, white tails hanging down to the ground. Rodney explained that the lamb trade had two peak seasons. They shipped frozen carcasses to the United Kingdom for Christmas and boatloads of live lambs to Saudi Arabia for Ramadan. Actually, Rodney got it a little wrong—the holiday on which Moslems are supposed to kill and eat a lamb, preferably slitting its throat inside their own house, was called Aid al-Adha. But he was right that for the religious holiday the sacrificial lambs could not have any human marks on them, which is why their tails had not been docked and they lacked the ubiquitous tags punched onto other lambs ears.

Back at the house Rodney reminded me that since his wife was away a gourmet experience was not going to be a part of my stay. From what I had heard, I missed a lot, but Rodney need not have apologized. He sliced several excellent cheeses, opened a bottle of Chardonnay that I had brought from Hawke's Bay, then went into the kitchen where, with a craftsman's economy of moves, he grilled fresh fish and roasted vegetables. I swirled wine in the glass, nibbled on cheeses, and fingered a basket of historic stone axes. When Europeans had brought metal axes to New Zealand, the Maori threw their old stone axes away, and kids would find them lying on the ground for years to come.

Rodney was descended from one of New Zealand's original missionaries. His great-great-great-grandfather was Henry Williams, who had translated the Bible into Maori. In the process he helped create the written Maori language and compile its first dictionary. He was the man who translated the Treaty of Waitangi from English into Maori before the chiefs signed it. Saving souls did not prevent missionaries from having a keen eye for real estate, and to this day many descendants own substantial properties. Rodney grinned—"We have a book called *Faith and Farming*. We call it our stud book." I began telling him that something similar had happened in Hawaii, where missionaries got the best land and the most valuable water rights. I had a friend in Connecticut who was still getting payments for water in Hawaii because his distant forebear took some profitable time off from saving souls. The expression on Rodney's face made it clear that this was not a promising topic for an after-dinner conversation. Rodney told me his property had been originally bought through the land court. Individual Maori did not own land—tribes did. The courts had their work cut out for them because the tribal boundaries were always changing, as the Maori fought over land.

We were in one of the most historic areas of New Zealand, just a few miles away from the site of Captain Cook's first landing. A promontory called Young Nick's Head was just across the road. For the past several weeks local newspapers had been writing about the Young Nick's Head controversy. The station that included that promontory had been sold by its absentee Australian owners to an American from Wall Street and Maori radicals were protesting the sale. They argued that the historic land should not be sold to a foreigner.

The American offered to cede parts of the station, including Young Nick's Head, to the people of New Zealand, but demonstrations continued even after the government approved the sale. Rodney, who shared a boundary with Young Nick's Head station, thought the demonstrators were only looking to stir up trouble because after the sale the public would receive free access to the promontory, which it did not have before.

The irony of the situation was that the promontory called Young Nick's Head was not the land seen by Cook's cabin boy. After Nick had first spotted land, the ship sailed for two more days before reaching the shore, and the curvature of the earth was such that he could not have seen a low coastal hill from that distance. What he saw was some tall mountain deeper inland.

Captain Cook had landed in what is now downtown Gisborne, but his first encounter with the Maori went badly. The landing party was met by a warrior group that performed a *haka*—a ritual greeting that looked extremely menacing. I saw a *haka* performed several times and found it disagreeably aggressive. It included a display of weapons, threatening gestures, sticking out of tongues, and finally, a ritualistic throwing of an object, such as a branch, at a visitor's feet, challenging him to pick it up. Today you can see a *haka* at cultural centers, during televised welcomings of foreign dignitaries, or before international rugby games. Facing a group of warriors advancing in a menacing *haka*, Cook stood and glared, which was a good response, but his marine sergeant, seeing a Maori approach with threatening gestures, raised his musket and fired. He killed a chief's son, and after that the locals would not trade with their visitors. Cook named the area Poverty Bay and sailed away without obtaining anything he needed. After rounding the East Cape he came to a new area where the marine sergeant was kept in check. Cook traded for the supplies and named that area the Bay of Plenty.

I asked Rodney whether he had considered buying the neighboring station when it came up for sale, and he said he had, but the asking price was too high. The guy who bought it paid four million dollars and he would get only a three precent return from it, but unlike a local he did not buy it just for the return. Rodney's former manager was running that station. "He is the best man for the job," said Rodney. "He'll make money for the owner. It's just that the percentage is too low for an economic operator to buy at that price."

After dinner Rodney brought out two deep dishes of homemade ice cream. He paused, looked at them and then at me, went back to the cupboard and returned with a container of a heavenly concoction, ladling a few spoons on top of each dish. It was sweet, with a strong fruity smell and a kick of alcohol. According to Rodney, it was called rum pot, and had four ingredients. You put equal weights of plums and sugar into a glass container, filled it to the top with rum, sealed it, and stored the concoction in a refrigerator for six months. The fourth ingredient was the willpower that you had to exercise to leave your rum pot in the refrigerator for half a year before opening.

It was getting late. "Land is a strong magnet, and if you're a farmer your anchor is your square mile of land. Where you live, if it is a reasonable place, you become attached to it. The home is not the house," Rodney said. "It's knowing your grandfather is buried under that tree, or on that hill you had your first date." As a young man Rodney had traveled around the world on his motorcycle with a tin of petrol, a tin of oil, a bag of rice and a few dollars. He camped along the roads in Africa and India, but all the while he knew he would return to this piece of land.

37 The Rules for Whale Encounters

Rodney had laid out our breakfast in his large sunlit kitchen—homemade cereals, mounds of fruit, fresh bread, jars of jellies, a deep dish of fresh yogurt. He wanted to fry some eggs or make an omelet, but I begged off. Outside the window the meadows gently rolled down to Young Nick's Head and a deep blue Poverty Bay glittered in the sun. The house, built in 1905, had expanded over the years in several directions, adding rooms and terraces. Earthquakes had jammed a few windows and bent a few doors, but it was a comfortable, bright, well lived-in place that looked like an old rancher—wrinkled in places, with a few broken bones, but healthy enough to tackle his deer or spend a day on the tractor.

Rodney talked about the history of the area, probably the oldest in New Zealand. Polynesians who first arrived here had sea sense. Captain Cook had a compass and read the stars, but they read ocean swells and the flight of sea birds.

They brought dogs and rats—this country had a native marsupial, but no other mammals. When the Maori discovered how to keep kumara for a year—in trenches dug on hilltops under a roof—their food supplies improved and the population went up, leading to wars that intensified just prior to the Europeans' arrival. Afterwards, if a little tribe got a whaling station, it protected it and in return received axes and muskets, with which they could take on much bigger tribes and rearrange the ownership of the land. The Europeans also brought diseases against which the Maori had no immunity. Those whalers were the scum of the earth, said Rodney. The first whaling station was set up in 1827 by Australian ex-convicts. Whalers spread sickness, guns, and whiskey. That's when the missionaries came to help. I listened, took notes, and wanted to stay another day, but Rodney said no. His wife was away and he had a meeting that night.

By now I was used to starting my mornings with a call to Dell. Today's news was that my paperwork had been approved and I was told to fax a credit card so an engineer would come over to examine my computer and give me a quote for repairs. It sounded absurd. I was driving through the country, moving almost every day, and the idea of paying hundreds of dollars to sit on my butt and wait for a day or two until some clown came to tell me what I already knew—that the screen was busted and had to be swapped—made no sense. They would not let me ship the computer in, would not even give me the phone or address of the Auckland depot. I remembered that Adrienne, the woman who sat next to me at Bay and Shona's party, had a son in Auckland with a computer repair business. It turned out that Rodney not only knew him, but was related to him. The young man was a friend of his son and had a reputation as a serious expert. I called Adrienne and got Sam's cell phone number. The idea of having my computer fixed by a descendant of the man who translated the Treaty of Waitangi had a certain poetry to it.

After leaving a message on Sam's voice mail, I rang up Adrienne again— "I got your boy's voice mail, he is probably in a pub." She retorted that he had 20 employees and was probably in a meeting. I said it looked like she was failing to supervise her child. She shot back that the child was six-foot-six, 33 years old, and married. It was fun to tease Adrienne—whatever you threw at her came back twice as fast. She had me in a corner, and we laughed. Sam called back in a few minutes, listened, and then essentially took the problem off my hands by telling me to ship the computer to him. He had no Dell parts, but would buy the screen from Dell and get the machine fixed. No, he didn't want a credit card in advance. I took a deep breath and Rodney directed me to an express office in Gisborne. We shook hands, I put my gear in the car, and promised to be back.

A young clerk at the computer store gave me an empty cardboard box and some leftover Styrofoam, but when I also asked for some tape he packed my computer himself and refused to charge me. I carried the neat package to an express office, and while there also shipped a kilo of coffee to Shona that I had brought her from Gino, but kept forgetting in the back seat of the car with all the excitement. Mission accomplished, I drove across the city's compact little downtown to a museum on the riverbank, which looked like a beached ship. One of the many things New Zealanders tend to do well is run museums, and I anticipated a very pleasant morning.

By the entrance was a traveling exhibit of photos from nineteenth-century China. An English photographer had taken exquisite pictures of the world that existed for centuries and was about to disappear in a few years under the tide of modernization. Further down the hall another exhibit took a strikingly original look at the history of Gisborne. Dozens of twin sets of photos hung side by side, taken on the same spot one hundred years apart. Someone found a lot of old photographs, then went to the spots where they had been taken and took new pictures from the same angle with a color camera. You could see not only changes in buildings, but how people looked inside schools, factories, and shops. Each pair highlighted both change and stability.

A passageway led to the wheel house from The Star of Canada, a freezer ship that ran aground outside Gisborne. It had been removed from the wreck decades ago and attached to a local house to serve as a room before being donated to the museum, giving the building its ship-like appearance. There was an exhibit on surf lifesaving—Gisborne had some of New Zealand's best surfing beaches and several rescue stations. Lifesaving was not only a community service, but also a sport, with national and international competitions. I thought of Rodney while looking at an exhibit on whaling—150 Europeans and 300 Maori worked at the station, killing whales so efficiently that they kept running out of barrels for storing whale oil.

The museum's Maori wing was superb. The original settlers of this area had come in ocean-going catamarans from Polynesia and gradually their culture evolved into Maori culture. Some roads in New Zealand still follow the tracks of the extinct giant moa birds. The Maori used to chase them along those tracks, travelers who walked in their footsteps helped flatten the trails, and that is where European settlers laid some of their roads. This reminded me of New York, where Broadway follows an old Indian trail. The position of the Maori received a boost after World War II, in which many of them volunteered. The Maori battalion at Monte Cassino took the highest casualty rate of any New Zealand division—649 out of 3,578 volunteers were killed, and 70 percent wounded.

An exhibit on Maori tribal life centered on their *marae*—meeting houses, which were given the name of a common ancestor of the tribe (*iwi*) or subtribe (*hapu*). The *marae*, regarded as having a life-force of their own, were meeting places for all descendants of a tribe, where they gathered to discuss important matters, celebrate, or mourn. Those intricately carved structures dotted the countryside, but the exhibit neglected to mention that women were not allowed to participate in the discussions that took place in the *marae* of most tribes.

The gift shop sold crafts by local artisans—museum shops were among the best places to buy quality souvenirs in New Zealand. Leaving my car at the museum, I crossed a bridge and sat at an outdoor table in a riverfront café. The lunch special was a delightfully firm grilled deep-water fish served on a bed of couscous with a tamarind sauce and fresh greens. I opened a newspaper and read while eating and sipping dark beer. In local news, a feral pig had ran into a suburban yard and was munching on flowers when a housewife saw it from the kitchen window and ran out with a kitchen knife. Assisted by her nine-year-old daughter, she cornered the captain cooker, stabbed it, and twisted the knife to cut the innards. The photo showed a good-looking blonde of about 30 with a girl next to a serene dead pig. The irony of it was that while this was happening, the woman's husband was out pig-hunting with his mates and came home empty-handed.

After lunch I went for a walk along Turanganui River, the shortest in New Zealand, counting six bridges along its twisting three-quarters of a mile, although there may have been more. Near the beach a statue of James Cook stood astride a globe, legs wide apart, a stubby cannon pointing up between them. You could always count on a provincial chamber of commerce to put up a silly sculpture. The sign, probably by the same people, praised "A fine seaman, an outstanding captain, and an honest man." I remembered the saying that a camel is a horse designed by a committee. A little farther, at the very mouth of the river, was a surprisingly lively statue of Young Nick—a teenager holding on to a mast in the air, pointing forward, eyes wide open, crying out above the surf.

I crossed a bridge and walked back on the opposite shore of the river. At the recreation dock were sporting canoes—rowing catamarans with outriggers, made of modern plastics, gently propped up on wooden stands. The signs listed fishing and lobstering limits, as well as regulations for encounters with whales. It was forbidden to approach them closer than 50 meters (150 feet), and swimming with whales was not permitted, but you were allowed to swim with the dolphins. This was New Zealand at its best—you could go out in a canoe on your lunch break and encounter a whale before returning to the office for the rest of the afternoon.

Gisborne stood at the southern end of the East Cape which jutted out into the Pacific. Since I was headed north, I could either drive around the Cape or cut across. Had I been traveling with a companion, especially someone who could drive, I would have gone around the Cape, visiting its historical sites and Maori settlements. Driving alone, I would not be able to look around much and read about each little place as I drove. I decided to cut across and added the road around the Cape to my growing list of places to visit next time.

Bay and Rodney had told me there was a Russian woman who ran a homestay in Opotiki, a tiny town on the north side of the East Cape. They were amused that a young woman from a faraway huge country was living in the deepest of rural New Zealand, and Bay mentioned that she worked for a Russian newspaper. I dialed the number and a woman answered in friendly, almost unaccented English. Speaking to her in Russian and addressing her as Natasha, a diminutive for Natalie, I asked about room availability. She seemed not at all surprised that someone called to book a room in Russian. It was low season, they were completely vacant and I could come any time I liked. I had not spoken Russian since coming to New Zealand, except for that one call from a Russian reporter in Blenheim, and I was sure Natalie did not get to speak it often, but there we were, chatting in Russian across East Cape as casually as between two neighborhoods in Moscow.

The road from Gisborne to Opotiki went through the Waioeka Gorge, down an abyss, and up the other side. The gorge was 58 kilometers wide (almost 40 miles), and its depth made it dark and damp. The road, an engineering masterpiece, skirted the edges of ravines. A nearly vertical wall rose hundreds of meters above the car on the side of the road, bursting with tightly packed vegetation. Pines and leafy trees, palms and giant ferns, all reached out, fighting to catch the scarce sunlight. On the other side of the road were ravines, without guardrails. Skidding from this road would have meant certain death, and that chilly realization made me concentrate on driving.

At the far edge of Opotiki I drove up to a cluster of houses perched above the dunes. Natasha came out to greet me, while Jeff sat in an easy chair by the window, watching the sunset. He was in his early seventies, Natalie in her early thirties. He was an American photographer who had first flown to New Zealand to help his mother after she came here as a tourist and suffered an accident. He stayed here during her recovery, traveled around the country, and liked it so much that many years later, after his mother died, he bought a remote farm and came back to live. He repeated what I had already heard from other Americans here—this country was more relaxed, with fewer personal restrictions. Jeff told me that 10 years ago, on a tour of Russia, he met a beautiful interpreter who cried when he was leaving, "I will never see you again!' "That's OK," he replied. "I'll send you a ticket." They have been married for nine years, and when Jeff's children came to visit from the United States, Natalie got along great with the teenage grandchildren. They thought their grandma was the coolest. Jeff and Natalie were energetic and slender, with many intense interests, not the least of which was their interest in each other.

Natasha and I switched back to English because Jeff never learned Russian and it would have been odd to speak it in front of him. I carried my bag to a suite on the second floor of the guest cottage amidst the dunes running to the sea, then returned to the main house, where Natasha was cooking dinner, including a few Russian dishes. Books in English and Russian were everywhere, and I recognized many of my favorites. Jeff's easy chair was strategically placed to watch both the sunset and the kitchen, and the floor around it was strewn with the latest magazines, including the two to which I subscribe—*The New Yorker* and *The Economist*. Jeff never lost his rapid-fire American accent, while Natasha, who shuttled between the kitchen and the dining area of their open space, kept referring to Russian as well as local news. Their place felt more like a friend's apartment in New York than a house in a New Zealand village.

Jeff opened a bottle of wine before I had a chance to bring mine from the car. Natasha served *lobio*—a dish of ground nuts and beans with basil, popular in Russia, as well as borscht, next to several plates of local dishes. This was my first Russian food since a quick visit to Moscow before the flight to New Zealand. Natasha kept talking about the recent elections in New Zealand, in which she served as the district publicity manager for the National Party. She felt proud that her candidate, a novice, came close to beating the Labor candidate who had run for reelection. That's when I figured out the connection between her, Rodney and Bay. She showed me a local newspaper with a photo of Jeff playing racquetball in a community center and a Russian newspaper that came out once a month—there were few Russians in New Zealand.

Natalie's parents had recently returned to Moscow after an extended stay. Jeff chuckled about what he called New Zealanders' quiet bloody-mindedness —they would not be told by outsiders what to do. When a corrupt officer at the Russian consulate, angling for a bribe, held back documents that his in-laws needed for their residency papers, a New Zealand official said to Jeff, "They do not understand, no one tells us what to do" and issued the permits without the Russian paperwork. New Zealand had unilaterally declared a nuclear moratorium, even though it cost them a lot of business, because all U.S. Navy ships, whether nuclear or not, stopped coming to New Zealand. I remembered Rodney's pride the night before when he had spoken of New Zealand's Americas' Cup victory—"A wee little country beat the U.S.—a bunch of guys built a boat in a shed, working during the day, building at night."

The red sun had sunk into the ocean beyond the dunes when we moved to the armchairs near the terrace's open glass door. I ran down to the car and returned with a bottle of golden apple liqueur, bought earlier that day at a cider factory in Gisborne. Jeff was delighted to have a visitor who smoked cigars. He offered me a huge one from a box he ordered from Nicaragua, and I gave him a Dominican Churchill from the box that traveled with me from New York, sealed in a tube for perfect freshness. We clipped our cigars, lit up, and in a few minutes poor Natalie was smoked out of the room and went downstairs to work on her computer.

Jeff was curious what I thought of the age difference. I answered cautiously that back where I came from they had a saying: for an old man to marry a young woman was like an illiterate buying a book, hoping that his friends will read it. Yeah, said Jeff, that's what all my friends kept warning me about, but it doesn't seem to be happening, we are really into each other. Jeff and Natalie had an intense relationship—they interrupted each other, finished each other's sentences, snapped at each other, touched each other's arms. Blowing rich smoke, Jeff laughed, "It's not the age difference, it's not the religious difference, it's not the background difference. Our main difference is that I am a guy and she is a woman—that's where we don't see eye to eye."

He told me a story about a Norwegian fisherman who always sold the freshest, firmest fish from his boat, and everyone kept asking about his secret.

At his retirement he showed his friends that he used to throw a catfish into the holding tank. The predator kept the other fish moving, making them firmer and better tasting. "Natalie puts a needle in me," he said. "She keeps me moving." I went downstairs, where Natalie was working on her computer. She lent me a powerful flashlight with which I walked in the direction of the pounding surf. My cottage was very spartan, but I stood on its terrace, feeling the warm wind, watching a faint line of moonlight on the water, listening to the surf, unwilling to leave this magic dark space and go to sleep.

38   *Fight or Be Cooked*

In the morning Natasha let me work on her computer since mine had been shipped to Sam in Auckland, and afterwards the three of us had breakfast together. There was a kitchen with breakfast supplies in my cottage, but guests were welcome to eat in the main house with the family. I loved their hospitality. Jeff recommended a trip to White Island, which had New Zealand's most active volcano, but in winter there was only one boat trip per day, and it had already left. I decided to drive to Whakatane, the port from which the boat operated, and take it the next morning. Speaking of Maori place names, the combination *Wh* is pronounced as *F*. Say "Whakatane." Say "Te Whau." Now try this—"Whakapapa." You can find it on the map.

I could not believe my eyes when Jeff gave me the bill. It was the most underpriced stay of my journey. A waterfront apartment with a terrace, a delicious dinner with wine, a nice breakfast, to say nothing of the cordial hospitality and the fun of being there, cost me less than 40 U.S. dollars. New Zealand was inexpensive, but this was unreal. Jeff took me on a short hike along the beach, past a cottage where a man and a woman were hammering on the roof, doing minor repairs before the tourist season. I thought I heard them speak German, and Jeff said he had hired two travelers who needed the money to continue their trip. They waved to us as we passed—the informal economy was in full swing.

We walked on the flat, broad ocean beach, low waves lapping on one side, dunes rising on the other. Birds were everywhere, but no penguins. Jeff had mentioned at dinner that they nested under the floorboards of a nearby church whose sign read: "Please forgive the fish smell. Mother penguins feed their babies fish." He pointed to the roof of a house behind the dunes and said it was for sale for NZ$167,000, less than US$80,000. It took a while to get used to local real estate prices. A person who came to New Zealand with the proceeds of selling a house in the United States, like Jeff, was immediately ahead of the game. I treated Jeff to another Dominican cigar, and he presented me with a Nicaraguan. We blew puffs of aromatic smoke—my cigars were a little sweeter, his had a bit more of a bite. The wind had died down, the sunshine was warm, the ocean that pounded the beach the night before now gently rolled on the sand. We came to a stream that ran across the beach and turned back. It was good to be here during low season. Had Jeff's guesthouse been full, he might not have had time for such a leisurely walk.

I told him what I thought of his bill, but Jeff said he only recently opened his homestay and kept prices low to build up volume. He wanted Natalie to have something to fall back on "in case something happened to one of us." We stood in front of a throne-like chair in the dunes that Jeff's Russian father-in-law had built out of driftwood. I sat on it, and he took my picture. Back at the house Natalie came out to say goodbye and tried to return the unfinished bottle of liqueur. I told her to work on it with Jeff and backed my car onto the road.

Downtown Opotiki stretched for a few blocks of two-storied buildings. At one edge stood a tiny historical museum, where an old lady was trying to fit a key into the lock. The museum was run by volunteers, she had a lunch date, and the lady who was supposed to relieve her did not come to work because her husband had died the day before. I asked for permission to take a quick look, and she opened the door for me, encouraging me to visit all the rooms. It was like a tightly packed warehouse, but she said they had received a grant to add a second floor and expand the exhibits. I told her of a historian I knew north of Auckland who had gone to a week-long seminar on running a small museum. Perhaps they could participate in the same program. She offered me a basket of fresh lemons—take as many as you like. Lemon trees were full of fruit that time of year, and people stepped out from their kitchens into the yards to pick a few whenever they needed to make a drink or to cook. I helped her lock the door and she went to her lunch, while I crossed the street to the historic Hiona St. Stephens Anglican Church.

A woman at the rummage shop came out to unlock the door, and we talked about the gory history of her church. Their first minister had been hanged by the Maori, before being decapitated and having his head placed on the pulpit. The woman pointed to small dark stains under the varnish that she said had come from his blood. It sounded like a horrific crime, but the reality was much more complex. The Reverend Carl Volkner was a German Lutheran minister who volunteered for missionary work and was ordained in the Anglican Church. He came to Opotiki with his wife when the area was exclusively Maori and built a missionary church in 1864, Hiona being the Maori word for Zion. When war broke out in Waikato on the North Island, some Maori from that area came to Opotiki to enlist locals in the resistance.

The Reverend Volkner began passing information on Maori movements and fortifications to the government. He also spread rumors that his competitor—the Catholic Father Garavel—was a spy for the Maori, forcing his removal. When the Maori realized what he was up to, the Reverend fled to Auckland with his wife, but then, ignoring warnings, stubbornly decided to return with another missionary. A Maori resistance leader pronounced a sentence of death on Volkner, not harming the other missionary. After a prayer Volkner was hanged, which gave the government a perfect excuse to send in the militia for reprisals and land seizures. The church was converted into a fort, and by the time it was handed back, so many Europeans had settled on confiscated land that it was no longer a missionary—but rather a settlers'—church. Five Maori were arrested and four of them hanged, including the chief, whose guilt was that the rope from his horse was used to hang the missionary.

The surviving missionary buried the Reverend's body outside the church, which was later expanded above the grave. In 1989 the remains of four unfortunate Maori were exhumed from the prison cemetery and returned to their *marae*, and in 1993 the government issued a pardon, delivered to the *marae* by the justice minister. The tribe gave that paper to the church for safekeeping as a sign of reconciliation, along with a gift of special windows and tapestries.

While my guide was locking the church, I noticed a box for used stamps by the door. She explained that local Anglican and Presbyterian churches put up those boxes to collect used stamps from parishioners to sell to stamp dealers. It seemed like a frugal method of fundraising, turning something that normally would be thrown away into a source of income.

Driving out of town, I noticed strikingly colored carvings above the gate of a local elementary school, pulled over, and walked up to snap a photo. A group of little Maori boys with wide, alert eyes ran to the gate, and I photographed them under the carvings. They were curious about my digital camera, and I showed them how to click through several pictures in which they could see themselves. The little kids were fascinated, but I felt uneasy, expecting a teacher to come running out at any moment—who was this strange guy who got out of his car to take pictures and talk to little boys? I enjoyed being in a more innocent land, where a friendly stranger could talk with kids without provoking alarm.

The smooth, two-lane highway cut into the shoulders of hills and I drove quickly but very carefully, paying full attention. Up one side the earth rose, down the other it was cut, as if with a knife, down to a fast-running river about 20 feet below. The margin of safety came only from a five-foot-wide shoulder with no guard rail, so that a careless driver would soon have a short flight followed by a very long swim.

Whakatane basked in winter sun, so warm that I took off my jacket and sweater and found an outdoor table in a waterfront restaurant. The blackboard listed three scallop specials, it must have been their season, and I ordered mine grilled with lemon butter, served on a bed of salad with two thick slices of fresh sourdough bread, great for picking up the sauce. I finished a pint of full-bodied dark draft, went inside to pay, and asked the barman whether it was true that Whakatane had the most sunshine hours in New Zealand. He laughed and said, like a true New Zealander, "Our Chamber of Commerce would like you to believe this extension of the truth!" Then I remembered reading a similar claim about Nelson. Since there was no tipping in New Zealand, I thanked him, pocketed the change, and walked across the street to book my trip to White Island.

The tour office was in the lobby of a modern motel and since the boat left early it would make sense to stay there. They had one vacancy, I asked to see the room, looked inside for a moment and went straight back to the car. After weeks of staying in comfortable homes, a boxy motel room was no longer appealing. I pulled out my bed and breakfast book, marked a few listings that looked attractive and started calling. No one was at home on this gorgeous afternoon and I kept leaving messages. Just as I put the book down, my cell phone rang—one of my calls was returned and I made a booking for that evening.

The beauty of the day and the pleasure of the short hike on the beach with Jeff that morning made me feel like taking a longer hike by the water. At the information center—every town in New Zealand has one—a woman gave me a trail map and recommended a hike around Kohi Point that would take about three hours one way. She asked whether I had a cell phone, then wrote a number at the bottom of the map. It was a local taxi service that she recommended calling if I did not feel like walking back to the car after completing the trail. She must have seen a few tourists before me.

I drove to the Pacific beach near the trailhead. The tide was out, the beach was wider than the length of a football field, seagulls walked everywhere, lazily flapping up when dogs ran at them. The parking lot was almost empty. There were no tourists and since it was a workday most of the people on the beach were women with young children. They walked or ran without any fear of strangers, treating the huge beach like their own backyard, which in a way it was.

The trail climbed, became steeper, then dropped down to another cove with a stony rather than sandy beach. It charged up the next hill, steeper than the first, meandered a little, then picked up hard, and I began to sweat. A sign pointed in the direction of a petrel colony, one of the very few on the mainland. Those sea birds prefer to nest on small offshore islands, which offer better protection from predators. A warning sign mentioned the size of the fine for bothering petrels—it could have required taking out a small mortgage.

The path broke out into the clear at the top of Kohi Point, over 500 feet above the ocean. The blue water seemed on fire under the sun. Gulls cried and wheeled below my feet, following two fishing boats out to sea. A tall, almost vertical white plume rose above White Island on the horizon. The trail climbed again, and in the clear, under the warm sun, I was soaked in sweat from my shirt down to my socks. The path flattened after reaching a forested ridge and continued along the spine of the mountain, which felt like some enormous beast, overgrown with trees, sleeping on the beach.

A sign pointed to the traces of a *pa* and said it was one of the oldest fortified Maori settlements in New Zealand. That's how high you had to climb if you wanted to give trouble to its inhabitants, while they waited for you with their war clubs. Each *pa* is surrounded by moats and sharp spikes, and is highly compartmentalized, so that every little spot could be defended to the last drop of blood. It was better to go down fighting than give up and be ritualistically slaughtered and cooked. I recognized several long square indentations as the former sites of *kumara* storage, remembered Rodney, and thought about the law of unintended consequences. Learning to store *kumara* had led to a population increase, which in turn led to greater bloodshed. A whole lot of people got their heads bashed in because some smart women figured out how to store sweet potatoes from one growing season to the next.

The trail turned downhill and I saw a dirty backpack in the middle of the path. I stopped, looked, and listened—there was no one around. I picked it up and looked through its pockets, hoping to find a piece of paper with a name and an address. There was no name, but a shiny new cell phone, a stapler, pliers, a roll of a wire, and colored ribbons. It was an odd assortment, but I hoped to be able to find the owner if I brought the cell phone to a local mobile office. Then I heard someone climbing noisily up the overgrown slope. A big youngster of about 19, in workman's clothes, with a ski hat low on his forehead and a hammer in his hand eyed me suspiciously. "Is this yours?" I asked.

He was a possum trapper, which helped explain the strange collection in his backpack. His boss had won a contract for possum reduction in the area and had hired several kids to do the work. It was forbidden to use poison in populated areas, so they set traps, visiting them daily with a hammer to bash the possums' heads. The kid got paid by the hour, but in order for the boss to collect on his contract, a government inspector would come to the area, set up 100 traps and, if he caught fewer than 5 possums, pay the contractor. The kid had set up 50 traps in the morning and dispatched 5 possums. There was no way he could convert those numbers into percentages. He had left his backpack on the trail as a sign to his friend in case he walked by, which did not seem like the most brilliant signal.

We walked together and I kept asking him questions. No, they had no use for carcasses, just tossed them in the bushes. Pink ribbons served as trailside markers for the traps, they tied them to branches a certain number of steps away from the spot, so that people would not be able to find and pinch their traps. He lived with other kids in the boss's beach house, which was empty in winter but rented out for good money in summer. In his spare time he liked to fish or go to bars. I sweated keeping up with him and soon we saw a parking lot on a hill below. The kid's friend, another trapper, was already waiting in the truck. I thought of asking for a ride to my car, but the odor of death hung just a little too heavily around them. Also, my attention was drawn to a group of about 50 Maori who were getting out of their cars and assembling around a hillside marker, facing the ocean.

A man in his early thirties, quite fat, was giving a long speech. By now I had been in the country long enough to catch a few Maori words—boat, New Zealand, potato. The man was a great speaker, holding his group in the palm of his hand, as they roared with laughter and turned their heads. I was watching a woman with a one-year-old child in her arms. She had a *moku*—a Maori chin tattoo that looked as if she bled red and green from the entire width of her lower lip, staining her chin with an intricate pattern. The baby, laughing, kept hitting her face as hard as he could. She laughed and pretended to bite him, he laughed and bit back. It was a loving game but with a much higher level of aggression than I would have tolerated with my kids. The speaker switched to English. "They say this is where the *waka* landed that brought *kumara* to *Aotearoa*. Those two gentlemen where blown off course . . ." That group was marking the arrival of a canoe that brought sweet potato from the Pacific, but his choice of words was amusing, when he referred to stone-age people hurtling across the ocean as "those two gentlemen."

The sun was very low and it was getting cold. The Maori were bundled in jackets, but I had left my warm clothes in the car and my legs felt heavy after climbing that mountain. I pulled out my map and cell phone and called the taxi company, but they could not comprehend where I was. I asked a Maori driver to talk to them on my phone, giving them local landmarks. Back at the beach, my car was the only one left in the parking lot. I drove across Whakatane and into the country, calling my hosts for directions. When I told Lynne how tired I was, she assured me that a hot tub and a cold beer were awaiting.

A comfortable house stood at the end of a country road, where "lifestyle blocks" edged up on a farm. A very big boat sat on a trailer, dwarfing my car. Lynne showed me to a corner room, pointed to a hot tub outside and asked what brand of beer I preferred. Cold, I said. She was, as they said in New Zealand, "good as gold." I stripped off my sweat-soaked clothes, went outdoors, and stretched out in the hot tub, feeling the fatigue slowly leave my muscles. The first sip of cold amber beer felt like a musical chord.

Lynne must have overestimated how hungry I was, judging by the mounds of food she put on the table. Bruce returned from work—he was an assistant high school principal—just in time for appetizers, starting with a dish of fresh local oysters. Bruce opened a bottle of Sauvignon I had brought from Hawke's Bay and showed me pictures of their two sons. One of them was delivering a yacht at the time, sailing it from New Zealand to Los Angeles, and from there to the East Coast via the Panama Canal. We moved to the dining table for a huge main course of red snapper with all the trimmings. Bruce was a commercial fisherman until he turned 50 a few years ago, after which that work felt hard. He still had his big boat. "You come back in summer—I'll take you fishing." Now he worked as a teacher and assistant principal, but had filled out papers to be transferred to a program for one-on-one academic coaching. What he really wanted was to get a job as a DOC fisheries inspector. We finished our snapper and leaned back, full and satisfied, but then Lynne brought out a delightful chocolate pudding from the oven.

Bruce was a nationally rated croquet player and coach. Several months earlier some Americans had flown him to Napa Valley in California for an invitational tournament. It was his first time in the United States and he told me he loved the country and hoped to be invited back. After dessert, he turned on the outside lights and stepped out to practice croquet—he kept a full size court behind the house. Lynne asked whether I would like to try, but I told her my only request was that she please check the hallway after I had left the kitchen—if she sees a body on the floor on the way to my room, please cover it with a blanket. I made it to my bed, feeling every muscle in my body, and immediately fell asleep.

39 Between the Dolphins and the Gannets

There was a sliding glass door between my room and the garden with its hot tub. In the morning I swung open heavy curtains and laid back for a few minutes to watch a show more colorful and vibrant than anything on TV— huge flocks of multicolored birds pirouetted in front of my door. Bruce and Lynne had dug up a sizeable patch of their garden for replanting, and the birds were having a party picking bugs and worms from the freshly turned earth. Bruce had already left for work and I asked Lynne to limit my breakfast to just a few slices of fresh fruit and toast, which was all I could eat after the previous night's dinner. She was cooking and laughing, when I raised my hand to make a point, and suddenly my finger was gripped by tiny scratchy feet, like a circle of a thin wire. A cockatiel flying around the kitchen had landed on my hand and started stepping sideways, moving up my arm to the shoulder. I offered it a slice of apple from my plate, but Lynne said his favorites were boiled egg and cheese, which were not on the menu that morning. I felt sorry to leave this comfortable sunlit house after only one night; without having played croquet, gone fishing, or heard more of Bruce and Lynne's stories.

I stepped on the gas to catch the boat in Whakatane and climbed to the enclosed upper deck. The large cabin cruiser was designed to carry 44 passengers, but on this wintry day it had fewer than two dozen tourists and several guides. We crawled through the no-wake zone in the harbor, passed the statue of a woman opening her arms to the sea, and then the engines roared, pushing the nose out of the water. A 50-kilometer (about 30-mile) crossing to White Island across the choppy sea took 80 minutes. The morning was windy and grey, and a white plume rose from the island, widening as it hit low clouds, which made it look like a huge tornado, only it stayed in place instead of moving.

The White Island volcano was the most active in New Zealand, and whenever people could not see its plume from the shore, they worried that a buildup of pressure could lead to an eruption or an earthquake. The Maori used to hunt birds on the island before the arrival of the Europeans and laid a claim to it, but a nineteenth century court found they had never inhabited the island and reserved it for the Crown. This is how the ownership of land got established in New Zealand—the Maori kept their traditional lands, the government took vacant land, of which there was plenty, and the disputes ended up in court. The Crown sold the island to a local merchant for a couple of hogsheads of rum and other essentials.

New Zealand lies in one of the most seismically active areas of the Earth, at the southern rim of the great volcanic Ring of Fire that erupts in the Russian Far East, swings through Japan, crosses the equator, and roars in the volcanoes of Indonesia before reaching New Zealand. The early European settlers quickly found they had to build houses to resist earthquakes. I recalled an exhibit in Te Papa in which railroad tracks were twisted like two dress ribbons and another in which you could enter a small building whose shaking imitated the great earthquake in Napier in the 1930s. The boat was taking us into the crater of a volcano, and the release forms to be signed before coming on board were the most extensive of my entire journey. The last eruption had occurred only two years earlier, on a day when the boat did not sail because of bad weather.

We anchored in a bay whose water was too shallow for our cruiser to reach the shore. The crew launched a small inflatable boat that locals called a zodiac— hard bottom, inflatable sides, an outboard engine in the back. I was given a yellow hard hat and, just in case, a respirator. The zodiac shuttled a small group to a broken pier, where we climbed a vertical ladder and jumped over a foot-wide crack to join another group that had already come ashore. Our two guides wore red helmets, with a young woman leading the group and a man bringing up the rear. The environment was so destructive that our guides carried their walkie-talkies inside sealed plastic bags and wore boots with no metal eyelets because they rusted after a few trips. No one had lived on the island for the past 70 years, and everything made of metal had crumbled in the sulphurous air, but anything made of wood was remarkably well preserved.

The landscape was totally unlike the green expanse of New Zealand. Barren multicolored rocks rose hundreds of meters on all sides—we were in the crater of a volcano. Imagine a giant lying on the ground with his mouth wide open, some teeth intact, others broken. Imagine yourself walking on his hot tongue, feeling and hearing his hot breath, seeing some of his teeth rise above you into the sky, and noticing slivers of ocean where the teeth had been knocked out. Now think that he can belch at any time and clench his teeth around you. The guides pointed out seismic sensors throughout the island. Scientists were constantly monitoring the volcano and the boat sailed only when the danger ratings were low.

The island was dotted with hissing vents of super-heated steam. The woman warned us to stay away from the whitish-orangish circles on the ground. They were scattered along the trail, each at least ten feet in diameter, some slightly elevated, and hot to the touch. These spots signaled where the ground was heated from below and ready to collapse into a mud pot. Stepping on such a circle, you could disappear into the hot bowels of the Earth.

We walked up a ridge, and the guide warned us to stay at least three to five feet away from its edge because there was no grass holding the ground and we were walking on compacted ash. If you stepped closer to the edge and that ash crumbled, you would slide about 300 feet down an almost vertical face. At the top of the ridge we started inching forward, making tiny steps, mindful of the warning. Suddenly, everybody oohed and aahed, as a lake of piercing green came into view far below. I could not take my eyes off a hissing vent at its edge, blowing steam under huge pressure. That was the main vent on the island, responsible for the tremendous plume visible from the shore. How small it was! Its smallness, disproportionate to the huge plume it created, reminded me of the nuclear bomb — a twin of the one dropped on Hiroshima—that stands in the West Point weapons museum in New York. It stopped me cold; this thing the size of a small black car that had wrought such immense destruction and suffering. Superheated steam roared and hissed, sounding like some mad fireman's broken hose, deafening even from such a distance.

Below the ridge was a row of steaming vents surrounded by patches of yellow crystals, like the freshest yolk of country eggs, and the guide explained it was pure sulpha being blown up to the surface. The shades of yellow were immensely attractive, but as I stepped closer to them, a gust of wind blew steam into my face, and suddenly I felt as if I were in the hottest sauna and jumped back. The guide said the island used to have sulpha mining operations and the miners lived there. We passed Donald's Mount, where one of the miners had disappeared in a mud pot, leaving only his boots to be found at the edge. The official verdict was suicide, but people said perhaps he was pushed. A battery of gurgling vents was called Noisy Nellie, after another miner's wife.

Miners were brought here by entrepreneurs hoping to use sulpha from the White Island volcano as fertilizer. The yellow deposits around the vents were pure sulpha, but the quantities were commercially insignificant and miners crushed rocks from the crater to extract sulpha. Every attempt at commercial exploitation had failed, most dramatically in 1914, when one of the crater walls—the giant's teeth—collapsed on a workers' dormitory. No one knew of the incident until several days later, when a supply ship came on its regular weekly run to a vastly changed landscape. The sailors could not land because they had no boats for going ashore, but blew their horn for five hours. When no one responded and no boat came from the shore, they sailed back and reported the emergency, but could not return to the island for eight days because of stormy seas. There had been ten miners and five cats, who kept the rats under control. Rescuers found only one survivor—a cat named Peter, who was brought back and renamed Peter the Great. The rescuers dug trenches in ash and rocks but found no remains of people or buildings. When some wooden pieces washed up on the mainland, they figured that the dormitory was bulldozed by the rockfall and pushed out to sea. Standing inside the volcano, I thought of September 11, when so many people had disappeared without a trace.

The privately owned island had changed hands several times. During the last mining venture some 70 years ago promoters had floated shares, claiming in their prospectus that sulpha made up to 80 percent of the rocks. The promoters housed workers on the far side of the island, outside the crater, but the processing plant had to be inside, and miners went to work by boat when the sea was calm, by foot over the ridges when it was stormy. Their highest yield of sulpha was 40 percent, and the cost of running a remote operation made it economically unviable. I thought of the old Western saying—"A mine is a hole in the earth near which sits a man in a hat and a tie selling shares." The investment bankers who sold shares to the public made out a lot better than the blokes who bought them. After that mining company went bust, the island passed into the hands of underwriters, whose descendants still owned it, refusing to sell to the DOC. Trading on Wall Street, I always stay away from IPOs—initial public offerings—because I find it hard to believe that owners of businesses sell shares to the public out of the goodness of their hearts. Most IPOs sink below offering levels, where one can make a much more intelligent decision to buy or pass.

The thing that stuck in my craw was the private, for-profit ownership of a national landmark. Private owners had a monopoly—if you wanted to visit the most active volcano in New Zealand, you had no other choice. I would gladly pay to see something that a person had built or planted, but this island has stood since time immemorial, and collecting a fee from visitors seemed no different from a warlord in Afghanistan collecting tolls from those who had to pass through "his" gorge. Perhaps I should be the last person in the world to complain about such things because I came to the West from Russia with $20 in my pocket and made out well in the free market, but that is not to say the system could not be improved. The descendants of the original investment bankers charged NZ$20 per person landing on the island, which the tour company collected and forwarded to them. There was no water fountain on the island, no toilet, they did not have to pump steam, but they doubled the fee a few years ago—a monopoly is a wonderful thing. My grandfather used to say: "The single most important choice in life is to correctly choose your parents." The people who chose to be born into the family of those investment bankers were very smart. Since our boat could hold 44 passengers and made two trips a day in summer, they received a great and ongoing reward for having made such a wise choice.

The boat made a quick circle around the island and stopped for lunch. The crew had a beautiful large tray of sushi for themselves in the cabin, but the passengers were given small plastic trays with industrial sandwiches, bags of potato chips and cheap chocolate. I gave my food away to a skinny young man who looked like he would eat anything. The day before I had asked whether they would serve wine or beer and was told there would be none since it was an eco-tour. I could not see the connection between ecology and abstinence, but remembered it while listening to the crackle and pop of plastic packaging on all sides. Small groups of travelers kept to themselves, but one group from Northern Europe howled like hyenas on the way to the island and even louder than Noisy Nellie on the way back. The point of this tour for them was a shared sense of tribal belonging, bonding in their language in a foreign country rather than looking around themselves.

Irritated by the landing fee, the cheap operator, the egotistic crew and the loud company, I pushed my chair as far back as it could go on the open rear deck, practically above the propellers. I had found out too late that another firm ran helicopter tours to the island. I should have done better research and paid to fly. The landing fee could not be avoided, but I would be spared the eco-fakes and howling neighbors. As the sun came out and the day grew warmer, I leaned back in my chair and dozed off.

I woke up from a sudden silence, the propellers had stopped. Passengers were walking to the front deck and leaning over the railings. There were dolphins in the water, darting right and left, jumping out and slicing back in. As the boat moved again, they hung in front of it, pushed by the hull's water pressure, like kids catching rides on a streetcar. Further ahead was a cloud of gannets, large sea birds, flapping above the water. There were small water spouts—20 or 30 at any given moment. I never heard of dolphins spouting water—whales do that, but these spouts were too small. The dolphins grew more numerous: There were at least a hundred of them in the water, moving in small pods (packs) in every direction. The boat moved forward and I saw that there were not spouts but splashes from diving gannets. They were substantial birds, only a little smaller than albatrosses, with powerful elongated beaks, fearsome to the fish. We had sailed into a feeding frenzy.

There must have been vast schools of fish below, deeper than we could see. Dolphins, hitting those schools from below, were pushing them up, while gannets bombed them from above. Hundreds of gannets flocked 50 to 100 feet above the water, from where they could see deeper than any human from the deck. Suddenly two to three dozen birds would see a school of fish, turn, fold their wings and dive, following each other like naval bombers in a World War II movie. One after another, like bullets fired from the same gun, they flew head first, wings tight to the body, full speed into the water, creating splashes that looked like spouts. They disappeared for a minute, and then we saw a whitish splotch underwater where the entire flock was swimming up for air. They came up to the surface, still swallowing their fish, surrounded by pods of dolphins, while other gannets were gaining altitude and shooting into the water. So many birds hit the water at once that the blue ocean turned light green from being so churned up with bubbles.

The water was dotted with silver confetti—fish scales—and amidst them floated a few broken and damaged fish that had escaped from the beaks of gannets, only their escape did not do them much good. Three species played a part in the feeding frenzy—mammals, birds and fish—and two out of the three were having a grand time! Travel is such a lottery, I thought. Had I flown in a helicopter I would never have seen this. My cell phone rang—it was the boat company office. They reconciled their books for the day and noticed that they accidentally charged me NZ$990 instead of NZ$99 for the trip. I should be more careful checking my bills, it was easy to become careless in New Zealand. They said their card company would not let them process a refund for almost $900—would I be willing to take cash? Twist my arm, I said.

After collecting my refund I hit the road to Mt. Manganui, going north along the Pacific coast. My cell phone rang again—it was Sam from Auckland. He had gotten a quote from Dell for a replacement screen, and since the figure was high he called to ask for my approval. I thanked him, told him to go ahead, and offered to stop the car and read him my credit card number, but Sam said he would bill me when the repair was completed. He chuckled, saying that his employee had tried to call Dell when Australia was open because dealing with Malaysia was impossible.

My B&B book listed several attractive places in Mt. Manganui, but all were fully booked. This was the only night on my journey when I could not get the accommodations I wanted. A major furniture show in a nearby town had soaked up all the better rooms. I could either go to a motel or start calling homestays that were not my first choices. Earlier I decided to stay away from motels, and so dialed a place with a grand-sounding Manor in its name. Graham led me to his house by cell phone, repeating, "We'll take care of you." I pulled up to a large house on a tiny plot of land in a suburban development. A tall, broad-shouldered man with a pale puffy, face and an effeminate manner that belied his large size came out to greet me. He introduced me to two other guests and took my breakfast order on a piece of paper, the only time in New Zealand a host did that. The amount of sweetener Graham put into every phrase made me cringe. "We'll take care of you. This is my wife, she will take care of your breakfast. I used to be a builder, but hung up my apron to take care of people like you." On the walls were many photos of Graham and his missus and their two children, also with bland puffy faces.

I told Graham that my computer was broken and asked for permission to use his. I had continued to update my diary in Internet cafés or in people's homes, then emailed a copy to myself, which I could open again from any-where, and a copy to my New York office. "The B&B Association told us to be careful about people messing up our machines, you can't trust everyone these days, but we'll take good care of you, Alex." He connected his slow, ancient machine to the Internet and sat down next to me, watching my fingers as I typed the password, a little too fast for him. I opened my diary and Graham moved closer and started reading. I opened a blank page and waited. He sipped beer and also waited, leaning his head a little, trying to look beyond the blank page at the interesting stuff. I never met with such intrusiveness in New

Zealand, where people normally give you all the privacy you want. We waited. I was ready to write and he was ready to read. I closed the file and clicked off line. "Was that all?" asked Graham with a slight whine. I walked to the car and drove to a restaurant, sorely tempted to pick up my bag and leave, but it was too late in the evening to look for another homestay.

Coming into the restaurant that Graham said was the best in the neighborhood felt like entering the Twilight Zone. The place was fancy, but did not feel like New Zealand—an illiterate pretentious menu, a waitress screaming out cheerfully, "Yes, buy-base, Sir,' repeating my order for bouillabaisse and bringing out a scrimpy fish medley. Back at the house Graham showed me a hair dryer stored in a drawer in the guest lounge. I did not need a hair dryer, but placing one in a lounge that served several rooms did not feel hospitable. I made myself a pot of tea and munched on surprisingly good oatmeal cookies from a jar by the TV, finishing most of them. Graham appeared at the foot of the stairs and eyed the jar with a look of pain, but said nothing. I thought of asking for a refill, but decided not to push it.

There was no lock inside of my room door, and I felt uneasy—I did not trust this place. I pulled up a heavy luggage bench against the door, and took my time going through the B&B book to find an attractive place for tomorrow. I called a homestay whose owner offered tours of the Coromandel Peninsula and after a friendly chat made a reservation. I washed my boots, covered in White Island sulphurous ash, using Graham's hand towel and then got into bed. Reading Captain Cook's biography, I had to take the shade off the night lamp to get enough light.

40 Thrown Out for Misconduct

In the darkness the trucks began to roll on the road between the house and the beach. Graham and his missus might have been able to see the ocean from their second floor windows, but my view from the ground floor was limited to a floodlit cement wall and the tops of container trucks. Perhaps I should have checked a local dictionary to see whether in the homestay business the word "manor" meant a house by the highway.

I turned on the lights and read Cook's biography until it was light enough to see the treetops beyond the wall. I packed, moved the bench away from the door, and, after hearing steps on the second floor, called for Graham, then started carrying my things to the car. His wife came down and seemed shocked I was leaving without breakfast. The night before Graham told me it could not be served before 8:30, but she offered to have it ready in half an hour. I asked for the bill and gave her my credit card. Graham came down, and in his most sacchariny voice asked for cash, but I was not going to accommodate him. Many B&Bs belonged to a network that allowed them to fax credit cards instead of processing them on the spot. Graham took an eternity copying every single word from my card, including the emergency numbers. Finally he sent the fax and I could see him coming in for a handshake, but I was not going to give him that satisfaction and held the door with my right hand, extending only the left to take back my card.

I felt as if I were crawling out of a mud pool—that was the worst stay of my journey. A few minutes later, driving north on the ocean road, I began to notice the silver light of the early morning, the blue-grey expanse of the ocean on my right and the enormous palms fringing the beach. My mood began to improve. I parked at the foot of Mt. Manganui, a tall, conical hill that gave the town its name, and noticed people in swimsuits running from the parking lot to a low structure. Following them in my sweater and windbreaker, I saw behind the wall an open plaza with steaming hot pools. There were lockers and towels for rent, and I immediately decided to return here after climbing the Mount.

As usual in New Zealand, public trails crossed private farms. A sign asked hikers not to bother the sheep and there were several gates, which you had to open and close. There were special stepladders across sheep fences, designed so that a human could step on them, but a sheep would be anatomically incapable of using those steps. The trail to the top split, one arm going up in sharp muscular zigzags, the other winding leisurely around the hill. Dozens of people hiked in the early morning sun, chatting with strangers sharing a section of the trail. Near to the top the views became expansive, the ocean wrapped around the horizon, ships rode anchor offshore, a parklike town spread below. On the other side of the Mount a cruise ship steamed confidently through a narrow channel between the hill and the mangroves.

I worked up a sweat going uphill on the steep trail, but circled the Mount on the more leisurely trail going down. A small group of men and women were doing a speed run—up one trail, down the other, over and over again, carrying weights, sweating profusely. One sees a lot more runners, especially women, in

New Zealand than in the United States. Returning to my car, I found swimming trunks, rented a locker, and jumped into a hot pool. The air was cold, and steam hung in gauzy sheets above the water in which people soaked, swam, and talked to their neighbors. I met a very cute four-year-old girl who showed me how to dive from the side of the pool in her floaties and led me to a water fountain. She reminded me of my own daughters when they were little and I chatted with the grandfather who chaperoned her. The day that had started in Graham's saccharine pit had progressed first to the top of the Mount and now into a hot saltwater pool. If independent travel was a lottery, then I had pulled out two good tickets in a row before noon. That is what makes traveling without reservations such an adventure.

A Maori employee in dreadlocks explained to me that Mt. Manganui was one of the very few places on Earth with salty geothermal water. Seawater seeped underground through cracks in the ocean floor and returned to the surface heated to 46 degrees Celsius (115 Fahrenheit). In the old days they used that water to fill these pools, cooling geothermal water down to 102 degrees simply by letting it fall through the air. Then, about 25 years ago, there were two cases of bacterial meningitis in the country and the Health Department required all public pools to be chlorinated. Since chlorine turned geothermal saltwater black, the company built a heat exchanger. Geothermal water heated up water from the ocean, to which chlorine was added. The Maori brought out a book that listed almost a hundred public geothermal swims in New Zealand—one could plan a vacation around those spots. I wanted to buy it, but he had only one copy and would not sell.

Feeling clean and energized, I found an Internet café and caught up on my diary in a very pleasant environment, with no scoundrels trying to read over my shoulder. I stopped for lunch in Tauranga, a bland port town, where I lucked into the best fish and chips of my entire journey. It was past lunchtime, and the restaurant was cold and almost empty. I took a table by the window, opened a newspaper, pulled up an electric heater and ordered New Zealand's most popular dish. The bread crust on the fish was crisp and chewy, but when you broke it steam came out and underneath was a thick golden fillet, separating into moist, glistening layers under the pressure of a fork. The french fries were thin, long and perfect, while the bitter draft had a tinge of sweetness. I wanted to order more, but the cook had already left for the day. In the drizzle, I hit the road to Tairua on the Coromandel Peninsula further up north on the Pacific coast, stopping only to look at a neat and well-signposted open-pit gold mine.

Approaching Tairua, I crossed a causeway and drove up a hill whose conical volcanic shape was strikingly similar to the one I had hiked in the morning. Where Mt. Manganui had pastures, Tairua had very attractive houses with terraces. I tried calling my homestay, but got no answer—the mobile reception was not very good. With the hood of my car pointing skywards, I kept going through hairpin turns, trying to catch a glimpse of house numbers. When I stopped to ask directions from a woman in a jeep she told me to keep going. It was a joy to realize there would be no highway between my room and the ocean that night.

Near the top I saw the number on a mailbox. There were three houses—an older sprawling house with a Mercedes at its gate faced the ocean and two suburban boxy houses next to it. I went to the one with more character, but no one answered the bell. I sighed and knocked on the door of one of the modern houses, but a young man came out and pointed back to the older house. I opened its gate and walked on a short path through an explosion of flowering bushes. A tall, very stylish woman in black opened the door. Her name was Andrea and she led me into a hallway filled with art and antiques, then to a guest room with a big fluffy bed and a glass wall that slid open to the terrace with expansive views of the bay. A large catamaran was gliding towards the shore, but we were so high on the hill, we could not hear its engine.

It stopped raining, and I stood on the terrace, sipping a beer that Andrea had brought. The land fell nearly vertically from the terrace to the pearly grey ocean. It was absolutely quiet. I could see low clouds of a slightly darker pearl color running in front of the wind above the roof. The tops of the palm trees and pines gently swayed against the pale blue sky. I felt happy, at peace. A day that had started so badly was ending in a crescendo of beauty. I found the wooden box tucked away in my suitcase, pulled out a wine-red tube with pale gold lettering, unscrewed its top and took out a cigar with dark brown veins in its light brown wrapper. I lit up and soft Caribbean smoke wafted into the Pacific sky. I tried to read the book about Captain Cook, but the views of the bay, the islands, and the hill were too captivating.

As the evening grew darker, I closed my book, tossed the remaining third of the cigar into tall wet grass, and joined Andrea and James in their living room. Interesting people have interesting rooms, and this one reflected decades of worldwide travel. Jim, tall and strong, in a soft khaki shirt, was a retired policeman. Andrea worked as a nurse at a local hospital. Jim had served with rescue units and loved diving. He mentioned that his favorite dish was crayfish, but he never bought any and caught every one he ate. He especially liked diving in winter, wearing a seven-millimeter wetsuit, because the visibility in cold water could reach 70 feet and he could see the crayfish from afar.

Andrea brought out a tray of delicious appetizers, and I gave her a bottle of feijoa wine, made from local fruit; I had stopped at a winery on my way out of Whakatane, but they had only fruit wine. Andrea loved it, but it was too sweet for me and Jim. Looking out the window, Jim said that whales often came to play in the bay, but there were none this evening. He named the islands—the Slipper, the Rat, the Rabbit. The Maori who lived in the *pa* on top of Tairua had used the Slipper to hold their captives before eating them. To prevent them from swimming away, they broke their legs. The Maori had no pack animals and used slaves to carry goods and serve as walking meat lockers. Some tribes had worse reputations than others. Jim once arrested a Maori who had become very belligerent inside the precinct. A Maori cop said something to the man, after which he cooperated. "What did you say?" asked Jim. "I told him I'd eat him," laughed his colleague. "We used to go where his people live and have a picnic."

The Maori were great warriors and built better fortifications than the Europeans. Once in the early 1800s an English detachment spent three weeks dragging cannons to attack a Maori *pa*, and blew apart its palisade and towers. After the bombardment they expected a walkover, but instead walked into a wall of lead. The Maori had three defensive trenches, and as the warriors in one rose and fired, those in the other two reloaded. When it was over, there were 161 English and two Maori dead. The English were slow to learn and attacked another *pa* in a similar manner, with the score of 60 to 1. They eventually won because they had better guns and took advantage of the fact that the Maori abhorred night fighting.

Jim moved aside his glass of fruit wine and told me of his experience with a much more satisfying beverage. He once nabbed a local thief with some Russian goods and since there was a Russian merchant ship at the pier, Jim and a partner went to see the captain and take a statement from him. The captain called in several other officers and brought out vodka, the best Jim had tasted in his life. Leaving the ship early in the morning, neither he nor his partner could drive and had to call for a patrol car to take them home.

Andrea decided I should have dinner at a restaurant in a converted Auckland ferry at the bottom of the hill. I was not very hungry and did not feel like driving on a dark, narrow, twisty road, but she swung me down in her Mercedes. While Jim was mild, she was very firm—one could have thought Jim was the nurse and Andrea the cop. It was a slow night, and the woman who owned the restaurant was waiting on the tables. The firm white fish came from her husband's catamaran I had seen from the terrace only a few hours earlier. The pine nuts in the rice were like high notes in a symphony. She lent me an illustrated book about Auckland ferries, which I read while eating alone. Auckland was built around a great natural harbor, and ferries were an essential form of public transportation. As the newer models arrived, some of the old ones had been converted into restaurants. I asked the owner whether anyone was watching the sea ahead of our ferry. She charged me for less wine than I drank, and when I asked her to ring up Andrea to come get me, she picked up the phone and laughed, "Please come, your lad is being thrown out for misconduct."

41 A Blue Electric Charge

My bedroom had a glass wall and the bathroom had a large window overlooking the bay. Those of us who live in big cities rarely have bathrooms with views, and it felt strangely exciting to be soaping up under a warm shower, naked in front of the wide expanse of the Pacific. I got dressed, picked up a camera and sunglasses, and went to the living room where Jim was waiting to take me on a day-long tour of the peninsula, which I had never visited before. Andrea had spread fruits, breads, yogurt, and jams next to a pitcher of frothy freshly squeezed orange juice and a silver pot of coffee on an antique table by the window. She wanted to cook something hot for breakfast, but I begged for a reprieve. There was so much good food that I had to watch myself if I did not want to turn into a butterball by the end of the journey.

Jim had started his little tour company after retiring from the police force. He knew local geography and botany inside out, loved history and drove tourists in his diesel minivan around the Coromandel Peninsula, one of the most picturesque areas of the North Island. I thought of Natalie in Opotiki, whose Russian father, younger than Jim, had a hard time adjusting and returned to Moscow. He took pride in being a good employee, always the first to arrive in the morning, doing exactly what the boss told him to do. When no boss in a small town needed him, he grew morose and floundered. Jim, on the contrary, took charge of his retirement and started a nice little business. The two men, one of whom had grown up in a free country, another in a totalitarian society, ran their lives in hugely different ways.

Jim glided down the hairpins and across the causeway. This used to be an island, he said, and the word Tairua meant two tides in Maori; there was water on both sides. He pointed to a cluster of small, festively painted shed-like houses by the causeway. Those were baches—weekend shacks built from Fiberlite and plopped down in scenic areas, usually without a permit, where people put furniture they no longer wanted in their regular homes. Lots of those went up in the 1950s, when postwar prosperity first came to New Zealand. No one could explain the origins of the word bach, but a dictionary suggested it came from the word bachelor, because of their simple lifestyle. Few remained, as people knocked them down and built more substantial holiday homes, and I could see that a day would come when a preserved bach would be put in a museum.

The Coromandel Peninsula jutted out from the North Island into the Pacific, its broken coastline a haven for sailors. The proximity to Auckland, New Zealand's largest city, made it a popular location for second homes. The drive to Auckland took about four hours, while a flight in a private plane took less than an hour. In recent years many artists and craftsmen have moved to the peninsula, opening galleries and shops and staging cultural events.

It was winter, but the hills were green with forests and pastures. "All native trees are evergreens," said Jim. There are no native deciduous trees. When Europeans brought them here, they found that everything grew faster. A pine tree could grow to maturity in 20 or 25 years, compared to 45 in the United Kingdom. He pointed to several fields where a cheery yellow was splattered on top of green—"Gorse, Scotsman's curse." The weed was so tough that animals refused to eat it. Gorse grew slowly in Scotland, but thrived in New Zealand, and to get rid of it you had to spray gorse-killing chemicals, plough the land, and wait for two years for the weed to return. Then you had to spray for the second time and plough again, and then finally seed the field with grass. It took about three years to reclaim your land.

Jim pointed to ponga trees—huge ferns that stood like ribbed construction beams with green explosions on top. The Maori grew them close to each other to create the walls of their *pas*, and the early settlers built their shacks that way, which is why on some old photos you saw miners standing in front of a shack, with smoke coming out of the giant ferns on the roof. The manuka tree was famous for its honey, but outdoorsmen used it mainly for kindling. You could tear off a piece of its bark and start a fire even when it was wet. The kahikata, or white pine, was the tallest tree in New Zealand, called a butterbox tree because its odorless wood was good for making boxes for storing butter. When Jim was a boy in Scotland, his aunt used to bring home those boxes for kindling, and years later he had a jolt of recognition when he saw his first butterbox tree in New Zealand. We drove to a kiwi plantation, with Jim sneering at the fools who sold those trees abroad, creating their own competition. "Sell the product, not the tree," he growled. Low bush-like trees leaned on wire supports like grapevines, and every fifth tree was male, with flowers but no fruit. Strangely enough, the bees that pollinated kiwi trees produced such a foul honey that it was used only for industrial purposes.

Jim gave me a condensed but lively course on local botany. He pointed out some leaves whose antiseptic properties were similar to antibiotics, which people used for treating injuries when hiking in the wilderness. Silver fern, the symbol of New Zealand's All-Blacks, had a silver underside of such brilliance that you could see it from afar if you laid its leaves upside down. Outdoorsmen had a list of emergency signals using silver ferns, and Jim once flew a rescue mission where he found a person by noticing them from a small plane. He pointed out the deadly tut vine, whose leaves quickly killed anyone who tried to chew them. He told me how once a visiting Australian circus pulled over for a break in the shade during the four hour drive from Auckland to Rotorua. Two elephants reached through the bars of their cage and munched on the vines; they were dead by the time the circus reached Rotorua.

We passed several beautiful dark blue pukeko birds, smaller than pheasants, pecking at the grass by the side of the road. When Jim came to New Zealand as a teenager, he went shooting pukekos with his brother. On the way home they showed their bag to a neighbor who praised them, and they did not pay attention to his chuckling. The next day Jim's mother tried cooking the birds, but they were so tough, the family ended up eating hot dogs for dinner. The next time Jim ran into that neighbor, he gave him a recipe for cooking pukekos—"Take a large pot, fill with water, add salt and spices to taste, put in an axe and a pukeko bird. Boil. When the axe gets soft, throw out the bird and eat the axe."

We turned towards the sea. While most of New Zealand is tectonic, created by the uprising of the Earth's crust, the Coromandel Peninsula is volcanic, created by eruptions. Where the road skirted exposed rocks, you could see gold, red, yellow, orange and black surfaces. The cuts in the volcanic hillsides were daz-zlingly beautiful, but in order to control erosion, pump trucks drove slowly along the exposed stretches, blowing a liquid mixture of grass seeds and fertilizer from high-pressure nozzles. We stopped at the water's edge near a large red box with rescue gear, and Jim gave me a quick rundown on local beaches—some were safe for kids, others had more interesting waves for surfers but you had to watch for riptides. He pointed to a small rock he believed should be dynamited because it created a rip that took several lives. He felt at home on this area and standing next to him you knew that no poisonous vines or deadly riptides would get you.

A cluster of nearby islands was named the Aldermen by one of Captain Cook's officers who thought they looked like a group of aldermen outside church on Sunday. The water around them was six degrees warmer than in nearby areas, thanks to geothermal heat, making them a great place for fishing and diving. Turataras, the lizards that were the last surviving dinosaurs, live on the Aldermen; they are about six inches long, with a single sharp tooth. When Jim tried to touch a turatara, it bit him right through a lobstering glove, but he pried its jaws open and let it go. The shore on which we stood looked like the white cliffs of Dover in England, only Jim explained this was compressed vol-canic pumice rather than limestone.

The weather kept changing from sunny to drizzling every half hour. Fur-ther down the coast, at Cook's Beach in Mercury Bay, Jim spoke of his admira-tion for the man who had sailed here around the world and measured the distance between the Earth and Mercury by triangulating that planet from two heads a few kilometers apart. His work was so precise that it took scientists over 200 years to improve his measurements. On a low hill behind us a Californian was getting ready to produce Cook Beach wine. He was building a restaurant that looked like a corporate lobby, clashing with soft green environment. We drove by stables with a sign reading "Horse treks. Pub crawl on horseback." Jim explained that the only pub in the area was several miles away and a pub crawl consisted of a ride, a pint and a return to the stables. After a pit stop near some bushes he started the engine and said, "A carrot is a vegetable, but a pee is a relief." In Whitianga, one of New Zealand's oldest European settlements, a real estate company was building a canal to drain the wetlands and selling small canalfront lots for NZ$280,000.

Many places on Coromandel Peninsula had Indian names, such as Bom-bay or Khyber Pass. Back in the colonial days the government encouraged retired soldiers from India to settle here, to be available for the defense of Auckland. Their inducements were 10 to 20 acres of land plus a home on a payment plan. The attitude of New Zealanders towards England has changed dramatically since Jim arrived here, with the country developing its own Pacific identity. Jim remembered being told by his neighbors in the 1950s and 1960s "We are going home next year," meaning they were going to England, even though their families had lived in New Zealand for two or three generations. Now they no longer played "God save the Queen" at public meetings.

We kept passing volcanic hills where the Maori built their *pa*, making them easier to defend. All their combat was hand-to-hand, and the main weapon was a *patu*—a club of very heavy wood. A chief's *patu* was carved from even heavier greenstone. The Maori used no spears, only long fighting sticks, which they never threw. When a *pa* was overrun, the men were eaten, women used for breeding, and young children assimilated into the winning tribe. Archeologists continue to find broken human bones with the marrow sucked out of them. Maori activists have demanded a return of dried-up chiefs' heads from British museums, but it is far from certain that all of those belonged to the chiefs. The Maori were smart traders. When they saw prices paid by collectors for highly tattooed chiefs' heads, they started tattooing their slaves. When a slave got a chief's *moku* (tattoo), his future was pretty clear.

Jim parked in front of one of his favorite cafés and we went in for lunch, starting with half a dozen oysters from the bay we had passed just a few minutes earlier, still carrying the aroma of the ocean. They were served on half shells, on a bed of rock salt, with wedges of lemon and a small dish of balsamic vinegar. The day grew grey, and we warmed ourselves with steaming bowls of curried mussel chowder, then shared a plate of bright orange potato wedges with cheese. I had a glass of cold, flowery Chardonnay and then another, but Jim drank only water and coffee on the road.

He raced to catch the last ride of the day on the narrow-gauge Driving Creek Railway. A sculptor who owned a large land area on this peninsula built it to ferry clay to his workshop. When his friends started using the railway to go into the woods and party, others started asking for rides, and he opened his railway to the public. I saw him scurrying between pot sheds, looking shy and eccentric, avoiding tourists. He was a bachelor and willed this property to the people of New Zealand.

A tractor engine pulled a string of little cars, while the driver played an audiotape of a steam train over the public address system and laughed, "Not bad for an old diesel, eh?" We entered a thick forest and the driver warned us to keep our arms and legs inside the tiny cars and hold on to our trail maps in case we fell out. The track zigzagged uphill, which the driver navigated by stopping, switching tracks and changing between two small diesel engines, one at each end of the train. Children squealed as we rode above the ravines. Ceramic sculptures by the owner and his students dotted the track. In summer the train stopped for picnics, and there were so many empty wine bottles stuck head first into steep hillsides that several areas had walls of glass.

The track came to an end at a hilltop platform that jutted out above the valley like some unfinished bridge. In the forest below, the sculptor had planted kauri trees. "You should come back in 300 years," said Jim. "They'll be enormous." I wanted to make an appointment for another tour at that time, and Jim said, "Make it in summer because at that age I won't be getting out much in winter." The driver told us to look for a new restaurant in what he called the Eiffel Tower. We saw an oddly shaped structure in the valley which looked not at all like the famous tower in Paris, and the driver spelled its name—I-Fool Tower. It was hokey, but fun. Starting the engine for our return, the driver moved in the wrong direction, closer to the abyss. Several women screamed. "Oops!" he said. "Almost lost it. Thanks for reminding me. Still got your maps? Now you know what you can use them for." Back at the station I told him I had only two complaints about the trip—the maps were too small and the paper on which they were printed was too rough.

We drove back in the dusk, closing the circle on the peninsula. Sheep grazed on both sides of the road, and Jim said that while pastures in Australia were so dry it took two acres to support one sheep, here in New Zealand they could keep five to ten sheep per acre. There they watered them twice a day, here they could drink all day long. The sheep in Australia were dusty and dirty; tourists were surprised how clean they were in New Zealand. We passed a flock of black lambs. "You never used to see them," Jim said, "because they got slaughtered for meat. A handful of black hair would destroy the value of a bale of wool, but now craftspeople are breeding black sheep."

Our conversation drifted to police work and Jim described the fitness test he had to pass to join the force and then retake every few years. He had to sprint 200 meters (over 200 yards), run across some planks and through tires lying on the ground, climb over a wall, scale a chain link fence, sprinting between obstacles. He then had to pull a 90-kilogram (200+ pound) dummy 10 meters (30 feet), and push a loaded trailer that weighed as much as a small car for two meters (six feet). The course was timed, with a norm for every age. Anyone who failed was given time to lose weight and get fit, but ultimately, if he could not make it, was expelled from the force. Jim had taken his last test at 55, and scored well enough for a 45-year-old man.

He pulled off the main road and showed me a village where during recent torrential rains an old lady had been swept into the bay by a swollen stream running from the hills. A young woman was also swept away but managed to swim back. Around the corner he pointed to the house where he had lived with his first wife, a neat modest home in the shade of palm trees. As we sat silently in the van looking at it, I felt a level of sadness I had not noticed before in this tall, strong man.

We hit the road again, zigzagging on a narrow strip of flat land between a rocky hill and low jagged shore. Jim knew this drive like the back of his hand, having commuted on it for several years. He told me how one night a speeder passed him in a tight spot, pulling in front so suddenly that he had to brake hard. Watching the speeder's taillights, Jim remembered a sharp turn was coming up. The speeder missed it and shot straight ahead and into the shallow waters of the bay. Jim pulled over and watched him get out of his car. "Are you hurt?" He wasn't, but needed a tow. Jim saw several headlights in the distance—he would get help. "I don't give tows to assholes," he said and drove off.

We passed some deer paddocks, and Jim chuckled telling me about what he called "gentlemen's hunting," which he discovered while relaxing in a country lodge with friends after a day of deer hunting. One of them saw something through the window, and carrying rifles they got into a LandRover and drove into a farmer's deer paddock. There, mixed in with a herd of deer, was a wild stag munching on grain supplements. It was big and strong enough to jump over the fence that held domesticated deer. With the engine still running, they lowered a window and Jim killed the stag with a single shot. The trick was to keep the engine running to sound like a farmer bringing supplies. The farmer did not mind hunters in his paddock because the wild deer ate his feed and carried illnesses. "That was gentlemen's hunting," laughed Jim—"in your slippers!"

We bought wine and smoked fish and stopped at a house by the edge of a lake to pick up Andrea, who was visiting a girlfriend. A low modern building with huge windows was tucked under tall trees by the lake. A petite blonde came to the door. We shook hands and held them as our eyes locked. I felt like I was back in physics class where we had turned a crank that electrified two silver balls, and a blue electric charge shot crackling between them.

The air appeared to have changed, tingly and fresh like after a thunderstorm. We could not take our eyes off each other. Annie moved with the easy grace of a gym instructor, dancing more than walking through her spacious living room. Jim opened the wine and she brought out a tray of appetizers, but I could not remember a word we said or what was on the plate. Annie sat down at the piano and sank her small strong hands into it, playing classical jazz. We kept looking at each other, feeling the force like two magnets. She asked us to stay for dinner and there was small talk at the table. When Andrea and Jim moved to the couch with their coffee, I helped Annie carry empty plates into the kitchen—our first chance to be alone.

We dropped our plates on the counter and clung to each other, groping, hugging, feeling. "I'll stay," I whispered. "It'll look awkward," she whispered back. "I am leaving tomorrow, but I'll come by early to say good morning." "You do that," she beamed. Walking from the kitchen to the living room, I knew that nothing could force me to leave. "I'll stay to help with the dishes," I said. "Annie will give me a ride back later." Andrea was perfectly poised. "You come for breakfast together tomorrow," she said.

The moment the door closed we started tearing off each other's clothes, as Annie led me up the broad stairway of her split-level house, littering it with jeans, sweaters, camisoles, socks, panties. Naked in the bedroom, we fell into bed and turned towards each other.

It must have been about three in the morning when Annie finally drifted off to sleep, but I was still wide awake. I felt happy, electrified. I tiptoed to the door, opened it, and stepped out on the balcony, screened by the orange trees on two sides, under the silver light of a full moon. It was winter, but the air was still, and I stood naked, enjoying the coolness against my superheated skin. It was very quiet. After a few minutes I cooled off, tiptoed back into the room, crawled into bed, snuggled up to Annie and drifted off to sleep.

42 A Farmer and a Scholar

We woke up early as the sun streamed through the open curtains from above the lake across the terrace and into the room. We held each other and talked. Annie's long marriage had unraveled and 10 months earlier she had asked her husband to pack up and leave. She had been alone ever since, partly by choice, wanting to regain her balance. And partly because she lived in a small community where many men tried to hit on an attractive woman, but nothing was simple—everyone knew each other and there were strings attached. We got out of bed, took a shower, collected out clothes from the stairs. Annie put on another one of her tight gym-scxy outfits, and I had to wiggle into yesterday's clothes.

The dark blue lake glistened through brown pine trunks and clouds of green needles. Annie spoke of feeling closer to nature in New Zealand than in any other country in which she had lived. We got into her small car and she drove across the pastures, over the causeway and up the hill, pouring forth the story of her marriage when suddenly I had to yell for her hit to the brakes—cows were crossing the road. Annie got upset when the farmer gave her a dirty look. "You come to New York," I said, "and you'll miss that farmer. If you make a mistake driving in the city, they won't give you a dirty look, they'll spell out your entire mental diagnosis, complete with a paternity evaluation."

Andrea and Jim were still asleep and did not answer the doorbell, but Annie, who knew the house well, led me in through the terrace. When Jim came out I asked him to take our photo, then went to pack while Andrea prepared a light breakfast. We drank coffee, chatted and looked at the bay through the open glass door. I asked Andrea for the bill and resisted the temptation to joke whether she was going to charge me for one night or two. I repeated to Jim how much I enjoyed his tour and was eager to repeat it before the kauri trees grew tall. He did not like credit cards, and I gladly dug into my pocket, still bulging with the White Island cash refund.

Annie and I walked out and got into our cars. She led and I followed for about 20 minutes until she pulled over at a fork in the road. She had to turn and teach a class in her studio, I had to drive straight to Taupo, halfway across the North Island to meet Tony who was flying in from Sydney later that day. Annie stepped out of her car. I came up to her and we hugged, standing silently by the side of the road. Not a single car drove by, cows munched on the other side of the wire fence. Everything that had to be said was already said. We did not know whether or when we would meet again. We kissed, and I walked back to my car, stepping sideways, never losing sight of Annie. I started the engine and leaned on the horn. The cows raised their heads, I pulled the car back onto the road and drove past Annie. I could not see her face, and soon the road turned and I could not see her car either.

The road twisted and turned, passing gold, red, and black volcanic rock-faces. It began to drizzle, and I concentrated on driving. It distracted me from the never-ending tune of what-might-have-been. What might have been if we lived in the same city? Would it have lasted? I drove for hours, watching the road, thinking, occasionally popping in a CD, stopping once to refuel the car. The sun tried to break through the clouds as I neared Rotorua. It felt strange to be approaching it from the west—I always drove into this town from the north.

Over the years I had developed a system for visiting New Zealand—fly into Auckland, pick up a car, drive to Phyllis' house for breakfast and leave extra luggage with her, hit the road to Rotorua, approximately four hours' drive south. Reconnect with the country on the beautiful drive and have lunch at the Pig and Whistle, a pub in a converted police station. They used to brew their own beer in the basement, and even though they expanded, opening other locations and brewing elsewhere, the place remained charming. Then take in a show at the Agrodome, check into a hotel, walk over to the Polynesian Spa and soak in its geothermal pools. Go out for dinner with a bottle of local wine, before finally crawling into bed for a night of blissful rest. Follow up by a big breakfast the next morning to fortify myself for another exploration of the North Island.

Rotorua is one of the most geothermally active areas of New Zealand and plumes of steam hiss throughout its downtown. Some areas have such a sulphurous odor that for a moment it seems you have arrived in hell. People come to Rotorua to soak in its famous hot pools and fish in its lake. It is one of New Zealand's great Maori centers and Alan Duff, the author I had met a few days earlier while visiting Bay and Shona, spent his youth there. As the road hit the lake, I wanted to turn right and drive downtown, but my time was limited because Tony was probably already in the air and I had a lunch date with Lachlan and Heather, who owned a nearby farm.

I had first met Lachlan a year and a half earlier, when Phyllis put me in touch with him after hearing I wanted to show a New Zealand farm to the small group with which I was traveling. Lachlan had come out of his milking shed in coveralls and mud-splattered boots, but it quickly became apparent that he ran his farm like a scholar. He explained the science of his milking operation, took us to see a commercial forest he had planted and a native forest he was restoring with some friends, before taking us to visit his neighbor's deer farm. The group was mesmerized, and when I asked Lachlan what I owed him at the end of the afternoon, he smiled and said, "You could say thank you." I invited him and Heather for dinner with our group and sent him a signed copy of my book.

Whenever I came to Rotorua with children or friends, I took them to see the Agrodome, a farm show with fascinating demonstrations of sheep shearing and working dogs and a very nice gift shop, but this time I drove past. Lachlan's house was surrounded by sheds with farming equipment and three cows munching on what might have been called the front lawn. A pony-sized cow was the smallest in the herd and Heather's pet. The other two were being watched by Lachlan while they recovered from some veterinary problems. We talked about the news, and Lachlan, like many farmers in New Zealand, was deeply concerned about the plight of commercial farmers in Zimbabwe, under murderous attacks from government-incited thugs. This could never happen in New Zealand, but he said, "Our property rights are being whittled away. I need a permit to build a cowshed on my own land, an environmental permit to put effluent on pasture, as well as building permits. No subdivision of farms is allowed, and soon they may start regulating how many animals I may put on my pasture. Twenty years ago I could do pretty much anything I wanted on my farm, but the government is changing that."

"The New Zealand farmer is the most competitive in the world. We export over 1,000 milk products—milk, butter, cheese, casein, ethanol from milk, and so on. Ninety-five percent of our income comes from exports. We receive no subsidies whatsoever. Our government's only expense is funding research and regulation. Its seal of approval makes our products easier to sell in Europe. Our main problems are tariff barriers. We are not allowed to bring milk or cheese into the United States. The U.S. slaps a tariff of US$1,800 per ton on our butter, and we are so efficient that even after paying up we remain profitable, but it means that the American consumer pays 90 cents more for a pound of butter than he should. Whenever the European Union comes out with a subsidy for its farmers, the world price of that commodity falls by the amount of that subsidy."

A truck clanged across the metal bars on the driveway that prevented cows from walking out. We put on our boots and went outside to help Lachlan's worker hoist a heavy farm tool into his truck. When we returned, my cell phone rang—it was Wally, a friend who had helped organize the fishing trip I would be taking with Tony. When I told Lachlan who called he said Wally used to be his lawyer. It was amazing how many people in New Zealand knew each other. Heather set the table for lunch. She baked a fish pie and Lachlan brought out several bottles of local whites, letting me choose a very pleasant Sauvignon. I kept cutting more and more slices of Heather's freshly baked bread, stabbing the brownish crust, moving the knife through the soft inside and smearing the sweetest yellow butter on each slice. It tasted better than most pastries.

Lachlan had earned a degree in agricultural science and set himself the goal of being able to retire at 40. He got a job at the Ministry of Agriculture and Fisheries (MAF) and worked there for four years, advising farmers on increasing their production. One day he helped a farmer increase his income by as much as his own annual salary, and that day he knew he was ready to go out on his own. His initial capital came from buying a house as a young man, renovating it, and selling it at twice the purchase price. After quitting the MAF job he leased a farm—"I got cows, rats, mice, cats, dogs, bloody chocks (chickens)—one hour the owner walked out, the next I walked in. In a leased business there was no cost—pure cash flow. I married that year, went to Europe with Heather, boated in England. After three years of leasing, I bought 80 hectares and converted them to dairy farming. Prices crashed in the 1980s and the price of the farm fell by 50 percent. I was technically bankrupt but used cash flow from milk to expand; prices came back. I bought my first milking shed for $10,000 from a farmer who was expanding and was going to throw out his old shed. Increased production as fast as I could. Leased more, got cash flow up, increased capital, bought more land.

"My mother milked 30 cows, in 1987 I milked 60, today 600. My parents made a good living from 50 cows, but today you need a lot more. Based on a 15-year inflation-adjusted average, commodity prices fall 2 percent per year because of improving productivity." That helped explain some of the behaviors in the commodity markets that I liked to trade. Lachlan had no choice but to become more efficient each year if the price of his product was in long-term decline. I mentioned to him that I had stayed on another farm where cows were milked on a slowly rotating carousel, standing with their heads in and udders out. Walking onto the carousel they crossed a fountain that washed their udders and walking off they crossed a stand that sprinkled glycerin. On my son's first visit to New Zealand he had come too close to the carousel just as one cow raised its tail, with a sad impact on his personal hygiene. Lachlan said that a herringbone pattern was more efficient. If lightning knocked out the electricity, the cows got stuck on a carousel and one needed a tractor to rotate it. "I have 40 sets of cups in the shed, one man can operate 20." Two men could milk 40 cows because the duration of the milking cycle was such that by the time a man attached the 20th cow to the machine the first cow was finished.

Lachlan had increased his staff to three since my last visit—two milkers and a milker/manager. The farm required two people working seven days a week, which is why he had three employees, to give them some time off. They milked twice a day for three hours at a time, plus four hours of other work. Working 10 hours a day, a milker put in about 3,000 hours a year, earning NZ$40,000–50,000, with the manager making more. "We get paid for the amount of solids in milk. A farm is valued in dollars per kilo of milk solids. If you can increase the amount of milk solids, you will receive a higher price for your farm." Lachlan had more than doubled production, while feeding his cows only grass, with no expensive supplements. I asked about the trees he had planted—I had been seeing a lot of tree farms, most of them owned by foreign investors. "The only place where it pays to grow trees is on bad land. If it is not suited for grazing, then it is essentially free and you get an immediate tax savings for expenditures." It cost Lachlan NZ$60,000 to plant 42 acres, and he estimated the value of wood he would harvest in 25 years would be between NZ$600,000 and NZ$1.5 million. "Buying land to plant trees makes no economic sense," he laughed.

A farm bureau recently valued Lachlan's farm at NZ$5 million, and he had a NZ$600,000 mortgage. I asked him the same question I put to Anders and Emily—didn't he feel tempted to cash out and live off tax-free bonds? Lachlan and Heather loved living on their farm, but having a manager and two workers allowed them to travel anywhere in the world, while monitoring the farm daily via email and earning 12 percent on their capital. "I have more control over the outcome here than with a bond," said Lachlan. I glanced at the wall clock—Tony must be in Auckland by now, getting ready to change planes. I got up, inviting Lachlan and Heather to stay with me whenever they came to New York. "There'll be no cows within at least a 20-mile radius of my apartment, but we'll find some other local wildlife for you."

I shot over to Taupo, a town less than an hour's drive from Rotorua, next to the biggest lake in New Zealand. A cop clocked me with a radar gun and wrote a speeding ticket—he was patrolling alone and unarmed. The weather turned so cold that I shivered getting out of the car at the tiny airport. Tony walked across the tarmac, tall, smiling, and looking comfortable in his light windbreaker. We drove to the best hotel in town, where I had reserved two adjacent rooms overlooking the lake. It became dark, but whenever the moon broke through the clouds, you could see anchored sailboats. This was the only night I spent in a hotel on my journey through New Zealand. It was more comfortable than some farmstays, less comfortable than others, but it was predictable and boring. I missed the lottery of homestays, where there was always a chance of staying in a spectacular place with interesting people.

At dinner Tony spoke about the main hazard of fly-fishing in Australia—poisonous snakes. He once stayed on a country farm with his family, where they were advised not to go near the old milk barn because it was infested with snakes. One day his daughter almost stepped on a tiger snake and Tony killed it with a shovel. Then he turned around and saw what he described as that snake's grandfather. A shovel would have been useless, and he went inside to get a shotgun. He knew a professor who drove over a tiger snake on a gravel road trying to kill it, but driving over a snake on gravel does not kill it, it only makes it very angry. The professor stepped out to take a look, wearing thongs, and the snake bit him five times. The paramedics pumped him full of antivenin, but they did not have enough. Tony did not fly fish in February and March because that was the snakes' mating season, when even peaceful ones became aggressive.

My hotel room had warmed up by the time I returned from dinner because I managed to trick the heating device that shut off automatically once the room was empty, by using several pieces of plastic. The corporate box refused to be defeated by the old trick of sticking a credit card in it, and figuring out how to beat it reminded me that cold had been one of the great driving forces in the development of civilization.

43 Where the Queen of England Goes to Fish

Early in the morning I came down to the business center and worked on a computer next to a visiting executive from Auckland. He sounded angry and miserable after a night in a cold room, but I kept my mouth shut. I learned long ago that when you told people how to defeat the system they often became even angrier. A grinning man in a thick windbreaker strode into the room, his slightly graying moustache pointing forward like whiskers on a tomcat. This was Wally, an old client of mine who lived in the deepest of rural New Zealand. Phyllis, who had relatives in the area, told me after a few drinks that's where they invented sheep shagging. Wally was a lawyer, a businessman, a pharmacist, a coroner, and perhaps a few other things I did not know about, but most of all he was a fisherman. Once I knew that Tony would be joining me on the North Island, I called Wally for advice on fishing.

Wally had a large boat, but it was out of the water for maintenance that winter, and he called his contacts to find the best sports fishing charter on the lake. Knowing little about fishing, I had a ton of questions and as Wally answered them, he became even more enthusiastic and finally announced he was going to join me and Tony in our charter. He said he would bring his gear and show us some miraculous and mysterious casting moves that few people knew about, and then he would grill our catch according to his secret recipe and serve it with some superlative local wines. All that Wally wanted in return was for me to bring some of my cigars that he had sampled on my last visit and had never forgotten.

Tony came down for breakfast and the three of us took a table by the window overlooking the lake. Sailboats bobbed in the rising sun—the day was going to be warmer than the day before. The moment Tony and Wally realized they were both lawyers and businessmen with many shared interests, they switched into such high-speed lingo that I missed much of the content. Many professional guilds—lawyers, criminals, physicians, and others—each have their own lingo, allowing them to communicate with insiders at a great speed, while being poorly understood by outsiders.

Tony and I checked out, locked most of our luggage in the trunk of my car and left it at the hotel. We got into Wally's top-of-the-line Australian car, and Tony had many questions about its performance and reliability, since he was thinking of buying the same model. The legal guild was going strong. Wally drove us to his favorite wine store, whose manager invited us down into the wine cellar. He discussed the finer points of their stock with Tony, while Wally did a lot of damage to the contents of that cellar with his credit card. I carried an armful of bottles to the car and we drove to the dock, parking in front of a 55-foot boat. A big, gruff bear of a skipper came out to take our bags, assisted by a slender young woman who was to be our cook and an all-around helper during the overnight trip. Tony and Wally gave me the master cabin with a queen-size bunk and a porthole window, while they shared the big cabin in front—that was our legal department.

The skipper crawled out of the harbor, then shoved the controls forward, and the boat roared towards the far end of the lake, where the fishing was supposed to be the best. The air at this speed was so cold that it cut through our clothes and we climbed to the fly bridge, enclosed on all sides, trying not to spill our beer. To our right, cliffs overgrown by forests flew by while on our left, across the blue chop of the lake, stood majestic Mt. Ruapehu, covered in ice and snow. It might have been the only place on Earth with a ski resort on the slope of an active volcano. I went to ski there once with Danny but the season was ruined after a volcanic eruption dusted the snow with ashes. Today skiing would have been perfect, but we had bigger fish to fry.

I asked Wally about the fishing season. "It starts on July 1 and runs through June 30. Some rivers, where the trout go to spawn, are sometimes closed to fishing, but you can fish in the lake anytime you want." I told him about my lunch with his former client who complained about the erosion of property rights. Wally disagreed: "We've got to protect this lake for future generations by limiting the number of animals on surrounding farms. Their effluent affects water quality. Today the water is so clean, you can scoop it up with a cup over the edge of the boat and drink it." I finished my beer. "Don't the fish pee in it?" Wally tipped his bottle. "No," he said. "They swim out of the lake and upstream to do that."

Farther from town there were almost no houses along the shore. Most of the land around the lake belonged to the Maori tribes, which meant it could not be sold without every tribe member's consent, making a sale essentially impossible. A few farmers had long-term leases, but recently a tribe threw people off their land after a 30-year lease expired. "Some tribes are more difficult to deal with than others. Their ruling system is based on age. Say a tribe had some funds invested in shares, and there was this young share trader just back from New York. Well, it wouldn't be him deciding what to buy or sell, but some old man who may have never gone to school."

The waves grew bigger in the middle of the lake, and at this speed their spray hit the windows of our fly bridge. There was a hatch between the bridge and the cabin, put there, according to Tony, for the purpose of passing beer bottles. A head appeared in the hatch, and our skipper climbed up, settling into the seat near the controls. He came to drive here because he could not see where we were going through the waves that hit the cabin windows. Wally said the entire lake was an enormous flooded volcanic crater, created by an explosion thousands of years ago. Rocks the size of a Volkswagen, tossed by the explosion, were found as far away as Huntly, a more than three-hour drive away. There had been no human habitation in New Zealand when the thing blew, but ancient Chinese chronicles reported a glowing sky in this direction at that time.

At the far end of Lake Taupo the skipper pulled back the throttle. The engine roar softened to a purr, a little louder than breathing. High, almost vertical rocks protected this part of the lake from the wind, and the rising sun made it warm enough to unzip our jackets. The skipper and his helper went to the rear deck to set up the fishing gear. Since the best fishing in that area was in 50 to 90 feet of water, the line from each fishing pole was clipped to another, much thicker line with a lead ball that sank to the needed depth. With the boat crawling, the hook and the lure trailed behind the lead ball. The moment the trout struck, the clip released and you could play the fish on the line, while one of the crew pulled up the lead ball with a small electric motor. We stood on the rear deck, watching the three fishing rods in their nests. They bent gently as the lines trailed behind the boat, but suddenly one of the lines tightened, bending down the tip of the rod. Strike!

Within half an hour, each of us had reeled in a rainbow trout weighing about five pounds each. Each had put up a good fight, going right and left and even jumping above the water before being scooped up in a net by our helper. A blackjack about two-thirds the size of a New York cop's nightstick hung near the opening in the back of the boat. The girl threw each fish on the deck and smacked its head twice so that you could hear the bones crack. Wally said the stick was called a priest because it gave the fish its last rites. "Wait 'til you eat 'em," he said. "They taste differently from farm-raised trout because fish farmers feed 'em chicken pellets." Clasping a bending rod must have awakened some deep atavistic hunter instinct in me. In talking about the fight of my trout, I mentioned that after breaking above water it seemed to stand on its tail. Wally laughed, "That fish walked on water? Alex, you're becoming a real fisherman!" He pondered, "Are all fishermen liars or do all liars fish?"

The girl asked whether anyone wanted another beer, but in Wally's opinion, since it was past 10 AM, it was time for a Chardonnay. He briefly consulted with Tony whether the sun was over the yardarm and went to the refrigerator, where he had offloaded his stash. He returned with a first bottle of blindingly beautiful wine. We poured and breathed in its slightly grassy aroma mixed with the fresh lake air. We drank slowly and stood, silently savoring our wine, then poured another round, killing the bottle, and went back to fishing.

The skipper pulled up to within touching distance of the vertical rocks. There was a waterfall, a narrow cascade of several hundred feet. The scene felt surreal—a vertical rock with a waterfall, a deep blue lake with a white boat suspended on it like an insect, and three lines trailing behind. It was breathtakingly beautiful—and Tony had another strike, reeling in a heavy silver trout that fought all the way to the boat. Then the fish stopped biting and the skipper decided to move to another spot. With a gleam in his eye, Wally asked whether

I had remembered to bring my cigars. I opened the box, helped him clip a cigar and held out a gas lighter. It was not yet 11 AM. A cigar before noon was one of the great luxuries of life. It took more than an hour to smoke, and since you could not smoke it in a hurry, it meant that the day was starting out very well.

Rebecca—the skipper's helper—popped up on the rear deck again, offering us beer, but Wally had a better idea. Grinning from ear to ear and clenching his cigar, he made another trip to the refrigerator, and returned with another crisp and elegant bottle. "My boat is called Chardonnay Tours," he said, "and no one can get aboard without a bottle of Chardonnay. Coming back from a fishing trip we may waver a bit walking back to the house. We like to fish, but we couldn't give a fat rat's ass whether we catch fish or not. Catching a fish is incidental to being on the lake with friends." Tony told us about his friend, another solicitor in Sydney, who liked to sail to the first cove in the morning and drop anchor. "Sitting in that cove with a cold beer and a kilo of fresh prawns you do not need to sail any farther or fish any harder." I knew I was in the company of two serious fishermen who were going to set me straight about this sport. "There are only two things worth being passionate about," said Tony. "Fishing and red wine." He noticed I was taking notes and asked "Are you going to attribute this to me?" Yes, I said, and he added, "Then add the third—my wife."

Rebecca kept putting some cream on her hands, which did not seem to help — they stayed red and swollen from being constantly dipped in cold lake water and handling fish. I gave her a jar of lanolin, bought on my previous visit to the Agrodome. It came from sheep's wool which was always so greasy that the hands of the shearers who used it—big strong guys with bulging muscles who manhandled sheep all day—were softer than a young girl's.

The skipper had filleted two trout, and Rebecca grilled them for lunch, serving them with fresh salad and bread from a local bakery. The table was laden with condiments and appetizers, and of course Wally visited the refrigerator, picking up a bottle of a more robust wine to accompany our fresh pink fish. I had a second helping of grilled trout, then a third, then leaned back on the soft leather couch and imperceptibly drifted off to sleep.

When I woke up, the boat was gliding through a deep cove with a string of Maori shacks on the shore. Tony and Wally were out in the back, and I asked whether the fish were biting. Wally said there was a big trout in the cove with my name on it: the Alex trout. As soon as I cast there was a strike, and I fought my largest fish to the boat, feeling a little sorry when it failed to escape and

Rebecca met it with her priest. Wally said this was the cove where they had taken the Queen of England when she came to fish in New Zealand. A cold river that fed into the warmer lake attracted the fish here.

The boat glided past a thick rock slab at the water's edge, which locals called Flat Rock Café. It had a vertical wall in the back, with 60 feet of depth in front. The skipper said that when the Duchess of Kent chartered this boat, she pulled up here, had a picnic and a swim. As Wally went on another hike to the refrigerator, it became pretty clear that we would never get a chance to see his secret casting method. Now, instead of cooking fish, he gave us a quick rundown on his secret recipe. "Here on the ledge, we make a fire and then spread the ambers," he said. "We take a trout and wrap it in six layers of wet newspaper with a little spice, butter and lemon. We put the wrapped package on top of the ambers and when the newspapers burn through, we turn the package over and wait until the newspapers on the other side also burn through—the fish comes out just perfect, it is fantastic eating." The ledge glided into the distance.

I went inside to chat with our skipper. The charter company hired him to drive the boat, which had been leased from a local deer farmer. It cost the farmer over NZ$20,000 to have his boat certified for public charters and make the required modifications. This was New Zealand—clean, technologically advanced, with scrupulously enforced standards. The skipper said it was possible to fly out to the ledge in a helicopter and meet the boat there, saving a couple of hours' crossing time. I enjoyed the crossing and would not have wanted to skip it. The skipper grinned and said that another luxury was to bring in the entertainment in a float plane. "You mean professional girls?" I asked. That was the only time on my journey this service was mentioned. I told him that both Tony and Wally were happily married, and while I looked for top professionals in every field, this was the only area in which I had zero interest in professionals and a total preference for amateurs. The skipper's face grew a little longer as the idea of a float plane with professional entertainers sank to the bottom of the lake.

Back on the rear deck Wally was saying, "In my town we have two traditions. The start of duck hunting season—guys get pissed and shoot. Then the opening of the fishing season on our lake. We have a Scotsman who took over the restaurant on a landing a few years ago. He blesses the boats with whiskey and makes haggis for everybody." Tony had brought along a bottle of exquisite aged single malt Scotch and we took small sips, puffing our cigars. I took out a camera, asked Tony to hold his arms as wide as he could, and snapped his picture. He smiled, "The ones you don't land are the biggest." After he had bought a lot of gear and come home after his first fishing outing, Julie, his wife who is a chartered accountant, said to him, "You know, this fish cost us $1,873. They are about $6 a kilo in the shop."

For dinner we had the best and freshest fish, expertly grilled, with every shade of pink under the fork. Rebecca baked a vegetarian lasagna and the skipper grilled thick steaks on an outdoor cooker. Wally kept opening bottles of wine whose very names sounded like poems. Wither Hills Sauvignon Blanc. Oyster Bay Chardonnay. Clear View Chardonnay. He even bought a bottle of Obsidian, a red I had enjoyed during my stay on Waiheke, but by then I was a confirmed white wine drinker in New Zealand.

We anchored in a quiet cove, protected from the wind. There was no moon, but the sky looked as if someone had thrown handfuls of shiny pebbles up in the air, there were so many bright stars. Tony and Wally talked quietly in the front cabin. I took a long hot shower and went to my cabin, enjoying its coziness, its neat compartments using every inch of space. The idea of an Antarctic cruise, mentioned by Bob at Mt. Cook, began to look more attractive. I woke up several times from what sounded like a loud slap on the wall of my cabin, realized it was a wave, and went back to sleep.

44   The Polynesian Spa

It was still dark when we got up, drank hot black tea from thick mugs and stepped out to the rear deck for our first cast of the day. As the sun went up the trout went lower, from as shallow as 16 feet to as deep as 160 feet. Wally had a strike and handed me his rod—this is Moby trout! I reeled in his fish, fighting all the way. The clutch prevented the line from breaking and very few trout got away, but I was glad whenever little fighters succeeded. Rebecca scooped up the ones we caught and cracked their skulls, and the skipper filleted them.

Wally raved about Taupo, so close to the attractions of Rotorua, Mt. Manganui, Auckland, Mt. Ruapehu, and the Waitomo caves. Tony and Wally discussed Australian real estate, a topic in which both, especially Tony, had a great deal of experience. The morning grew warmer. "One of the best things about the sun," said Tony, "is that it's free. Our politicians in Australia haven't yet figured out how to make us pay for it by the hour." At about 10 AM he went into the cabin, brought out a bottle of aged single malt, and I took my first sip of the day—it was sheer decadence.

Our boat moved in long soft sweeps from one end of the cove to the other. The only other people on the water were two Maori in a rowboat close to shore. There was a lot of activity in the settlement, centering around the *marae*, a combination church and community hall. Carloads of people kept arriving, a bunch of kids played soccer on the beach, broke into a fight, then picked up the ball again. Wally thought it was a *tangi*—a Maori wake that lasted several days, with the body laid out in the *marae* prior to the funeral and tribe members coming from near and far to stay a few days and pay respects. A *tangi* was such an integral part of Maori life that many labor contracts included a *tangi* leave. A business owner had to set limits because a member of a large tribe could spend a major part of the year going to funerals.

We had to return to shore a little early because Wally had to drive to a board meeting. The following week he was going to Sydney and exchanged phone numbers with Tony. In the cabin, Rebecca spread out our last feast of grilled trout. Fiery pink slices of fish with black specks of freshly ground pepper were interlaced with green leaves of salad and red tomato slices, circled by yellow lemon wedges. We savored our food, grilled fish that was in the water an hour earlier. We split a single bottle of Chardonnay because both Wally and I had to drive within a couple of hours. All the trout that did not get cooked were put in a bag with ice and Wally said he would give them to his cousin, who owned a restaurant.

At the dock the skipper produced the bill and we tossed our credit cards on the table. I thought how differently male and female groups split their bills in restaurants. Women were likely to pull out a calculator and discuss who ate what. Men were more likely to throw too much cash on the table and not worry about the exact change. I glanced at the bill—it was about right: the day's charter plus a few extra hours, the meals fee, the overnight fee, a few beers from the boat's stock. I handed the three cards to the skipper and told him to split it three ways. After we signed, Tony and Wally picked up their bags and carried them to the pier, but I put some cash on the table in front of both Rebecca and the skipper and told them to split it. A tip was not expected in New Zealand, but I could not resist because we had received such great personal service; also,

I could blame Tony for setting a bad example because he often broke the no-tipping tradition.

Wally drove to Auckland for his meeting, but Tony and I had five hours until our flight. We were going to fly north, to the historic Bay of Islands for some ocean fishing, and I suggested we use our free time visiting Rotorua, an hour's drive away. The grey ribbon of the road twisted between the hills with forests and pastures on both sides. White plumes of steam hissed from the paddocks, rising between the trees, sounding like broken water mains in the city. Tony, who had never been to New Zealand before, greatly enjoyed the views.

In Rotorua we turned towards the lake and parked in front of the Polynesian Spa. I had missed the show at the Agrodome and lunch at the Pig and Whistle, but now I was going to complete at least one-third of my Rotorua program by soaking in its geothermal pools. The floor and walls of the changing room were paneled with an attractive light wood and powerful showers whipped up a rich lather. We walked out onto the shore and lowered ourselves into the first hot pool. Several of them were near the lake, one hotter than the next, and we kept moving until we found the one that felt just right. We stretched out in the hot water, with the low sun shining in our faces, looking at the blue lake. White splotches of geothermal salts specked the shore, birds flew above the water, green hills with pastures dotted by white plumes of steam rose on all sides. It felt very peaceful, yet time was ticking ahead. We went to the lounge, where Tony had a beer, and returned for one more dip in the pool. Then we showered, dressed and got back in the car, feeling light and fresh. We drove back to Taupo, passing the hotel and the dock, parked at the tiny airport and dropped the car keys into a slot. The luggage allowance was 50 pounds per person, but between the two of us we had 200 pounds, mostly mine. The airline agent let it slide after I showed her my transpacific tickets and explained it had been a long journey. "Try to go lighter next time," she said.

The propeller-driven plane had 10 rows of two seats each, with an aisle down the middle. The cockpit had no door and one of the two pilots doubled as a ticket taker and a seatbelt checker. He told me he had been flying for 10 years and I asked whether he had any interest in moving up to transoceanic flights. No, he said, the money would be better there, but he loved the scenery and went home every night. "I've never worked a day in my life," he laughed. "I get paid for my hobby. Don't tell the airline." Our flight from Taupo to Auckland stopped over in Rotorua, and on that short hop the plane flew very low, never gaining much altitude. We flew over an amazing checkerboard of green pastures and white plumes of geothermal steam. Flocks of sheep whizzed back, as the plane flew over groves of pines and a crisscross pattern of small streams that I had not seen from the road. I should fly more on my next visit to New Zealand, I thought. Chartering small planes was inexpensive and the views were intoxicating. I craned my neck trying to find the Polynesian Spa.

Local commuters got off the plane in Rotorua and a group of Koreans returning to Auckland from a golfing camp got aboard. Great numbers of Asians came to New Zealand to study, play sports, and enjoy its wide open spaces, but most came in large noisy groups, making no attempt to connect with the people among whom they moved. On our hop to Auckland the plane flew higher, and in the dark I could see the sprawl of the city. Auckland had felt small when I flew there from New York, but returning from the country it looked like a huge metropolis. Christchurch and Wellington had much more human dimensions, with livestock near the city center. I leaned into the aisle and watched the lights of the landing strip over the pilots' shoulders.

We walked to the terminal and waited for our flight to Kerikeri, near the northern end of the North Island. I tried calling Phyllis, but got her answering machine. Tony and I sat in the semi-dark terminal, comparing notes. He said, "This Taupo trip was great for scenery, relaxation, food, and company—but it certainly wasn't sport. Once that fish is hooked by a boat trailing hooks at the right depth, with a clutch on a reel, that fish has almost no chance. If you want sport, try fly-fishing. If between the three of us we landed two small fish, it would have been a good day. If we had landed a five-pound fish, it would have been a trophy for the wall."

I wondered aloud why in New Zealand society, with so many smart people and all practical things so well organized, there was no literature to speak of and not much art. Tony thought that people tended to focus on the gratification of their immediate needs. Life was comfortable—old age was taken care of, health was taken care of, children's education was taken care of, unemployment benefits never ran out, and beaches were good and free. It was easy to enjoy life and focus on the practicalities of daily living.

Our flight was called and we flew over the dark land to Kerikeri. There were just a few people at the tiny terminal when we arrived, among them a heavyset older Maori woman with the keys to a rental car for us. It had a stick shift and was fun to drive on the empty dark roads. Several weeks earlier Wally had put me in touch with a woman whose husband had a fishing charter in the Bay of Islands, and Wendy was a gem. She took care of every detail of our stay, from the car to restaurant reservations. Our homestay was supposed to have been closed for the month because the owner went skiing with her kids in Queenstown, but she had her girlfriend open it for us. Tony and I found the house, had a drink, and said good night to each other.

45 *How to Catch a Barracuda*

We got up before dawn for our fishing trip. The hills had begun to glow purple by the time we got into the car. We drove to the village of Paihia and walked to a pier that jutted out into the harbor, squinting at the rising sun. In winter, the better boats were off the water being serviced, but Wally found us a guy with a smaller boat who operated all year. He waved to us from his open cabin cruiser and we boarded, heading into the Bay of Islands. There were 144 islands in the bay, some big enough to support a farm and some with summer homes, but most were nature preserves. The lacework of channels and coves made this bay a haven for boaters and fishermen. This had been the first major area of contact between the Europeans and the Maori. Next to Paihia was Waitangi, where the Treaty of Waitangi was signed, and across the inlet was the town of Russell, the first capital of New Zealand.

I found a spot on the boat protected from the wind and stood next to Steve, our skipper. He was a short skinny guy with jerky movements, slicked grey hair and a big earring. His weak chin, sharply receding to the neck, was shaved on both sides, leaving a narrow vertical strip of long grey hair running down the middle. I tend to distrust anyone who has crazy hair past the age of thirty. Crazy hair is OK on a kid. When my teenage son colors his hair blue and puts a stud in his tongue, I am pretty confident he'll grow out of this adolescent nonsense, but the crazy appearance of a grownup tends to be a sign of some unresolved personality issues.

Steve steered to the far end of the cove to catch small fish for live bait. There were several other boats on the water; it looked like the choice of charters was bigger than Wally had thought. The day was quickly becoming warmer. A dolphin crossed our path, then another, and soon a trio of them were jumping out of the water and slicing back in total harmony. Those dolphins must have been fishing, but Steve's fish finder drew a flat line, like the EKG of a dead patient. He called other skippers on his radio and steered close to their boats. Tony and I pulled out a couple of whitefish, about twice the size of anchovies. Steve moved to another spot, then another. He grew agitated. "Catching fish is hard. Don't think it's easy. If you were catching more, we'd be OK." Now there was a brilliant thought. We got about a dozen between the three of us when Steve proclaimed we were running late. He gunned the engine, shooting for the Hole in the Rock—a huge cliff in the water between the bay and the ocean with a hole so big that big boats could pass through when the water was calm.

I had first come to the Hole in the Rock a year earlier with Nika while staying in Waitangi to check out a hotel for a conference. We boarded a mail boat, similar to the one I had taken in Picton on the South Island—down to the bag of crackers that the captain carried for the dogs of the people to whom he delivered mail. It felt exciting to stop at Captain Cook's first anchorage in this area and I thought of the contrast between today's cultivated pastures and the wild appearance of this bay described by Charles Darwin in *The Voyage of the Beagle*.

The owners of many expensive holiday homes lived far away, while their caretakers got paid to stay in this pristine environment. We passed an island where in the early days a Maori farmhand had killed a coworker. When the lady of the house told him he might get hanged for it, he murdered her and her children, becoming the first Maori to be tried and hanged under British law after the Treaty of Waitangi. When we approached the Hole in the Rock, the waves were so high that those of us who stayed on the front deck had to hold the rails with both hands, riding up and down like in a high-speed elevator. There was a lighthouse on the headland operated by remote control, with an old lightkeeper's cottage converted into a backpackers' hut. It took several days to walk there from Paihia, taking in fantastic views. New Zealand had a network of famous walking trails, and while most were free, you had to buy a ticket for some of the most popular ones.

I asked Steve about the places we passed, but kept drawing blanks. It was pathetic how little he knew after 24 years of working in the bay, living with his eyes closed. He anchored in the channel between the headland and the Hole in the Rock that loomed above us. The sun was brilliant, dark blue swells rolled in from the Pacific, breaking into white sheets of foam as they hit the shore and the rock. Steve baited our hooks and we cast. Almost immediately I had a strike and started working the fish. This was much sportier than Lake Taupo. I had to hoist the rod high in the air, drop it, reel in the slack and then repeat the procedure again and again. There was gold and pink below the surface, and a snapper appeared, larger than any red snapper I had ever eaten in any restaurant. It was a gold snapper, corrected Steve. He reached for the large fish and took it off the hook. But his hand slipped and he dropped it overboard, my gold sinking in the water. "Don't you have a net?" I asked. "I don't use nets," said Steve, "because hooks get caught in them." What about a gaffe (a sharp hook on a handle used for piercing and lifting heavy objects)? "I don't use them because they spoil the eating appearance of the fish." The guy had an excuse for everything, but the eating appearance of this snapper was no longer my concern.

Tony reeled in a 3½-foot barracuda with vicious teeth that Steve released back into the water. Tony had another strike and took an eternity working the fish to the surface. It was an enormous yellowtail that weighed nearly 40 pounds. I took out a camera and snapped Tony's photo holding the fish. I could not take my eyes off its glistening yellow sides—I had never seen anyone catch a fish that big. Steve crushed its skull, tied a rope around its tail, plunged a knife into its neck to get the blood flowing, and put it overboard to drain. Then I had a strike, and from how it fought, Steve told me it was a barracuda. One minute it fought viciously, and then another it was coming in like a lamb, only to start fighting again. When I pulled it out, the fish was two feet long. With the 'cuda twisting on the line, Steve kept trying to jab his finger into its gills, while the fish tried to snap off his finger. Steve won and hoisted the fish by its gills, released the hook, and tossed the barracuda back overboard.

The channel grew choppier and we started dragging our anchor closer to the rocks. Steve announced he would move us farther out to sea, but his anchor refused to come up—it had caught something on the bottom. Steve said that was the first time that had happened to him, and he tried to release the anchor by running the boat in circles, dangerously close to the rocks. The three of us got in line behind each other and pulled the anchor rope. It turned out Steve had hooked up an old calcified net, overgrown with mollusks. He freed the anchor but the experience unsettled him and instead of going farther out to sea he pulled back into the sheltered bay. We kept casting, but only baby fish came up—little snappers, smaller than the half-pound regulation size. One look and overboard they went. Steve was prancing in the boat, "I can't believe it! I don't know how it happened, it's not as if every day is like this." "I come to fish for the scenery and the pleasure," said Tony. "Catching fish is a bonus."

I started asking questions and found that Steve had swapped a bigger marlin boat for this smaller one eight years ago—more activity, less seasonal—and three years ago he also returned to his original craft as an electrician, continuing to run charters part-time. He complained about the changes in electrical work, where most young guys now used computers. It sounded to me like his life was one long, slow, backsliding failure, even though he kept getting his chest full of air and posturing. Then he pulled out a pie baked for us by his wife. It was so kind of her, and the crust was perfectly crisp, with fluffy stuffing full of flavour. I told Steve what a gem Wendy was, how she took care of every detail and how without her we would not have been on this boat. He shrugged his shoulders—she picked up the phone, that's all. A good woman kept him afloat, but this Rambo wannabe could not see that.

We tried casting again, but it was pointless. A mail boat sailed by, with tourists gawking at the seals on the rocks and then at us. The seals were sunning themselves without pretending to fish. I remembered the ditty about a worm at one end and a fool at the other and asked Steve to head back. He revved up the engine, still mumbling how fishing was hard and today was not a usual day. Back at the dock he put on an unexpectedly dazzling display of expertise, expertly filleting Tony's yellowtail on the deck, surrounded by a cloud of screaming gulls. We took the choice parts and he kept the rest. We brought about 12 pounds of yellowtail fillet to a nearby restaurant that took half for our dinner and carried the rest home. Our large hillside house had a two-story living room that spilled out onto a deck. We sat there in the sun at a wooden table, watching ferries in the distance, drinking good beer, cutting slices of local cheeses, and putting them on slabs of fresh bread.

In the afternoon I showed Tony around Waitangi, where I had stayed twice—once with Nika and once for a week-long conference. An old resort on Maori land had been expertly restored and run by a Singaporean company, with many Maori employees. The hot tub where we liked to hang out was the size of a swimming pool. During the conference we went for a daily run across Waitangi Treaty grounds, with its small colonial house, a *marae*, a flagpole, and a huge war canoe. It felt strange to be running on soft grass between the buildings that marked the birthplace of a nation, and I thought of the historic district in Philadelphia where the Constitution was drafted by the Founding Fathers. There were large houses, off-limits areas and guards, but here you had two single story buildings, a guy who came out to hoist the flag at sunrise, while in the afternoon another guy would sometimes drive a large lawn mower around.

Here on this hill, on a summer day in 1840, nearly 50 chiefs that ruled many of New Zealand's tribes came together. The battle-hardened men with facial tattoos and scars carried greenstone war clubs and were resplendent in their bird-feather cloaks. From Her Majesty's man-o-war, anchored in the bay, rowed a boat bringing Captain Henry Hobson to sign the treaty for the Queen. It had already been translated into the Maori by the good Reverend Williams, a missionary with a keen eye for real estate, who was on hand to help with the proceedings. The man-o-war sailed back to England, the chiefs returned to their tribes, and the Treaty was taken around the country, where over 500 chiefs signed it. A new colony was born and 134 years later a tribunal was convened to make up for past iniquities, but here we were, running on the ground that was not even fenced in.

Returning to Waitangi with Tony, I discovered that our admission used to be free only because we used to run early in the mornings, before the ticket takers arrived. That was one of the annoying things in New Zealand—while most attractions on public land were free, the Maori tribes usually charged admission. I did not feel like paying for a few minutes' look at something I had seen many times for free and that was fine with Tony. He bought earrings for his daughters in the gift shop and we headed to Paihia, from which we took a ferry to Russell.

The little town of Russell, running uphill from a sheltered harbor, was one of the first European settlements in New Zealand because the Bay of Islands was a natural stopping place for arriving ships. It had a mild climate, plenty of fresh water and wood, and an enormous protected anchorage. Since there had been no central authority, Russell teemed with merchants, pirates, smugglers, whalers, whores, and rum runners. Its lawlessness made it famous as "the Hellhole of the Pacific." After the Treaty of Waitangi the new colonial administration made Russell its capital, and by the time it moved to Auckland (and thence to Wellington), the situation was well under control. Today Russell was a charming town of waterfront cafés and galleries. Unfortunately, on my previous visit I had run into a shopkeeper who must have been the descendant of some original smuggler or whoremonger. He sold me a pewter flask that leaked when I brought it to New York, but I forgot to take it with me for exchange or refund when I flew back to New Zealand.

Back in Paihia, Tony and I returned to the restaurant where we had left his yellowtail fillet. They prepared us a three-course dinner—an appetizer of

yellowtail sashimi, followed by a main course of steamed yellowtail with vegetables and ginger, and a dish of lightly breaded yellowtail. We drank a bottle of
Chardonnay, and Tony, who had recently returned from Tokyo, said that our
sashimi alone would have cost us $100 in that city. We drove back home for cof-
fee and the last few drops of Tony's single malt—it was surprising how fast that
bottle evaporated in the fresh air. We packed our suitcases and put them by the
door because we had to get going very early the next morning.

46 Stud Lambs Get Crotchety

We had breakfast at a table in front of dark windows, paid, and loaded our
car. Wendy had made arrangements for us to charter a small plane and
fly to Cape Reinga. Touching down on the Cape, the northernmost point of
the North Island, would complete the journey I had begun near the southern
tip of the South Island almost two months earlier. That tip was called the Bluff,
and the expression "from the Cape to the Bluff" has the same ring to a New
Zealander's ear as "from the Atlantic to the Pacific" has to an American's. I could
have driven to the Cape and back in a day, but Tony had to leave around midday
for Sydney, and flying would give us more time.

Driving through endless pastures in the first light of day, we overshot the
airport by several miles and had to track back. The road, as usual, was well built
but poorly marked, and the terminal, the size of a small suburban house, easy to
miss. Jerran, our young pilot, waited for us in front of the airport and led us to
his four-seater plane. He had already phoned the woman on whose farm he
hoped to land and she had told him the airstrip looked dry enough for the first
time in weeks. The morning was brilliant, cloudless and increasingly warm,
but Jerran said he was going to fly over and take a good look before deciding
whether to land or turn around and fly back. I told him that while I would like
nothing better than to land on the Cape and drive a four-wheeler to the tip, the
final decision was his. I recalled a recent disaster in Russia, when a former pres-
idential contender pushed his pilots to fly against their better judgment and
they all bought the farm.

We squeezed into the tiny plane, put on headphones, wobbled down the runway, and in a few moments were suspended in perfectly still air. Shades of green flowed back under our wings, pastures separated by rows of trees planted as windbreakers. We saw beige clumps of sheep, black and brown cattle, groves of orange and kiwi trees, sparse native bush and tightly packed commercial forests. Slanting light from the rising sun exposed countless horizontal ridges on the hillsides—tracks from generations of sheep. We flew above a highway that had shortened the trip from Auckland to Kaitaia, the northernmost town in what used to be called the roadless North. The drive now took 6½ hours instead of 18. Flying low over shallow bays we saw neat rows of buoys—oyster farms. Next to a harbor, craggy and dark blue like in a science fiction movie, Jerran pointed to the roof of what was considered the best fish and chip shop in the country.

The Maori tribe that lived in this area was one of the wealthiest on the island. They used to live much farther south more than a century ago, but were losing a war with their neighbors and did not have enough young men left to fight. The tribe escaped north under the cover of darkness, leaving only the old men behind in their *pa*. When their enemies attacked the next day, filling the trenches and climbing over the palisades, the old men set their *pa* on fire and took off in a boat. They rejoined their tribe, which went on to prosper in the previously barren far North. I said to Jerran that's how it worked in much of the world—an escaping tribe tended to do better than those who chased it out, as long as it survived. Look at the *pieds noirs*—the French who escaped Algeria and went from the bottom of the economic scale to the top in two generations.

We saw very few houses. Only four or five thousand people lived in the Far North with its 400 kilometers of coastline. If you came to a beach here and saw another person, it was considered crowded. We reached the 90-Mile Beach, the northernmost finger of land on the North Island. In fact it was only 90 kilometers long, about 50 miles, a rare instance of name inflation in the country. We had been cruising at about 1,500 feet, but when the breakers came into view Jerran went to a higher altitude. He said that fishermen on the beach sometimes attached kites to their lines to get them over the breakers. Those kites were not supposed to fly above 300 feet, but Jerran had picked up a few on his wings and propeller at 1,000 feet.

Flying north above the beach, Jerran descended to a few hundred feet. The peninsula was four miles wide, its sandy soil good only for growing pines. We saw a herd of wild horses running amidst the trees. The water was the color of dark greenstone, lined with rows of white breakers. Driving was permitted on the beach, but we saw only three vehicles, fewer than the number of wild horses. The only time this beach was crowded, said Jerran, was during the annual fishing championship, the biggest land-based fishing event in the world, which offered a $50,000 prize for the biggest fish. We flew over the Bluff—a cluster of flat rocks jutting out into the Tasman Sea. Each year several people got swept from them and drowned, and we saw angry waves foaming at the rocks even on this sunny windless day.

Jerran made several low passes over a grass airstrip, leaning right and left, peering from the side windows. He pronounced it fit to land and brought our small plane down like a feather. We rumbled to a stop on uneven ground, Jerran shut off the engine and we climbed out. A blonde in her mid-twenties drove up in a substantial four-wheel drive. Tony and I hopped in, while Jerran went off to visit a friend who lived in the area. Anne-Marie was born to Swedish parents and lived on a farm with her father and brother. She had grown up in Kaitaia among the Maori at a time when there was only one other European family in the area. She was a walking, breathing encyclopedia of local knowledge and went on about local history and pointed out trees and animals as she drove confidently down the dirt road to the tip of the Cape.

Anne-Marie parked her four-wheel drive at the end of the road and took my picture at the northernmost mailbox in New Zealand. We walked a short trail to a lighthouse on a cliff above the tip of Cape Reinga. Below us the waters of the Tasman Sea, which separated New Zealand from Australia, collided with the waters of the Pacific, which separated New Zealand from Latin America. Even on this quiet day you could see the line of turbulence where the two bodies of water met. Both had some of the most powerful waves in the world, and the area where they collided was boiling. Anne-Marie said that people tested local waters by tossing empty sealed 50-gallon metal drums from the beach below—the riptide pulled them underwater and they resurfaced a thousand feet away. This was definitely not a swimming beach.

The waters of two seas boiled below our feet in two shades of gray while another gray colored the sky above. Tony, Anne-Marie, and I were the only humans as far as the eye could see. I had the powerful sense of being in an eerie place. Far below the cliff on which we stood a short finger of land jutted out north, with two rocks and a clump of trees. Anne-Marie told us that in the Maori religion the souls of the dead flew to the Cape along the 90-Mile Beach, stopping momentarily on the Bluff to drop a final earthly reminder, such as a flower petal. They came to the cliff on which we stood and leapt down to the trees below. One of the rocks had a cave facing north and the Maori believed the spirits had spent three days howling in it while those left behind held a *tangi*—the open-casket wake. When the body was lowered into the ground, the spirit leapt into the sea and the turbulence took it out to the Three Kings Islands, about 30 miles offshore. There the spirits had their last drink of fresh-water, took their last look at *Aotearoa*, and again leapt into the ocean, which carried them to *Hawaiiki*—the mythical ancestral Maori homeland, a tropical island paradise.

I wanted to hike down to those gnarly trees, but Anne-Marie nixed that idea. First of all, the hike would have taken us several hours, but even more importantly, that area was *tapu*—taboo—as sacred to the Maori. A friend of hers who thought that *tapu* was rubbish hiked down and several days later was washed off the beach by a freak wave and never seen again. I was not sure that proved anything, but Anne-Marie was so at home in this area that arguing with her was the last thing I wanted to do.

We walked back to the four-wheel drive along a high ridge between the vast silvery ocean and low grey sky. Anne-Marie drove to a nearby cove with a swimming beach, and I asked what she and other young people did for nightlife here. She laughed—well, there was a bar in a nearby village, but mostly people visited each other, went fishing or hiking, had barbecues and beer. There was no nightlife, people liked to spend a lot of time outdoors, alone or with friends. Tony and I walked along the beach while Anne-Marie spread a white linen tablecloth on a table and opened her food hamper. She offered us tea and home-baked chocolate muffins with pale manuka honey. I asked how she got into guiding. She said she had mates who wanted to fly to her farm, and she got into a bulldozer and made an airstrip for them. Soon a plane from Salt Air landed and the pilot asked whether she could guide passengers. She enjoyed the diversion. Had we not flown in today, she would have been drenching cows. She laughed and said that showing us around was more fun than forcing antiparasitic medication down calves' throats.

We drove to a shallow stream that twisted behind the dunes, and soon there was water instead of sand under our wheels. The stream ran for several miles over sandy plains, constantly shifting and moving. Silvery yellow dunes loomed above us on one side, sparse green bushes ran towards low hills on the other, a few inches of water the color of the dunes splashed underneath, and a pale blue sky enclosed it all. The sand patterns on the dunes were hypnotic.

Anne-Marie said when she was a little girl she used to sand-surf the dunes with her friends. She drove through twists and turns in the shallow stream at a steady pace, explaining that people got into trouble when they stopped to take pictures. As soon as a vehicle stopped, it began to sink in the soft wet sand, and once the wheels sank deep enough, there was no getting out. It took about three hours from the moment a car stopped until its roof disappeared. It was sad to watch, she said. The cars sank fast at first, but then, with only their windows and the roof above the sand, they slowed down. So far that year, five cars had been swallowed up. The sand kept moving, and those cars reappeared several years later at the mouth of the stream, near the ocean beach. Anne-Marie grinned—by that time their mileage was low, but they were pretty much shot. The only way to save a vehicle was to get a quick tow. Anne-Marie had pulled out plenty of cars with her 4WD, but for any vehicle bigger than her own she went to her farm and returned in a tractor. Last summer she was flagged down by a guy who had stepped out of his motor home to snap a photo and when he turned around his new motor home had sunk half-way to its axles and would not move. He was so upset he looked as though he could cry and it took three tractors to pull him out.

Anne-Marie swerved out of the stream and drove onto a blindingly expansive ocean beach that extended in both directions like the wings of some giant bird. The sun had reappeared, the tide was out, the sand was littered with shells and sea birds flitted everywhere. The Maori had been coming here for centuries to gather shellfish and threw the empty shells into piles. Grass grew on them, and those piles turned into mounds up to 100 feet high which dotted the beach. This was a dangerous area for swimmers and a friend of Anne-Marie had been swept away by a riptide that pulled him almost a mile offshore. He knew it was useless to fight and only paddled to keep his head above water. Several hours later the tide turned and brought him back to the beach, depositing him a mile away from where he had entered. When some Maori gathering shellfish saw him emerge from the water, they thought he was a ghost and ran away. They had seen the sea take people away but never return them.

On our way back to the airstrip, Anne-Marie pointed to a paddock with her stud lambs. "They have a great life," she laughed. "Eat all the grass they want all year long and spend about three months a year visiting their girl-friends." She kept them for about five years before "putting them on a truck," because at that age they developed antisocial tendencies—they wanted to be left alone or fight rather than mate. "You mean they'd rather sit in an easy chair, watch TV, and be crotchety instead of going out?" "That's about right," she laughed. I asked Anne-Marie whether her farm offered a farm stay because I wanted to return to this area and learn more from her. They did not have a formal farm stay but had plenty of room, and whenever people turned up, they accommodated them. The best time to visit was in March when summer was over—the crowds gone as well as the mosquitoes—but it was still warm enough to swim on several safe beaches.

Getting into the plane, we flew back so low above the water that we could clearly see the black sleek dolphins swimming in the pale green bays. Jerran said that in summer sharks came to sun themselves in shallow bays, with hundreds of them dotting their favorite beaches. The locals knew which beaches to avoid. We flew over small islands in the bay, then over a golf course recently built by an American investor and called the best course in the world by a major golfing magazine. We flew over the flagpole on the Waitangi Treaty grounds and Jerran pointed out some of his favorite fishing areas in the Bay of Islands. There was a bit of a chop for the first time on our flight as we headed inland, with warm air rising from the orchards below. After a short roll on a grass strip we walked towards the car; our 45-minute flight felt like it had lasted less than 10 minutes.

Tony had to fly to Auckland and then back to Sydney later that afternoon. We checked the "esky" in the trunk—a Styrofoam cooler with half of Tony's yellowtail fillet. It held the cold surprisingly well—the ice had not begun to melt—but of course it could not be carried on the plane back to Australia. I called the people I knew who ran a homestay near Auckland and booked a room for the night, telling them I was bringing fresh fish for dinner. Tony took his suitcase out of the trunk and I helped him carry it into the tiny terminal. We shook hands and talked about taking another trip together. Tony mentioned taking a train through the Scottish Highlands to visit single malt distilleries. I could not think of a better companion for that trip.

I got into the car, tapped the horn, waved, and pulled away from the curb. Turning south to Auckland at the main road I suddenly felt very tired. I had reached the northernmost point of my journey and only a few days remained before flying home. It was the end of August and I could feel the winter giving way to spring. The sun was so warm I took off my sweater. Mobs of sheep dotted both sides of the road, their lambs trailing behind them. The beaches looked inviting even though the ocean was still too cold to swim. The road climbed and dived, twisting around hillsides, with very light traffic. It was fun to drive a stick shift and I remembered driving here a year earlier with Nika in a BMW Z3 roadster. You could rent them in Auckland, and the trunk of a little two-seater held only two small flight bags, making it wildly impractical but fun to drive. We took the top down and Nika did the Audrey Hepburn thing, swinging a scarf over her hair and around her neck. People turned their heads, girls smiled, and some young men glared, but I could not show them a birth certificate to prove that the pretty young girl with me was my daughter. Some of them tried to race me, but while any fool could step on the gas on a straightaway, our little roadster held the road beautifully and I beat everyone by going through the turns without slowing down. In one village a kid passed us in a big loud souped up car and a minute later I saw the flashing lights of a police cruiser behind me. I slowed down and was about to pull over when my daughter, her lips suddenly very thin, said, "You don't know he's flashing at you." I kept going, the cop passed us, and a minute later I saw him pulling the kid over.

I stopped at a winery to pick up a bottle for dinner. A chipper lady in her eighties with elaborately coiffed blue hair presided over tastings and sales, dispensing wisdom to all comers. It was a pleasure to watch her operate, so active and in charge at that age. I asked about her accent. She had come to New Zealand from Croatia before World War II to visit her uncle—Croatians were big in New Zealand's wine industry. After the war broke out, civilian shipping stopped and she never went back. I thought about the horrors of the war in her country, followed by nearly half a century of communism, then another war as Yugoslavia fell apart. Had she stayed in Croatia, she probably would not have survived, but if she did, she would be all bent and wrapped in black clothes instead of standing here, beautifully groomed and running her peaceful little business.

In the village of Kawakawa I paid a quick visit to a facility recommended by several locals—a public toilet designed by Hundertwasser, a famous Austrian architect. I toured only half of the structure and found it very colorful and funky, but the village would have done well to clean its marvel a little better and not skimp on the deodorant. Further down the road I picked up a hitchhiker, a teenager who told me he always wore bright clothes and no hat when hitching rides. Suddenly I hit the brakes and pulled over—the driveway of the farm on which I was going to stay came up sooner than expected. I dropped the kid off, made a U-turn and pulled into the driveway, passing some sheep and a sign that read "A Weaving Studio." Colleen came out to greet me; her husband Tony was still at work.

I had first stayed here the year before with Nika, attracted by the fact that Tony was a local historian. It came as a surprise that Colleen was a weaving instructor, and she spent the evening and a good chunk of the next morning teaching Nika to knit. She gave my daughter a starter kit of needles and yarn before we left and never charged us for it, but of course we bought many things she made, and to this day Nika's girlfriends ask where she found her black wool hat. The house stood along the highway between Auckland and the Bay of Islands, and during the visit with Nika I told Colleen that in six months I would be driving by her house with a group of people on the way to a conference. She invited me to bring them in for a cup of coffee, showed them her farm and fed us cakes with coffee and tea. The women in the group grew restless—they wanted to see what Colleen had in her studio. Have some more cake, she said. Finally, the women could not stand the suspense, got up, and headed to the second-floor studio, buying up pretty much everything in sight. Tony was away at that time, taking a week-long course on running a museum. He was a bus driver for the local school district, but also served as the archivist of the local historical society and the curator of the Albertland museum. One of New Zealand's very attractive features was its egalitarianism—it would have been unlikely for a bus driver in the United States to have a position of such importance.

I went to my room and took a nap, which I needed after several days of rising before dawn. After I woke up, Colleen showed me her new lambs. She was bottle-feeding two very cute ones—one white, another black—because their mother refused to nurse them. A few days earlier Colleen and Tony had gone out on a rainy evening and when they returned that sheep had given birth to two lambs, but was so heavy and its wool so wet that she fell and could not get up. After Tony and Colleen lifted her to her feet, she refused her lambs. Colleen enjoyed bottle-feeding them and planned to keep one and give the other to her grandson. Rural elementary schools had lamb contests with prizes for the biggest, the cutest, and the first to come when called. I was about to ask what she thought about the psychological damage wrought by being rejected by a mother, but then realized, wait, we're not talking about human beings here.

Tony and Colleen had restored one of the oldest houses in the area. Stripping away layers of paint and wallpaper, Tony had returned their house to its original living, breathing look. The first local settlers had come from England in 1861 in several ships chartered by a religious group and called their settlement Albertland after the prince who had just died. Leaving England they didn't realize they would be split into two groups because the Auckland government gave them two separate blocks of land. "We are in the midst of one, which had 3,000 people on 70,000 acres. My great-grandfather owned land on that hill," Tony said and invited me to join a boat trip his group was organizing to visit both settlements. "Historically the only way to get around was by water. We will sail around the Kaipara Harbor, the biggest in the Southern Hemisphere. This boat trip has never been done before." I would have loved to join them, but would be out of the country by the time they sailed.

The great-grandfather's framed indenture document hung on the kitchen wall. He had apprenticed for several years to a watchmaker who pledged to teach him the craft while providing food and accommodations. In exchange the young man pledged not only to work, but "...not to waste the goods of his master, nor lend them unlawfully. Not contract matrimony within the said term. Shall not play at cards, or dice, or any other unlawful games whereby his said master may have any loss. Shall not haunt taverns or play houses." The clause "shall not commit fornication" had been crossed out. The young woman who would marry the great-grandfather was following him on another boat with their lovechild.

Sitting in their wood-paneled living room, its walls lined with family memorabilia, I asked Tony whether it was true that the eruption that had created Lake Taupo could be seen in China. He went upstairs to his library and returned with several books. Yes, that eruption had occurred approximately 1,800 years ago, was strong enough to toss the rocks just as Wally had said, and was mentioned in Chinese chronicles. Colleen called us to the table. She took the yellowtail from the esky and cooked it with saffron that her daughter-in-law had brought from India. It was a valiant effort, much improved by the bottle of wine from a Croatian vineyard. The whipped cream on the dessert was outstanding. After dinner we returned to the living room, where Tony and I talked about history, while Colleen brought out her antique spinning wheel and started processing wool from her sheep into yarn.

Tony spoke of Maori cannibalism, which emerged whenever overpopulation became a problem. We talked about the great Pacific migration and Tony said that the next generation of historians, instead of relying on oral histories, would perform genetic testing in New Zealand and on the Pacific islands to find who came from where. I was surprised when he told me that in the course of his research into family history he discovered that he was $\frac{1}{16}$ Maori. He had the chiseled attentive face of a Roman centurion, but one of his great-grandfathers had a Maori wife, and their family photo hung on Tony's wall. That lady married twice, once to a Maori and once to an Englishman, but it was not until Tony did his research that the two branches came in contact.

Colleen's spinning wheel produced a quiet and repetitive sound with gentle clicking and soft hissing, as she rocked, working the pedal. I could no longer keep my eyes open and she laughed saying that the sound of the spinning wheel was better than any sleeping tablet. I went up the restored wooden staircase, past family photos, stepping on fluffy sheepskin rugs and fell asleep before my head touched the pillow.

47   *The City of Sails*

Waking up to the sound of birds in the garden, I drew open the curtains and watched Colleen's small flock of black and white sheep graze in the meadow that curled up the hill outside their home. Tony had already left to drive his bus and after breakfast I ran up to Colleen's studio to buy some mohair scarves for my daughters. Last year, after leaving here, I drove with Nika to Dargaville to see its huge Kauri Museum. Much of the North Island used to be covered by kauri trees, almost as big as the sequoias in California. Unlike the sequoias, kauri wood was well suited for woodworking. Most kauri trees had been chopped down to clear land for pastures, cut into beams and boards. After the lumbermen left, gum-diggers moved in, poking their long spiky implements into the ground where the trees used to stand. They were looking for "gum"—yellow and red clumps of petrified sap, called amber in Europe and the United States and prized for making ornaments. Now kauri trees were recognized as a national treasure, and instead of cutting them down people planted them, which was why Jim, who drove me on a tour of Coromandel, had invited me to return in 300 years.

I drove south, with only two quick stops along the way: the Sheep World, a smaller version of the Agrodome, and the Honey Centre, where beehives were on display and honey and beeswax products were sold. I returned to the car without spending a dollar in either place, suddenly feeling restless to reach Auckland, my final destination. Phyllis had sold her house there several months earlier and was shopping for a new one, while living with Jenny, her adult daughter. Jenny had invited me to stay with them in Remuera, a nice residential neighborhood.

The road widened into two lanes in each direction, with shopping centers on both sides. That and many familiar store names made it look like the

United States, only everybody drove on the left. The needle of Auckland's TV tower, the tallest building in the country, appeared on the horizon. There were fleets of sailboats on both sides of the harbor bridge. If New York is called the Big Apple and Chicago the Windy City, Auckland is called the City of Sails. Its huge harbor, strong ocean winds, relatively warm waters, and many coves and bays make it a haven for sailors. New Zealand has held the America's Cup for several years—the most prestigious prize in sailing. For a country whose population was less than two precent of the United States, winning that Cup was a source of great pride. During the first successful attempt the entire country was involved in fundraising by buying red socks with the proceeds going to the sailing syndicate. Even the prime minister pulled up his pant legs in parliament to show off his pair of red socks.

I took the exit into downtown Auckland, its gleaming business district hugging the harbor. Auckland is the largest city in New Zealand, with over one million people, but most of them live in single-family houses, surrounded by gardens, giving the metropolis a park-like appearance. The city runs up and down low volcanic hills that used to be dotted with Maori *pas*—someone had counted 28 of them in the city. I drove past America's Cup Village, crossed Queen Street, the main shopping avenue, and pulled up to the car rental office. I could not believe how much stuff I pulled out of my car—two suitcases, a case of wine I had been hauling from the South Island, a flight bag, shopping bags with gifts, and more loose stuff.

Phyllis drove me to her daughter's house. Jenny was at work, but had prepared a guest bedroom that opened into a charming little garden. Bear, a big black dog with gray whiskers, came out to bark, making sure we knew he was a serious guard dog, before doing a little dance around Phyllis. He did not care what the ownership papers said, he knew who fed and walked him. Phyllis was staying in the apartment above the carports, and Bear had taught himself to press down her door handle and let himself in.

My computer still had not been fixed. I had been talking to Sam regularly and he told me that the local Dell office refused to sell him the screen, keeping its small stock in reserve for customers with warranties. The service centers in Malaysia and Australia were hopeless, and Sam's employee was now talking with India's, which promised him a screen. I had worked out a system for keeping notes on the road, using my hosts' computers or going to Internet cafés but needed a computer in Rarotonga, an island in the Pacific. I was going there for a few days to warm up after the winter in New Zealand and to begin writing this book. Sam, kind as ever, told me to come and get a loaner unit. He would lend me an old Toshiba, fix my Dell when the screen arrived and give the repaired computer to Phyllis, who would swap it for his Toshiba when I stopped over in Auckland on my way back to New York.

Phyllis drove along tree-lined streets to Sam's substantial office. Adrienne did not kid me—her son was very tall, six and a half feet. He asked one of his employees to hook an external screen to my broken machine, allowing me to back up my files, then gave me his loaner unit. He still did not want to take my credit card number until the repair was completed—everything was on trust. That was pretty much the style of New Zealand. Earlier that morning I had had a call from Salt Air, asking for my credit card number to pay for the flight to Cape Reinga. They did not charge the card in advance, and in the flurry of thank-yous and good-byes after the flight Jerran forgot to take an imprint. I gave them the number, asking them to charge me half the fee, and gave them Tony's email in Australia so that they could get his card number for the balance. They had no worries—everyone was perfectly relaxed.

Later in the afternoon Phyllis drove me back across the Harbor Bridge to the North Shore. We met with a group of friends for a discussion of the markets and a potluck dinner. It felt nice to be driven for a change, after so many weeks behind the wheel. On our drive back the harbor was dark, and the bright needle above the casino looked like a rocket taking off into the black sky.

48   *A Stack of Sheepskins*

The Auckland Museum, surrounded by tall columns, stood in the middle of a large park atop a low hill, where a *pa* used to be. It faced a busy harbor and a row of antique cannons at the bottom of its wide steps pointed towards the sea. I tried to look through one of them at a cargo ship being loaded at the docks below, but it was stuffed with trash. Entering the museum, I turned into the gallery of Pacific exploration. Large models of outrigger canoes left one in awe of the people who felled huge trees with stone axes, used sharp rocks to carve out canoes, attached outriggers with strips of bark and set out on the vast ocean with no compass, following only the stars and migrating birds.

There were intricate wood carvings—the Polynesians as well as the Maori were expert carvers. I heard the muffled sound of drums that grew louder as I approached the great hall with its intricately carved *marae*. A huge war canoe, built for carrying more than a hundred warriors, reminded me of the whale suspended from the ceiling at New York's Museum of Natural History. Most of the Maori artifacts kept in glass cases were implements for cracking men's skulls and otherwise killing and maiming them, along with a few feather cloaks. The drumming grew louder. Many museums had Maori groups affiliated with them and this one was about to give a "cultural performance" amidst the exhibits for an extra fee. I had seen it before and would not pay to see it again. The dances were designed to threaten and intimidate. Semi-nude tattooed men, many clad in slithering slabs of fat, stick out their tongues so far that their innards seem to come out. They advanced, yelling, brandishing weapons and locking eyes with the viewers. I could see how this greeting fit into a society with endless intertribal wars, but did not feel like paying people to stare at me and wave sticks.

Skipping the second floor with its flora and fauna, I walked up to the third, devoted to New Zealand's history. Two fighter planes bracketed the landing—a Japanese Zero and a British Spitfire—a loser and a winner in the Second World War. The Zero had been fitted out for a kamikaze attack in the last weeks of the war, but the Japanese war machine was already falling apart, and while the plane sat on some Pacific island waiting for a missing part Japan capitulated. The man who was assigned to fly the plane survived and returned to Japan. Some quick-thinking New Zealanders fixed the plane and flew it home, and several decades later the Japanese pilot, by then a professor, came to visit Auckland and donated his flying scarf and wartime photos to the museum. One could not avoid thinking how little would have been gained and how much would have been lost had that missing part been delivered in time.

New Zealanders, so mild in their daily dealings, had one of the most warlike histories in the Western world. I missed the New Zealand Army Museum in Waiouru on this trip, but the Auckland Museum did a great job of covering the country's military history. The exhibit on the Maori Wars was sensitively presented—one side of the hall showed that history from the Maori point of view, the other from the British. After New Zealand became a colony, whenever the British Empire went to war, this tiny nation jumped in with both feet. It lost a higher percentage of its population in action in World War I than any other country in the Western Alliance. Its contingents had deployed to the Boer War, the First and Second World Wars, and saw action in Malaysia and Vietnam. The walls in the memorial gallery had photographs of the war dead, many with flowers pinned to them. There had been a sea change in this nation's identity—

from loyal British subjects to a Pacific independent nation, from a war-filled past to a staunchly antinuclear peaceful stance. Considering New Zealand's military history, its peaceable choice was made not from weakness but out of deeply felt principles.

Handicrafts by local artisans, jewelers and weavers in the large gift shop of the Auckland Museum were certified authentic, their quality an order of magnitude above the kitsch of Queen Street. I bought a carving of a household altar from Leti Island in the Moluccas, which I was going to use as a candle holder in my bedroom in New York. I could imagine how soft candlelight would play against this nude black figure on the fireplace. Waiting for it to be wrapped in layers of soft paper, I picked up a paddock-full of toy sheep made of wool for my friends back home.

Phyllis met me in Parnell, a stylish neighborhood chock-a-block with boutiques and eateries. There were several guest houses in the area, where I probably would have stayed had Jenny not offered me her guest bedroom. The day turned overcast and we dove into a tavern recently opened by Guinness, the Irish beer company, decorated with old photos on dark wood-paneled walls. We took a table near the fireplace and ordered dark draft beer that came with a head of foam—"a blonde in a black skirt." We shared a dish of fried herring with crisp green salad and a dish of grilled John Dory—a firm white fish from the depths of the Pacific. We watched the people in the street through the wide open doors and caught up on each other's news. Parnell was one of my favorite areas of Auckland, but when I came with Nika last year she preferred Ponsonby, with its art galleries and younger, funkier crowd.

We drove to Queen Street, but the broad main thoroughfare, running uphill from the harbor, had changed a great deal in recent years. Downtown traffic had passed some critical level and seized up, moving painfully slowly. The memory of easy driving through downtown was just that, a memory. The street was lined with solid English-looking buildings but the faces in the street and behind shop counters made it look like any large Asian metropolis. The entire country welcomed foreign tourists and students, but it looked as if most of them had come to Queen Street, displacing the locals.

We turned on Customs Street and stopped in front of Breen's Sheepskins to buy a few of those soft throw rugs that never wear out and feel like the most genuine mementos of the country. We could not find a parking spot, and Phyllis dropped me off at the door. I strolled between stacks of sheepskins and bins of sheepskin slippers and gloves when Phyllis walked in. The sheepskins came in different sizes, and I asked the owner to give me three in the size I wanted. "Please choose the better ones," I asked. "I won't," he said with a straight face. "We like to treat our customers badly. They must be masochists because they keep coming back." Grant had remembered me from my previous visits. We traded jokes and laughed, slapping the counter, when we heard a baby cry. Grant went to the back room and returned with a beautiful Asian infant. He had recently married a Korean woman and had just returned from a visit with his in-laws.

In the evening I borrowed Phyllis' car and drove to a restaurant in Mission Bay. Her sporty black number was a gift from Jenny, and a golden bow was still tied to one of its windshield wipers. A couple I had met a few days earlier had a son in Auckland and when I called Henry and invited him for dinner, he said he knew another "famous American writer" who was writing a book about New Zealand. My competitive curiosity was immediately piqued, and I asked Henry to invite him to join us. I recognized the man's name from a huge scandal on the fringes of psychiatry many years ago. Knowing that someone else was writing a book on the same topic spurred me to speed up my work.

I was the first to arrive at the restaurant and sat at the bar, ordering a beer from a barmaid who remembered me from previous visits. People kept coming in and I was trying to recognize the two men I had never met before. Henry was young, tall, high-strung, and guileless. He used to be a partner in a second-hand bookstore, where he had met Jeff. Jeff, also tall, very smooth, with silver hair, presented me with a copy of a book he had written about his scandal. He had inscribed it to me, writing diagonally across the page, and I immediately remembered what the great Russian poet Anna Akhmatova had said—inscribing diagonally was a clear sign of pretentiousness in a writer. We went upstairs, found a table, and opened our menus. Jeff was a strict vegetarian and could not find anything suitable for him. "Let's go," I said, closing my menu and getting up, "we'll find another place." "But you already ordered a drink," Jeff said, surprised by the speed of my decision. "This is like trading," I said. "The first loss is the best loss. If a trade is not going your way from the start, get out." I paid and we walked down the block to another attractive restaurant with a menu that satisfied everyone.

All my worries about another American writing a book on the same topic were quickly dispelled. While I was writing "on a spec," without a contract, just because I loved this country and liked to travel, Jeff would not start writing without an advance. He had bought an expensive house, lost a small fortune in the stock market and needed the money. In a recent brainstorming session with his New York publishers he suggested several topics for his next book, including why an American would want to move to New Zealand. His publishers nixed the idea, saying it would be a financial failure. I happened to disagree, but kept my mouth shut.

Jeff was a dazzling conversationalist, but I quickly realized he had only one topic—Jeff. Granted, he had a big personality, making it a big topic, but it became a little monotonous after a while. I continued to listen, sipping a superlative Chardonnay, and at times chatting with our Croatian waiter, an extremely good-looking gay kid who would stand by the table holding the bottle by its bottom, imitating the posture of an antique statue. Henry, Jeff, and I shared a heavenly dessert of fruit, chocolate, and pastries, and Jeff made a weak gesture to split the check three ways. I waved him off, paid, and we went across the street to Phyllis' car where I had an extra copy of one of my books, which I signed to Jeff. After he left, Henry and I found a table in an outdoor café under a heater, just like in Paris. We ordered cognac and smoked cigars, talking about books, his parents, and his plans for the future. I gave Henry an extra cigar to take home and we parted in the best of spirits.

49 A Tunnel through a Fishtank

Jenny's kitchen had a glass gallery extending into a sunny garden, and I sat there at the counter, eating breakfast and watching her flutter about, talking about the boat she had sold a few days earlier. It was too big and expensive to maintain and she got more money for it than she had paid, but she already missed going on the water and was trying to decide whether to get a smaller boat right away or wait. It looked like a case of seller's remorse and I wondered why a pretty woman in a boat club with hundreds of members would have any difficulty sailing as often as she liked. Jenny said the guys in the club were old and interested only in beer; she laughed when I told her about Anne-Marie's stud lambs. As soon as she heard I was going to dive in Rarotonga she told me she did not trust island rentals and led me to her huge SUV, which held two sets of diving gear and the rest of her stuff from the boat. It looked like she did not feel like unpacking and storing everything, as a concrete reminder that the boat was gone.

I was hoping to fly to Cook Islands with a small carry-on but Jenny threw a large dive bag on the floor and started tossing gear into it: vest, regulator, girl's pink weight belt, her ex-husband's mask and fins, the works. I drew a line on carrying the tank. She threw a diving knife into the bag—"Shark protection. If you see a shark, stab your buddy and swin back to the surface."

I put her diving bag, my flight bag, and Sam's laptop into Phyllis' small car. We had plenty of time before my flight and swung down to Mission Bay along the waterfront drive. The green mottled expanse of the bay was dotted with whitecaps, flags fluttered in a stiff breeze, and several windsurfers, including a kitesurfer, zigzagged to and fro. A broad walkway ran for several miles between the beach and the road, and hundreds of people were strolling, running, or rollerblading on that sunny warm winter morning.

We drove to Kelly Tarlton's Antarctic Encounter and Underwater World and Phyllis laughed when she heard how six months earlier I had taken a small group there, teasing them that I was going to drag them down into the sewers. Kelly Tarlton was a local explorer and entrepreneur who leased from the City of Auckland its old unused storm sewers. There, he built an Antarctic habitat, museum, and huge aquarium. A people mover, made to look like an Antarctic snow cat, glided past colonies of penguins in water that was cooled near freezing. All around us penguins preened on blocks of ice, swam, and snacked on fish. Suddenly, a killer whale's head popped out of the water, a bloody penguin in its teeth—but both were made of plastic.

I kept looking at a recreation of Robert Falcon Scott's hut, used by the polar explorer as a base for his team at the edge of the Antarctic between 1901 and 1904. The camp felt like a small island of the British Empire, complete with a printing press for producing a regular English newspaper in the Antarctic darkness. A moving sidewalk, encased in a narrow tube of air, moved through a tunnel filled with water. The enormous old storm sewers, flooded with salt water, teemed with local fish, sharks, electric skates and tropical island fish. Being surrounded by water, with schools of fish swimming on both sides and overhead, created the illusion of walking on the ocean floor.

We drove for lunch to the restaurant in Mission Bay where I had wanted to eat the night before. We parked near the sea wall and Phyllis talked about the days when her son was a teenager and had a small sailboat. One evening the wind shifted offshore and her son with another boy could not return. When it became dark, the other boy's father drove to the sea wall, parked facing the water, and turned on his headlights to show the boys where to aim. We walked into De Fontein—a beautiful two-story wood-paneled space where a McDonald's had gone out of business and the new owners opened a Belgian restaurant. It was dark and cozy on the first floor, where I had sat at the bar the night before, with floor-to-ceiling windows opening to the harbor on the second floor.

I had two rules while traveling with my kids—no TV and no fast food—and expected to get a chuckle when they heard about my lunch "at McDonald's." There was poetic justice in this upscale conversion. A few months earlier in the Estonian capital Tallinn in northern Europe, I was appalled to see a mansion anchoring a medieval street converted into a golden-arched fast-food joint. Here, in Auckland, the process had been reversed. Phyllis and I shared a pot of mussels with crayfish and brandy sauce, drank Hoegaarden White and afterwards she drove me to the airport for my flight to Rarotonga.

Flying north below the equator is like flying south from New York, towards greater warmth. I had developed a system of ending New Zealand winters with a few days on a Pacific island when I first came here with my son. We spent five days skiing on the South Island, ten days touring the country, then five days warming up in Fiji, an archipelago of two large islands and several hundred small ones. At the international airport in Nadi we transferred from a huge 747 to a plane so tiny that each person had to be weighed before boarding. At a resort we stayed in a beachfront *bure*—a hut with a thatched roof that was, nevertheless, air conditioned. We walked under palm trees, swam and Danny took waterskiing lessons. I went scuba diving each day, making two of the most interesting dives of my life. Once I dived to the remains of a U.S. bomber that went down during World War II, its bits and pieces strewn on the ocean floor and marked by a steel cable stretched along the coral. I swam slowly over its landing gear, a piece of the instrument panel, and the rudder. Another time local dive boats assembled above an underwater amphitheater where they fed sharks bloody fish and meat, and we watched a feeding frenzy, with each diver holding on to his or her rock, trying not to make any sharp movements. Back on the main island we met a local park ranger who left the national park in the care of his wife and took us into the mountain ranges where cannibals used to live.

Fiji had been put on the map by Captain Bligh, who sailed between its islands in a lifeboat after the mutiny on the Bounty. He outran the natives who routinely ate shipwrecked survivors, believing that they had fallen out of favor with the gods. Missionaries did a fantastic job of turning these cannibals into the kindest and nicest people on Earth and I enjoyed talking with the Fijians, always picking up local hitchhikers. Many were poor, but all seemed proud and happy. Returning to New York, I took up a collection of clothes and sent the box to the ranger's wife. I had gone back to Fiji and also stayed on Vanuatu, a Pacific archipelago where bungee jumping was invented—local tribes had a rain-making rite in which men jumped head first from tall trees, tying their ankles to the branches.

On this year's journey I decided to go to Rarotonga in the Cook Islands, because that archipelago had an especially close relationship with New Zealand. The local currency was the New Zealand dollar and all Cook Islanders had the right to live and work in New Zealand. Scholars believed that the Cook Islands were the last stop in the great Pacific migration before New Zealand, and I looked forward to staying at an original Maori island home. I was going to do a bit of exploring, but planned to spend most of my time in front of the computer, beginning to write my book about New Zealand.

SECTION
5

Cook Islands

Goodbye
New Zealand

The Cook Islands occupy a huge rectangle in the Pacific, over 850,000 square miles—almost a quarter the size of the United States. Amidst this watery vastness lie 15 tiny pin pricks, coral atolls with a total land area of about 100 square miles, the size of a small town. The biggest of them is Rarotonga, the seat of the government and the archipelago's main tourist center. Its impassable mountainous center is ringed by a strip of fertile land with palm trees, and a coastal road along its 20-mile perimeter. A few hundred yards offshore the island is encircled by a coral reef, a huge living organism that grew from the bottom of the sea to the surface, protecting the land from the onslaught of the ocean.

We came in at midnight and I was the first off the plane, walking to the low terminal building under a tropical drizzle. My diving gear came out almost immediately and I rolled the luggage cart into the waiting area. A young man from the transportation company put a flower garland around my neck and pointed to one of two waiting vans. They expected eight passengers at the hotel where I had booked a room, the only four-star hotel on the island. No one moved very fast; we were on Pacific time. I got into the van and waited. After a while three more people got in and I went to the transportation office to ask when we would be leaving. The locals smiled and directed me to a beady-eyed, heavy-set, young white woman who ran the office. She ordered me to wait back in the van. "Look," I said, "you're expecting eight people and have two vans. You have four people already—let's go, and have the second driver wait for the rest." When she saw me question her commands she started screaming, telling me to take a taxi if I didn't like waiting. This was the first time I had heard anyone scream in the Pacific. Rarotonga sure had a strange welcome. I hailed a cab, took my bags out of the van, and went to the resort ahead of everyone else.

50   *Writing in Rarotonga*

In the morning, my head still on the pillow, I heard a muffled roar. It undulated softly, growing louder one moment, softer the next, but never ceasing. It was a low, deep, powerful sound, as if huge planes were taxiing at a major airport. Then I remembered the long ride the night before and realized we were far from the airport. I drew open the curtains and stepped out on a wide wooden balcony above the beach. The wide lagoon, with a few tiny islets overgrown with palms, was perfectly calm. In the far distance I could make out the swell of the Pacific. Between them was a dancing white line of breakers, where the coral reef held back the power and the rage of the ocean, protecting this island. The dull muffled roar of the ocean hitting the reef never ceased.

I thought how our perceptions depended on the environment. Had I stayed near an airport or a highway, that noise would have bothered me, but coming from the reef it felt peaceful and calming. I put on a pair of swimming shorts—my uniform for the next few days—and opened a tourist brochure. After last night, more than ever, I needed my own set of wheels. To my surprise, one of the ads showed a spiffy convertible; half an hour later a woman from the rental company came to pick me up.

All traffic on the island used the shore road. The circle was 20 miles long, one lane in each direction, with no traffic lights. The mountains in the middle had no roads, and wherever you wanted to go, you went either right or left in that circle. There was a narrow strip of agricultural land with a few dirt roads between the shore and the mountain. In the pre-missionary days, when Rarotonga was home to several warring cannibal tribes, there had been swamps, in which the natives threw flat rocks creating a rudimentary beltway.

The rental place had two little Mazda Miata convertibles—red with an automatic and silver with a stick shift, both very ragged, with torn tops and non-matching replacement fenders. I did the paperwork and a few minutes later whizzed down the left side of the road in my raggedy silver two-seater. Its wide tires hugged the wet road, the five-speed gearbox was surprisingly smooth, the engine had a good torque, and the brakes worked. So what if the roof leaked? When I stepped on the gas in second gear, the little silver bug roared like a pride of wildcats and hurtled forward, with locals turning their heads and dogs scattering from the road. I made a full circle of the island before returning to the hotel, parking and walking up to my room to work on the balcony. I turned on Sam's Toshiba and started arranging my travel diary into a narrative. "In the Invercargill airport I saw a sign—four minutes to the world's most southern McDonald's. There was no security gate and I could sit next to the pilot. We flew south across the Foveaux Straight which Captain Cook missed in bad weather. At the end of the strip stood an empty shipping container. A huge rubber band was stretched to the max."

I worked all day with a few breaks. It drizzled on and off, and the lagoon did not look particularly inviting for swimming. Towards the evening the sky cleared and half a dozen locals rowed an outrigger canoe past the resort. I went down to the waterfront bar and had a drink, then put on a better pair of shorts and a polo shirt, threw a beach towel on the seat of the car, quite wet because of the torn roof, and drove into town for dinner. It was deathly quiet. The only place with a bit of life was a harborfront restaurant called Trader Jack's. The people at the tables—all white couples—ate in silence, but at the bar a small crowd of local businessmen and a few boaties were getting noisily drunk. I grabbed an empty stool and ordered sushi from the menu. No one else ate at the bar, but after a brief confusion they served me and I had my meal while taking in the local wildlife. I mentioned to the man who was playing the keyboard that my next trip was going to be to Moscow and he put on a dazzling Russian medley, from Doctor Zhivago to Moscow Nights. The local Captain Cook beer tasted salty, as if brewed from ocean water. I resolved never to drink it again, finished a cigar, and roared back to the hotel in my Miata.

The next morning I worked on the balcony again. "Doug told us he was an intellectual with a great sense of humor, while his wife was an esthetician. Margaret was a quiet, mousy woman who rarely left the kitchen. I asked Doug several questions and pulled out of him that he used to be a butcher—an Archie Bunker trying to impersonate Masterpiece Theater." Two cleaning women knocked on the door and I took my computer and a cigar to the waterfront bar, continuing to write there. A tall, athletic white man in long pants came by and I guessed he was the resort's general manager. Few men were formal enough to cover their legs below the knee on the island.

I complained to Greg about my incident at the airport and then we moved to the much more interesting topic of local history. He told me that ancient islanders had sailed to New Zealand from a nearby bay, following the shining cuckoo, a migratory bird. He pointed out where, at the far end of the resort, a European woman had been cooked by islanders in the old days. He told me to go see a man who ran a shell shop, a New Zealander married to a local woman and an expert on local history. Then he left for a Rotary club meeting with the Air New Zealand regional manager. It was the only airline that flew between the island and the outside world and all hotel managers were going to that meeting to beg for more flights and a better schedule.

I went back to the balcony and worked for several more hours, then got a paddleboard from the activities people and rowed towards the reef. The lagoon was placid with a few low regular waves, but closer to the reef the roar increased and suddenly the water became very choppy. With the board dancing in the waves, I turned as carefully as I could and paddled back fast. To lose balance would have meant to be thrown against the razor-sharp coral. The view towards the shore was breathtaking, with the top of the mountain lost in the clouds. A few ugly, boxy, white hotels spoiled the vista. I fondly remembered Costa Rica, which prohibited any construction on the beach that could be seen from the sea. After sundown I drove back to Trader Jack's. Garth was at the keyboard, sailboats bobbed in the harbor, and raindrops falling from the roof and catching the restaurant light looked like a shining glass curtain.

I ate breakfast at the resort while reading a book—there was no one to talk to. I have been to lively resorts and to dull ones, but this one was in a league of its own. Couples chewed in silence while egrets stood guard above the pond with fat eels. The only entertainment came from the birds with punky hair that flitted from table to table, pecking at crumbs. Once a chicken ran between the tables, probably arriving a little early for dinner. I brought Jeff's book to read at breakfast, and was entertained by his version of the scandal, but liked him less and less after every chapter.

Up on my balcony, facing the palm trees and the beach, I continued to work on the book. "Gerd, a professor of near Earth space physics from Bonn, came to Stewart Island to photograph birds. He looked like an exotic bird himself—long-legged, with a beaky nose. He told me the Earth was not quite spherical, and about the logistics of climbing Mt Kilimanjaro." Taking a break, I walked to an Internet café, housed in a green shed under palm trees. I asked for the bathroom and they pointed to the trees. This was Rarotonga—high-tech and low-tech side by side. I was surprised when an English girl who worked in the Internet café asked whether I wanted a cup of coffee. That was the most active sales approach I had seen on the island, where most help moved as if through a pool of honey. She was new to the island and I promised her she would slow down in a few weeks. An email came from Sam—Dell in India had agreed to sell him the screen, but it would arrive too late for my return flight. I would be flying back to the United States with a broken machine.

In a nearby shack a slender middle-aged man sold seashells. It did not look like a thriving business, but then no place on the island did. I had stepped in once before when his door was open, but no one was there. Terry sat behind a tiny table, facing shelves lined with dusty sea shells, priced surprisingly high. Next to Terry a plump, dark-skinned girl doodled on a piece of paper. She was about nine, and her childish scribbles hung on the walls, priced at several dollars each. Terry said he was a *papa'a*, a European. "Papa" meant skin, and "a" meant four—four-skin. When missionaries landed here, the locals were amazed they had four skins—an overcoat, a jacket, a shirt and an undershirt. "The natives went around naked and they threw some of those missionaries into the pot to see whether their fifth skin would also come off," added Terry with a grin.

In prehistoric times cannibalism flared up whenever food became scarce due to overpopulation. The weaker tribes put out to sea. They observed the annual migration of the shining cuckoo and deduced there had to be land down south since the birds flew across the ocean in a straight line and returned each year. They may also have heard the histories of explorers who had traveled south and returned. Terry answered a question that had been puzzling me—how the age of Pacific exploration came to an end. A thousand years ago small bands of desperate, skillful, and courageous Stone Age people had built sailing canoes and migrated from one archipelago to another, populating almost the entire Pacific within several centuries. Then they stopped sailing, and by the time Europeans arrived there was virtually no communication between the archipelagoes, with only small canoes used for coastal navigation, fishing, and raiding close neighbors.

Terry explained that the trees for making ocean-going canoes took about 300 years to grow and there were few such giants on the islands. Just as the last trees were being cut, many navigators and people with the skills to build and sail the canoes were eaten during intertribal wars. This reminded me of Western history, when the flowering of the Greek and Roman cultures was followed by the long Dark Ages, with communities hunkering down in poverty, ignorance, fear, and violence. When Europeans arrived in the Pacific, the islanders and the Maori were in the midst of their own Dark Age, isolated and cannibalistic. The Europeans' arrival had irreversibly changed the indigenous culture.

One of the results of the missionaries' arrival was a Babel Tower of tongues. When Captain Cook sailed here, most Pacific languages were so similar that he used a single islander as his translator. Missionaries of all denominations hurried to translate the Bible for the natives. The English and the French, Protestants and Catholics, went busily to work, and since different groups of missionaries dominated different islands, within a generation local languages diverged so much that islanders from different archipelagoes stopped understanding one other. Captain Cook did not believe he had done Pacific islanders any favor by discovering their lands. This far-sighted, dour navigator, revisiting the islands after several years, recorded in his diary huge social disruptions that evolved following his voyages of discovery.

The bigger archipelagoes, like Fiji, managed to preserve some local culture. Others, like the Solomon Islands, were mired in armed conflicts. The Cook Islands, as a protectorate of New Zealand, were in a league of their own—their citizens voted with their feet. The natives took advantage of being entitled to permanent residency in New Zealand and left in droves. The jobs, the incomes, the educational opportunities were in Auckland, not here. The native population of the Cook Islands declined from 24,000 to 12,000 in the past 20 years, with young adults especially disappearing from the islands and only old people and their grandchildren left behind. The archipelago was being depopulated and those who remained appeared to be in a state of grief and abandonment.

I went out for dinner and ended up at Trader Jack's again, the only place with a semblance of night life on this subdued island. Couples ate in silence in the restaurant, but at the bar were some loud alcoholics and a few gay guys. There were no single women. I talked with two expats, one from New Zealand and another from the United States, who were setting up an offshore ship registry. They mentioned that the Cook Islands were on the international financial blacklist. I had been to a few financial havens and saw some very sharp people there, but this bunch could not have laundered money if you put it in a washing machine and showed them the start button. Their noncompliance with Uncle Sam seemed to be due to lassitude rather than wickedness. I drank New Zealand beer, ate sashimi fresh from the ocean, and counted the days until my return to Auckland.

The next morning I was at the computer before the first swimmers hit the beach. "The farmhouse was comfortable and neat. As a child in Russia I had learned to expect poverty on farms, but here in New Zealand farmers lived in nice houses. A fire blazed at one end of the room, family photographs were everywhere. Murray went into the kitchen to make dinner and asked whether I wanted venison or lamb. We sank into comfortable couches." I wrote all morning and then took my little two-seater for a spin with its top down, swinging between two lanes, shifting gears, drinking in the roar of the engine, enjoying the push and pull of acceleration. At the tiny National Museum a group of young Mormon missionaries, wearing long black pants, white shirts and black ties, all with name tags, watched a video of the Constitution Day celebration. I stood behind them for a few minutes, looking at the screen on which nubile maidens in coconut bras and grass skirts undulated their soft hips in the most appetizing manner. I said without addressing anyone in particular that this was the most erotic Constitution Day celebration I had seen anywhere in the world. A couple of kids snickered, but quickly tightened up and returned to the screen in grave silence. I hopped into my convertible and gunned it for the diner where Garth worked as a short-order cook when not playing the keyboard.

He grilled some fish with rice and mango chutney and offered me a local newspaper. It reported that at the Rotary Club meeting, the regional manager of Air New Zealand had told the hotel operators, in so many polite words, to go suck on a coconut. They were not going to get any more flights because they already had all the business they could handle. I fully agreed and thought that the transportation office seemed particularly overloaded.

My return flight was drawing near, and I felt duty-bound to use Jenny's diving gear. The day before, spinning in my Miata around the island, I had booked a dive at a place she had recommended, next to sadly neglected botanical gardens. The face of the owner, an extremely short and fat New Zealander, was on the front of every tourist brochure on the island. Scuba diving always reminded me of what one of my teachers in medical school used to say about diabetes—it was a deadly disease for illiterates. With diabetes, if one kept testing and managing one's blood sugar, that person could have a nearly normal life expectancy, but someone without the intelligence or discipline could be dead within a year. Diving could be a lot of fun, but you had to watch the depth, the air, and the decompression.

I buckled Jenny's large gear bag into the passenger seat and stepped on the gas, downshifting to pass. At the dive shop five of us got into a van—an Australian woman, a Canadian woman, myself, and the dive master with his assistant, both Cook Islanders. When we arrived at the pier, our boat was limp. It was a zodiac-type boat, hard in the middle, inflatable around the sides. I was glad it lost air before we got in, rather than in the middle of the ocean. Jenny's warning about island rentals came to mind. We drove back, hooked up another zodiac to the van and crawled back to the pier.

The dive master dropped anchor halfway between the beach and the reef, and I got into Jenny's gear but could not equalize my ears on the way down. It felt as if someone was waiting for me with a sharp knife at 60 feet below the surface and whenever I tried to go lower, stuck a knife in my right ear and twisted. I swallowed, squeezed my nostrils through the mask and blew, but when I finally broke through and dived lower, there was nothing much to see. The dive master had taken us to a safe area with dead coral.

Riding back to the shore, I looked at the two women. The Australian was all excited about going to meet her boyfriend, but the Canadian was alone. She looked a few years older than me and said that she had sailed to Rarotonga from Tahiti with a group of women learning to sail. She had paid $6,000 for a three-week crossing during which she had to work. She had slept in an 18-inch high bunk, with five spare inches at her head and another five at her feet. The owners had the best cabin and grossed $36,000 in less than a month from six customers, a fortune in that part of the world. I always told my daughters to avoid courses "for women only" because they tended to be either low-grade affairs or rip-offs, or both. "Take a normal beginners' class, not for girls only," I always said to them.

Catherine had serious grey eyes and slightly graying hair. Her firm butt bounced up and down on the rubbery edge of the speeding boat, rivulets of salt water ran from her slender shoulders into the cleavage of a one-piece swimsuit. "What do you do for a shower on a sailboat?" I asked. She could swim in the ocean all she wanted, but showers were very sparse. She was still living on the boat, anchored away from the pier because the owners were too cheap to pay a small mooring fee and hook up to a water main. "At my hotel," I said, "I have this big huge shower and you can take the longest shower of your life, with all the shampoo you want." Catherine looked me seriously in the face, then ran me over with her eyes and thought for a while. "I'll come," she said.

On the drive from the pier to the dive shop our shoulders touched whenever the van hit a bump. "Damn," she suddenly slammed the back of her right hand into the palm of her left. She completely forgot it was the last night for several "girls" on the yacht and they had scheduled a farewell dinner. Our shower was off. The dive master parked in the shade, unhooked the boat and we washed our gear. I was walking back to the car when I heard a woman's voice yell my name. Catherine asked whether I would give her a ride to the harbor. I squeezed my gear into the trunk, she buckled in and her hair flew back when I stepped on the gas. On our drive she told me about her late husband, a scientist who had recently died in a freak single-car accident. We parked at the water's edge. A big fat guy dozed in a chair on the deck of a sailboat a few hundred feet offshore. I stepped on the gas and the roar raged above the water. He lifted his head, then jumped to his feet. Several women came up to the deck and stared. Somebody went to get a dinghy. We kissed and I drove back to my manuscript.

By now I knew all the barmen at Trader Jack's and ended up there again that night. John, a tall New Zealander who had served as a judge on the island for 30 years, held court at the bar. He agreed that the island felt depressed. Almost all locals with any energy or drive had left for New Zealand, and those who stayed felt abandoned and sad. The dive shop owner walked in with one of his employees, a young New Zealander who had signed me up for the dive; his glasses and thoughtful demeanor made him look like an assistant professor at a university. I bought him a beer and he complained that the hardest part of his job was sleeping with all the women divers that came through. He was longing for a peaceful night's sleep. I rode home along the dark road, noticing a sign "Slow down, dog crossing."

In the morning I was back on the terrace, a computer in my lap. "Four guys on the ultrasound team stood in the mud near the paddock. I told them I was a physician from New York, and the last time I saw ultrasound was when my ex-wife was pregnant. Each ewe running past the operator was momentarily locked in a pen, a hand-held scanner shoved under its udder." This was my last day on the island. I swung by both banks, trying to get a few local coins for a collector friend, but no luck—they had only New Zealand money. I went to the Cook Islands Museum and Library—a building the size of a four-car garage, its main exhibit some athletic medal won by a Cook Islander in the 1930s. I lunched at Garth's, looking at a car which illustrated the main rule of vehicle ownership in Rarotonga—never ever park under a coconut tree. When a coconut fell from a palm tree, it had the effect of tossing a large brick from a third floor window—it sounded funny until you saw the result. I stopped to take pictures at several local cemeteries—they buried people in crypts above the ground, just like in New Orleans, only here they buried them in the land useless for agriculture—the oceanfront.

Trader Jack's had a live band that night. An ocean-going motor yacht had come into the harbor and the crew was getting drunk, badmouthing the absent owner. I chatted with the mechanic and then took the yacht's cook—a Dutch woman nursing a broken heart—for a spin around the island. No crew member made much money, but working on a yacht allowed them to escape reality, not that it made them very happy. Judge John, wearing dress shoes but no socks, could hardly speak. I asked whether he needed help getting home, but he slurred that he had an arrangement with the police. Whenever they stopped him for drunk driving, they simply escorted him to his house.

Sitting at the bar, puffing a cigar, I watched the other side of the Cook Island coin. The fact that most natives had left stared you in the face from empty houses, undermanned businesses, and the pervasive sadness of those left behind. The other side of the coin was that these islands offered an escape to any alcoholic misfit in New Zealand. Anyone—from the grossly obese rude woman in the transportation office to the bumbling money launderers to the alcoholic judge—anyone with half a brain and one arm could come from New Zealand to the Cook Islands and earn a few dollars, enough to get by in its undemanding tropical environment. Nothing ever changed, nothing ever happened, and the beer taps never dried up. The hidden side of the coin was that the Cook Islands were the worst part of New Zealand. Fortunately, it was a part that was very easy to avoid.

On the last morning I drove to Garth's place, but the president of the Cook Islands Rotary club, who had promised the previous night to meet me for breakfast and bring some local coins, had stood me up. On the way back I saw that Terry had opened his shell shop. He left me to mind it, along with his fat brown dog, and rode a scooter home, returning with the coins. I gladly paid him double the price and we shook hands, both very pleased with the transaction.

I packed my bags. The flight bag and the computer fit into the trunk of the little convertible and I hoisted Jenny's bag with diving gear into the passenger seat. Driving to the airport I drank in the throaty roar of the engine, going slower than usual on the perimeter road that had become familiar by now. I wanted to take in the scenery for the last time. I knew I would never return to this island. On my next winter trip to New Zealand I figured I would probably go warm up in French Polynesia. Palms fringed the beaches, breakers danced on the reef, locals on motorbikes glided back on both sides, swathed in the powerful, subdued roar of the engine. I was leaving them behind forever.

At the car rental place I noticed the woman who had brought me there from the hotel on the first day. We shook hands and she told me the flight had been postponed for 16 hours; her husband was supposed to be on it. I swung down to the airport and sure enough, she was right. My connection to New York was out the window. The people at Air New Zealand told me to go back to the hotel. They had the monopolist's self-assured attitude—if you don't like how we fly, follow the shining cuckoo and row.

I returned to the car rental place, told them I would need to keep their roadster for one more day, and asked how to return it at 2 AM. The young woman told me to park it in front of the terminal, raise the roof, roll up the windows, leave the doors unlocked, and put the keys under the floor mat. "Remember not to lock the doors," she repeated. "It is safe. We will come for the car in the morning." I returned to the hotel, got my room back, called Phyllis in Auckland and my kids in New York, then went for lunch at a nearby sailing club and wrote all afternoon. I tried to catch a few hours of sleep before the flight. We landed in Auckland at 5 AM. Phyllis, bright and eager as always, was waiting for me in the airport. The sun was rising above the soft green hills.

51   Goodbye New Zealand

United had rebooked my flight and now I had 12 free hours. At Jenny's house Bear ran out, remembered me, and rubbed his muzzle against my leg. I had breakfast with Phyllis and Jenny, and after they left went back to writing for a few hours. Then I heard vicious barking and saw a gas meter reader standing frozen in the driveway. "Don't worry," I said. "The dog only shows he's earning his keep. Just watch, his most dangerous part is his tail. When he starts wagging it, he can break a bone." I asked the meter reader about his accent—he had come from South Africa two years earlier, escaping the hardships in that country. His kids, 13 and 10, were much happier in New Zealand. He had never been to the South Island and I urged him to go there, stay on farms and in people's homes, explore a bigger, less populated island with more opportunities. I felt like a local talking to a newcomer.

By then I had five hours until my flight. I took a shower and repacked, loading my suitcases, swollen with books, brochures, skiing and hiking gear, gifts and shirts that needed laundering, into Phyllis' sporty car. On our way to Mission Bay I asked her to stop at a bank and went in to pay a speeding ticket. I needed to take care of it if I planned to return to the country. The bank did not accept credit cards for tickets, and I handed it to Phyllis—please pay, I'll settle with you later. "Don't worry about it," she said. "You have given me plenty of free books." "No, I'll pay you for it, don't volunteer until you see the ticket." The amount depended on speed. Phyllis looked at it and laughed—"Oh! You do not do anything halfway. Mind if I show it to my daughter? She was upset about a couple of speeding tickets. I want to show her what a real ticket looks like." "Next time I'll bring a radar detector," I said.

We drove to Mission Bay, one of my favorite parts of Auckland, for our last lunch. Clear green water in the harbor was as flat as glass, with occasional ripples from light gusts of wind. Joggers and rollerbladers raced on the coastal trail. The air was so clear I could see single trees on the Rangitoto volcano and other islands in the harbor. We climbed up to the second floor of De Fontein, shook hands with a young Canadian waiter who remembered us and found a table in front of an open window overlooking the harbor. I ordered a draft of Leffe Blonde for Phyllis, a Leffe dark for myself, and a pot of mussels steamed with coriander and lemon. The mussels were succulent but spicy and I had a second Leffe. We enjoyed the pungent lemony dish and when we could see the bottom of the pot, I ordered a waterzooi—a Belgian salmon casserole. Then we got another round of beer and Phyllis kept on nibbling, but I moved the waterzooi closer to her and lit up my last cigar of the trip. Its soft, rich, complex aroma wafted out the window, towards the harbor.

"Are you glad to be going home?" Phyllis asked. I told her it was a good time to be leaving. I had accomplished what I wanted, collected material for the book, and started writing. My oldest daughter, whom I had not seen in months, was returning to New York from Paris the same day as me. An old flame was flying to New York from Florida to welcome me back. I had a ticket for Moscow in three weeks. It was a good time to fly back, especially since I knew I would be coming back to New Zealand.

I paid the bill and we walked to the waterfront basking in the sunlight. I put out the cigar before getting into Phyllis' car. She drove to the airport, crossing bays and bridges and passing sheep grazing next to the car rental places. "See you in January in New York," she said. Phyllis was coming to a conference and was going to stay with me in Manhattan. I grabbed a luggage cart and unloaded the car. We hugged and kissed, looked at each other, then hugged and kissed again. She got back into her car and pulled away from the curb. Waving to me, she nearly rammed a taxi. Its driver stopped, laughed, and motioned for her to go ahead. I waved and went into the terminal.

There were armed guards at every turn as I walked to my United flight to Los Angeles. It was September 9, two days before the first anniversary of 9/11. I told the young guard who scanned my hand luggage that I took this flight on the same date exactly one year ago. It was a different world. "It'll never be the same again," he said. I walked to the plane, stowed my luggage, put on noise suppression earphones, leaned back in my seat, asked for the first glass of wine, and opened a book on Abel Tasman, the discoverer of New Zealand.

The Practical Traveler

I have been reading travel books voraciously since childhood. After closing some of my favorites I was left with unanswered questions. How did the author get to that country? Where did he stay? How did he find his guides?

To help answer questions from my readers, I decided to add this chapter. If you read it, please keep in mind several important points. First of all, these are the choices of one man. I traveled without reservations, pulling names of places out of several guidebooks or Web sites or relying on friends' advice, and I am sure there were many great places that I missed. I kept a list of all the places where I stayed and services I used, but put only my favorites here; the bad and the indifferent I simply left out. Second, I paid for all of my accommodations and services exactly what anyone else would have paid on that day. No one could buy, trade, or finagle their way into these pages!

There are several directories of accommodations in New Zealand, and while I found many of them useful, I discovered early on in this journey that most of them collected fees from places they listed, ranging from a few hundred dollars a year in the B&B book, to several thousand in the more upscale publications. Then they turned around and sold their guidebooks to the public, without disclosing their financial arrangements. This reminded me of a friend who once said that the best business in the world was a whorehouse with separate entrances for men and women, with the owner charging entrance fees at both doors. I wanted to be absolutely free of conflict, which is why no one in this chapter gave me a penny's worth for their inclusion here. Almost none of them even knew I was writing a book.

Come to think of it, there is one thing that I want from every person mentioned here. If this book becomes popular, you may become very busy. Even so, I want you to always have room for me, at full cost, of course, because I plan to return.

Favorite Places

Most people arrive at a farmstay or a homestay expecting to be treated wonderfully simply because they show up at the gate and pay the set rate. Try to put yourself on the other side of that gate and think how you would feel if you ran a farmstay or a homestay. After seeing hundreds of guests, what would separate a new arrival from the crowd? A genuine expression of gratitude? A real interest in your farm? A small unexpected gift?

Early on in my journey I got into the habit of carrying several bottles of wine in the back seat of my car, most of them acquired while visiting wineries. Then, if I liked the people with whom I was staying, I would go to my car and return with a bottle. That small token of friendship showed my hosts I appreciated what they did for me. Remember, there are no hotels listed here, and these people are taking you into their own homes.

Looking at the phone numbers below, please keep in mind that the country code for New Zealand is 64, and you need to drop off the first 0 when calling from abroad (for example, you would call the first number listed below from the United States as 011-64-3-246-8843). Farmstays and homestays are listed in the order in which they appear in the book, and you can look up their details there. If you do stay with any of these folks, please say hello to them from me.

June and Murray Stratford
The Catlins Farmstay
174 Progress Valley Road
Catlins
www.catlinsfarmstay.co.nz
03.246.8843

A working farm between Invercargill and Dunedin. Ask June to take you on a drive to the shore and be sure to taste her blueberry muffins.

Klaus and Micha Lenk
Villa Sorgenfrei
11 Lake Hayes Rd
Queenstown
www.villasorgenfrei.co.nz
03.442.1128

Amazing hospitality in the Queenstown area. A good place for a longer stay because of a great range of activities in the valley. Be sure to ask Klaus to cook for you.

Evan and Heather Glass
Abisko Lodge
74 Main Street
Mt. Hutt Village
www.abisko.co.nz
03.302.8875

A lodge close to the Mt. Hutt ski fields. A very child-friendly place. I did not stay there on this journey, but had done so several times before.

Gino and Heather Rocco
Uno Piu
75 Murphy's Rd
Blenheim
www.unopiu.co.nz
03.578.2235
021.174.4257 (mobile)

Blenheim is in the heart of South Island wine country. Gino teaches Italian cooking in college—do not miss a chance to have him cook you the fish he catches.

Bay and Shona de Lautour
Tukipo Terraces
PO Box 114 Takapau 4176
Hawke's Bay
www.tukipoterraces.co.nz
06.855.6827
025.928.908 (mobile)

A working farm and now also a vineyard in the midst of Hawke's Bay wine country. Bay is a walking encyclopedia of farming and Shona a gourmet cook.

Rodney and Sarah Faulkner
Wairakaia Farmstay
1894 State Highway 2, Muriwai
Gisborne
www.friars.co.nz/hosts/wairakaia.html
06.862.8607

A working farm near Gisborne. Rodney is a descendant of the original settlers and an expert on local history. Sarah was not there when I visited, but if she cooks even better than Rodney, you will be in for a big treat.

Jeff and Natalie Jaffarian
Tirohanga Beach Holiday Home
P. O. Box 186
Opotiki
www.beachholidayhomenewzealand.com
07.315.8899

A homestay on the beach in Opotiki, at the opposite side of the East Cape from Gisborne. Both Natalie and Jeff are very interested in politics and you could ask Natalie to cook Russian dishes.

Lynne and Bruce Baker
Baker's Homestay
40 Butler Road, RD 2
Whakatane
www.bakershomestay.co.nz
07.307.0368
025.284.6996 (mobile)

Whakatane is the base for exploring White Island. Lynne is a generous cook and Bruce a nationally rated croquet instructor.

Andrea Patten and James Patterson
On the Edge Homestay
219 Paku Drive
Tairua, Coromandel Peninsula
http://ontheedge.tairua.co.nz
07.864.8285
025.736.176 (mobile)

Andrea runs a very stylish homestay—ask for the room that opens on the terrace. Jim's local knowledge is fantastic, and while he had sold his tour company soon after my trip, he still offers private guided tours.

Tony and Colleen Moore
The Retreat
RD 5, Wellsford
http://www.sheepfarmstay.com
09.423.8547

A country homestay halfway between Auckland and the Bay of Islands. Tony is an historian and Colleen is a spinning and knitting instructor who taught my daughter to knit in just one lesson.

Favorite Guides

I decided to list only the individuals with whom I had great personal experiences. Guides are listed in the order in which they appear in the book, and you can look up their details there.

Squisy
Boat Charter
Oban, Stewart Island

No last name, Web site, or phone—Squisy was a real eccentric who insisted that everyone on the island (population 350) knew him. I found him to be a very knowledgeable charter boat captain.

Wayne Steedman
Fergs Canoes
Franz Joseph Glacier Village
www.glacierkayaks.com
03.752.0230

Be sure to go on the first outing of the morning, when the fog still swirls above the lake. If at all possible, ask Wayne for a private guided tour rather than going with a group.

Barry Whitmore
Barry's Wine Tours
40 Warwick Street
Blenheim
www.yellow.co.nz/site/barryswinetours
03.578.1494
025.2644.704 (mobile)

Sit back and taste the wines instead of driving to the vineyards. Barry knows where the real connoisseurs go and he takes you there.

Paul Neame
Abel Tasman Air
Trent Drive
Nelson
www.flytasmanbay.co.nz
03.528.8290

A wonderful way to see the area is from the air. If you are lucky, Paul may trust you to fly his plane. I enjoyed taking him out for a beer after our flight and listening to his stories about local flying.

James Patterson
The Green Coach
Same contact info as On the Edge Homestay, page 257.

Jim is a great guide with deep knowledge of local history, geography, and botany. He is a born storyteller—worth a detour. He has sold his company but remains available for private guiding.

Chris Jolly Outdoors
PO Box 1020
Taupo
www.chrisjolly.co.nz
07.378.0623

An overnight fishing trip is highly recommended. They had several boats; ours was called *Pintari*.

Jerran Norman
Salt Air
PO Box 293
Paihia, Bay of Islands
www.saltair.co.nz
09.402.8338

Jerran is a good man to fly with and nothing compares to a ground tour with Anne-Marie after he lands you on her farm.

Background Reading

These are the books I enjoyed before and during my journey through New Zealand. They are listed alphabetically by author.

Anderson, Grahame—*The Merchant of the Zeehaen*
Te Papa Press, Wellington, 2001
A New Zealander retraces Abel Tasman's steps sailing along the New Zealand coast, putting his voyage into historical perspective.

Hough, Richard—*Captain James Cook*
Coronet paperback, London, 1995
A highly readable history of a great explorer who mapped New Zealand and spent 100 days there.

Hughes, Robert—*The Fatal Shore: The Epic of Australia's Founding*
Vintage Books paperback, New York 1988
If you plan to go to Australia, this is the best book on its history.

Lockyer, John—*A History of New Zealand*
Reed Books, Auckland, 2002
A brief illustrated history of the country, written at the high school level but very informative.

Sinclair, Keith—*A History of New Zealand*
Penguin, London, 2000 (fifth edition)
A brief, comprehensive and lucid history of New Zealand—first published in 1959 and currently in its fifth edition.

Guidebooks and Web Sites

I used these books and Web sites to find places to visit and to stay. Most of the books are updated annually—be sure to get the latest edition. The books and sites are listed in alphabetical order: New Zealand is a technologically advanced country, and most attractions and accommodations have their own Web sites.

Eyewitness Travel Guide to New Zealand
Book only
My main travel guide on this journey—more narrowly focused and better illustrated than *The Lonely Planet*.

Friars' Guide to New Zealand Accommodation
Book and Web site
www.friars.co.nz
A listing of upscale accommodations accompanied by beautiful photos.

Heritage and Character
Booklet and Web site
www.heritageinns.co.nz
A short free guide to upscale accommodations.

The Greenwood Guide to Australia and New Zealand
Book and web site
www.greenwoodguides.com

B&B, lodges, and farmstays that are attractive destinations. The only local guide with the integrity to disclose that it charges a fee to places it lists.

The Lonely Planet New Zealand
Book and Web site
www.lonelyplanet.com
My favorite travel guide provides plenty of historical information, while also covering many essential practical details, such as the opening and closing hours of various attractions. I used it extensively on my previous journeys in New Zealand.

The New Zealand Bed and Breakfast Book
Book and Web site
www.bnb.co.nz
To get into this book, a property must pass rigorous standards, including even such minor details such as lights controlled from the bed and 100 precent fruit juice with breakfast.

Southern Crossings
Web site only
www.southern-crossings.com
Luxurious accommodations—the agency staff is happy to help you design a personal itinerary, which can include a driver.

Bring with You

There are two approaches to packing for a trip—the minimalist way and the opposite. If you are a backpacker, you obviously need to pack very light, but if you plan to move about by car, the amount of luggage is not a problem. I carried my hiking gear, ski clothes, shirts and shorts for the Pacific beach, and so on.

Before you go, visit a Web site like *www.weather.com* to check the weather at your destination and pack accordingly. Keep in mind that New Zealand is very informal and you can go almost anywhere without a tie. I carried a jacket and tie with me on this trip because I needed them for a conference in Australia, but I did not use them even once in New Zealand. Another thing to keep in mind is that you will probably do a lot of hiking. Good running shoes will work most of the time, but for more rugged hiking I prefer Ecco Gore-Tex boots, which have the added advantage of being waterproof. For hiking nearly barefoot in hot weather I like Teva sandals.

Noise suppression earphones are very useful for long flights—I always wear them. They pick up the monotonous noise of the engines and rushing air, flip the sine wave and send out counter-waves, canceling steady noise. You can hear everything that is being said around you, but the background is much quieter and you tire less on long flights. There are several brands but I am perfectly happy with my old Brookstones.

There are two items you will need in New Zealand. The country operates on 220-volt electric current, as opposed to 110 in the United States, and even though most electronic appliances today accept either current, the plugs and sockets are shaped differently in New Zealand, requiring an adapter for most foreign plugs. You can buy these for a dollar at most electronic stores—you can pick them up on arrival in New Zealand at a chain called Dick Smith.

Also, some, but not all, phone plugs in New Zealand are shaped differently from those in the United States or Europe, and you may need to spend another dollar on an adapter for your modem. Another helpful item is a mixer for hot and cold water (its technical name is "fixed spout water mixer") because many B&Bs only have separate hot and cold water spigots. If you cannot find one at your local plumber, you can order it from F&M Plumbing Supply in New York (212-674-0545).

If you are bringing a computer, it may pay to set up a local Internet account. Since all Internet access numbers in New Zealand are toll-free, most places allow you to plug your computer into their phone line. I had an account with Maxnet—*www.maxnet.co.nz*—whose service was fantastic; I only wish I could find a similar provider in the United States. For any hardware problems, I highly recommend Sam Williams at Portables Plus in Auckland, *www.portables.co.nz* or 09.579.1095.

Flying in the Front of the Plane

Flying to New Zealand from the United States usually involves changing planes on the West Coast and then flying about 11 hours to Auckland from either Los Angeles or San Francisco. Locally, Air New Zealand has an excellent network of airports. It flies several times a day even to the smallest cities, but has a reputation for occasionally canceling underbooked flights, blaming it on technical difficulties, and putting passengers on the next available flight, but this matters only if you need to make tight connections.

Flying business class over the ocean is one of travel's essential luxuries. Those of us who used to fly in coach never knew how much we missed until we got to fly across the ocean in the front of the plane. This reminds me of the first time I bought a car in New York. Baking day after day in summer traffic jams, I promised myself that my next car would have an air conditioner, no matter what. Flying business class across the ocean is like having an air conditioned car in summer.

The better food, the rich selection of drinks, and most of all the comfortable seats and the hovering attention of the cabin crew make a huge difference in how you feel arriving at your destination. Flying business feels like going to a good club—I look forward to reclining in my seat, selecting a wine, and picking heated nuts from a porcelain cup as the plane gains cruising altitude and my dinner is being prepared. After several hours of sleep in a wide seat under a soft blanket I get off the plane, having experienced pleasure and comfort, looking forward to a new day on another continent. Stepping off the plane, I feel sorry for the poor huddled masses being held back by the flight attendants in coach, while the passengers in the front of the plane disembark.

At first, flying in business class may appear insanely expensive. A travel agent may quote you a price four or five times higher than in coach. Recently I wanted to fly from New York to Tallinn in northern Europe. My agent quoted $700 roundtrip in coach or $5,000 in business. Crazy, isn't it? That's how it looks until you discover the two great back doors to business class—frequent flyer miles and consolidator tickets.

Frequent flyer miles are the great parallel currency of America. You earn a point for every mile you fly, which is why it pays to stick to a few airlines, earning your way up to coveted elite status, giving you more perks. People earn more miles by using their credit cards than by flying. Years ago I read a letter in a magazine from a radiologist who charged a new $3 million x-ray machine on his AmEx and earned enough miles to take his girlfriend to Venice ten times in first class. What a great idea! A $15 charge for gas is not going to put you into a front seat, but it is amazing how many businesses accept credit cards for major payments. If you can run your business life on a credit card, you can fly in the front of the plane as a bonus.

There are two types of tickets you can get with frequent flyer miles—free and upgradeable. A free business class ticket from New York to New Zealand would have cost me 105,000 miles, without earning any miles for the trip. The sweeter deal was an upgradeable ticket, which is why the airlines put out so few of them. When I planned this trip, my agent quoted me $6,000 for a business class roundtrip ticket. I saw coach tickets on the Internet for as little as $1,100, but the cheapest tickets could not be upgraded. I called a couple of airlines and United offered me an upgradeable coach ticket for $1,700, taking 50,000 miles to instantly upgrade me to business. Flying on a paid ticket, I earned the roundtrip mileage of about 20,000, reducing my real cost of an upgrade to 30,000 miles. Since the market value of a frequent flyer mile is about two cents, the upgrade cost me $600, for a total cost of $2,300 for a very comfortable trip. At the same time, most of my miles were preserved for future travel.

Earlier, I had taken a trip to Tallinn by flying on what is called a "consolidator ticket." Airlines offload blocks of tickets to wholesalers or consolidators. You need to find an agent who is connected with them and is willing to wheel and deal. My gem of an agent[1] found me a consolidator seat on Finnair, via

---

[1]Rita Chistoni, Belmont Travel, 1.800.888.8660

Helsinki, for $2,000. I earned miles on American Airlines and the flight had other rewards. I discovered Finnair's heavy blankets encased in lily-white duvets, and became very friendly with a stewardess who at the end of the flight invited me to stay with her in Helsinki. But that's another story.

A nice thing about flying business over the Pacific is that most airlines fly a Boeing 747, a plane with a hump and second-story seating upstairs. The first class sits in the nose cone, but the pilots and business class are on the upper deck. They also have business seats downstairs, but the atmosphere is not nearly as clubby. Upstairs feels like a small cushy bus, with four to ten rows of seats and only two seats on each side of the aisle that recline almost flat. There is usually a snack bar with fresh fruit near the stairs and I love running up and down those stairs for exercise, keeping myself active on long flights during which many people become frozen in their seats.

Overcoming Jet Lag

This condition is familiar to all of us who cross the oceans by plane—you feel sleepy during the day, wide awake at night, hungry at the oddest hours. Jet lag occurs when your civilized self buys an airline ticket and flies across several time zones, while your primeval physical body does not want to follow and has to be dragged along, fighting all the way. Jet lag is generally less of a problem when flying west, into the sun—from Europe to the United States or from the United States to Asia—and worse after flying in the opposite direction. Jet lag can spoil the first couple of days of your vacation and make it difficult to return to work.

What causes jet lag and how can you minimize it? Your body has several internal clocks, more or less synchronized by the day-night cycle. Your sleep, appetite, many hormonal functions, and body temperature are tied to that cycle. When you travel slowly, by train or boat, your cycle has time to adjust, but crossing several time zones in an airplane within a few hours yanks your body out of its established cycle. You pay for fast travel in the form of insomnia, a sense of malaise, and poor concentration (it is better not to drive the first couple of days, but if you must, drive extremely carefully).

Once you buy an airline ticket and know you'll be jerking your body across several time zones, what can you do to minimize wear and tear? The solution is partly physical and partly psychological. The night before a long flight I try to get less sleep than usual. I want to get to the airport slightly tired and a little sleepy. Before going to the airport, I take a hot shower and change into clean, loose-fitting clothes. One of the advantages of flying business is that you have a separate, shorter check-in line, get aboard faster, stretch in your big seat and get a preflight drink—I prefer mineral water or a mimosa.

The first thing I do after buckling up is adjust my watch to the time zone of the city to which I am flying. It may be 6 PM in New York, but if it is 2 AM the following day in Moscow, where I am going, I want to lower my window shade and think about being way past my bedtime—then have a quick dinner and catch up on my sleep. No movie, no reading, no walking around the cabin or talking with my seat mate. I eat a quick dinner with a few glasses of good wine and a bit of a dessert with a sip of cognac. Then I put on noise suppression earphones (and an eye mask if the cabin is still bright), recline, loosen my belt, tuck in the blanket and fall asleep, ignoring the rest of the cabin. This way, I am on the arrival city's clock even before the takeoff.

Waking up prior to arrival, I like to begin my day with physical exercise. Flying upstairs in a 747 is the best—I go to the stairway and run up and down about 50 times and do a few pull-ups. On other planes, I just walk as briskly as I can without disturbing others, up and down the aisle. Then I carry my travel kit into the bathroom, line the floor with clean paper towels, strip naked, and hang my clothes on a hook. I soak a few paper towels in cold water and rub myself down, like taking a cold shower after a workout. Then I get dressed and return to my seat to open the window shade and have my breakfast. Refreshed and energized by the sun shining outside after a good night's sleep, I plan for the day ahead, because I have already been living in this time zone for the better part of a day.

The best cure for jet lag is sunshine. I try to catch as much sun as possible in the first few days—go to the beach or just stay outdoors. Try not to go to bed until at least 9 or 10 PM on the first day. Try not to sleep during the day. If you feel an irresistible urge to nap, set up an alarm or ask someone to wake you up after 45 minutes. The idea is to move into the local time schedule as soon as possible.

For the first three nights after flying across the ocean I take Melatonin. In general, I avoid taking medicines. With my suspicious attitude towards pharmaceuticals, it took me a while to try Melatonin, but now I would not travel without it. Falling asleep in a new place may be easy, but Melatonin prevents me from waking up in the middle of the night and I never feel heavy in the morning after taking it at night. Health food stores sell is without a prescription and you have to work out your own dosage—start low and move up if needed.

Recipes

I am a very occasional and minimalist cook, but some of the dishes I had on this journey have fired up my culinary ambition. The recipes I brought from New Zealand are listed here in chronological order, as I discovered them on my journey.

Daphne's Chutney
Chutney is a great condiment to enliven your main courses. You can also smear a little on a slice of bread as a dessert after a meal.

Apples	5 lbs
Raisins	2½ lbs
Pitted dates	2½ lbs
Brown sugar	2½ lbs
Salt	3 oz
Garlic	1¼ oz
Cayenne pepper	1¼ oz or more
Vinegar	3½ pints
Ground ginger	2½ oz
Allspice	2½ oz

Boil fruit and sugar in vinegar for three hours. Add the rest and boil for 15 minutes. Refrigerate.

Randy's Rum Pot
A marvelous concoction to pour on your ice cream or other desserts to launch their flavor into the stratosphere.

Pitted plums	3 lbs
Sugar	2.5 lbs

Put almost equal weights of thinly sliced plums and sugar into a glass container, fill with rum, seal, and put in a refrigerator for six months. Apply willpower and do not open until due date.

James' Pukeko Bird

This is the only recipe in this chapter that I did not test in my kitchen after returning to New York, but Jim is a man of abundant experience who swears this is absolutely the best way to enjoy a pukeko bird, should you ever shoot one in your neck of the woods.

Fill a pot with water, add salt and spices to taste, put an axe (the metal part only) on the bottom and when the water boils, add the pukeko bird. Continue to boil, and when the axe becomes soft, throw out the bird and eat the axe.

James' Fish Seasoning

Jim told me that after he gave this recipe to one of his American guests, the man mailed him $100 several weeks later to thank him for the best fish cooking recipe ever.

Mixed herbs	2 tsp
Ginger	2 tsp
Curry	1 tsp
Basil	¾ tsp
Paprika	¾ tsp
Cayenne pepper	¼ tsp

Put fish filets into the mix and grill or fry.

ACKNOWLEDGMENTS

Writing this page is like having a chocolate dessert or looking at favorite photos—sheer pleasure.

My greatest thanks to the New Zealanders who opened their homes and shared their stories with me, each of whom is mentioned in this book.

I feel intensely grateful to my friend Ted Bonanno who served as an agent for this book. Before he became involved I collected a folder of rejection letters as thick as a finger. Ted took this project in hand and found the book a home.

All of my three children, to whom this book is dedicated, contributed to its completion. Miriam edited the first version of the manuscript while working as a journalist in Paris. Nika, an art historian and a curator in New York, oversaw all aspects of book design and wrote the jacket copy. Danny, a student at New York University, edited the final version and came up with the book title.

My great friend Patricia Liu, direct as ever, told me to put a map in the book marking the location of every chapter. I do not think I've ever seen this feature in any book.

Carol Keegan Kayne ran the final check on the book, ferreting out errors that everyone else overlooked. I learned long ago to not dare release a book without her signing off on it.

My manager, Inna Feldman, enabled me to travel in the Pacific by confidently holding down the fort in New York.

Many thanks to the professionals at John Wiley & Sons and Fine Composition, Inc. who took my file on a CD and made it into the attractive book you hold in your hands.

Dr. Alexander Elder
Haciendas El Choco
Dominican Republic
January 2005